Charleston Furniture
1700–1825

Frontispiece BOOKCASE Height 10'9"; width 8'3¾"; depth 25¼"

Charleston Furniture
1700-1825

BY
E. MILBY BURTON
DIRECTOR, THE CHARLESTON MUSEUM

UNIVERSITY OF SOUTH CAROLINA PRESS
Columbia, South Carolina

© 1955 by The Charleston Museum

First edition published in 1955 as
Contributions from The Charleston Museum: XII
by THE CHARLESTON MUSEUM, Charleston, S.C.

This edition published in 1970 by the
UNIVERSITY OF SOUTH CAROLINA PRESS, Columbia, S.C.

Standard Book Number: 87249-198-6
Library of Congress Catalog Card Number: 73-120917

Manufactured in the United States of America

Acknowledgments

In the making of this book I have had the advice and assistance of many people, and I cannot regard the work as complete until I have expressed to them, in some fashion, my deep sense of gratitude. High on the list must be the name of Miss Emma B. Richardson, of the staff of The Charleston Museum, for her excellent work in preparing the manuscript, editing, reading proof, and in general making the book ready for the press. Her patience has been unfailing; her quick grasp of every problem, sure and accurate.

It is, I fear, impossible for me to make adequate acknowledgment of all those who have assisted me in searching out extant examples of early Charleston furniture. Limitations of space preclude a complete listing. I am particularly grateful, however, to those who have permitted me to come into their homes, often to the disruption of their households, to make photographs of their furniture. I was invariably received with courtesy, and in not a single instance was I refused permission to take pictures. I regret that I cannot show my appreciation of such generous co-operation by including in this book all the photographs I was permitted to acquire. The final choice has been determined by cost and space limitations, or by the necessity of avoiding repetition of the types of furniture represented. It should be understood, therefore, that the exclusion of any given photograph does not mean that the subject was unworthy of inclusion. It should be understood also that only by the collection and study of hundreds of photographs have I been able to write with confidence on the styles and types of early Charleston furniture; hence, every photograph I have taken has been invaluable to me, whether or not it occurs as an illustration in the book.

Institutions and societies as well as individuals have been generous either in supplying me with photographs or in permitting me to have the photographs taken. In particular I wish to express my indebtedness to the Baltimore Museum of Fine Arts, the South Caroliniana Library, the Henry Francis duPont Winterthur Museum, the South Carolina Society, and the Yale University Art Gallery.

I am equally grateful to those dealers who have supplied me with illustrations of Charleston-made furniture in their possession or have shared with me their technical knowledge. Among these have been Teina Baumstone, Benjamin Ginsberg, Joe Kindig, Jr., Joe Kindig III, Charles Navis, Jack Patla, William Richmond, and John Schwarz.

Nor may I neglect to thank those who worked with me in the taking of photographs. The work was usually done in the summer, either in the afternoons or evenings when the temperature, already high, was cruelly increased by the heat of the photographic lamps. The photographers—Benjamin R. Heyward and Robert Adamson Brown of Charleston,

A. K. Altfather of Columbia, and Henry Elrod of Greenville—were invariably cheerful and painstaking under those most trying circumstances.

For technical assistance in the identification of certain woods I owe my thanks to William N. Watson of the Smithsonion Institution and Dr. E. S. Harrar of the Department of Forestry, Duke University. Dr. J. H. Easterby, Director of the South Carolina Archives Department, and Dr. Clement Eaton, Professor of History at the University of Kentucky, have given me invaluable help in the solution of many historical problems; and Paul R. Weidner, of the Department of English at the College of Charleston, who read the manuscript critically during the process of composition, has helped materially in giving unity to the text.

Finally, I shall ever be indebted to Mrs. Henry Manning Sage, of Albany, New York, and Dover Plantation, Georgetown, South Carolina, who made this work possible. For her encouragement and advice, which I have enjoyed for many years, I cannot too strongly express my deepest appreciation.

E. M. B.

Contents

Acknowledgments   v

List of Illustrations   ix

Early Charleston   3

Sources of Furniture   6

Kinds of Furniture Used in
    Charleston   11

Kinds of Furniture Not Made
    in Charleston   12

Styles and Influences   13

Schools   16

Labels   18

Exports and Country Trade   18

Plantation-Made Furniture   20

Prices of Furniture   20

Dearth of Local Furniture   22

Conclusion   25

Woods   27

Charleston-Made Furniture   39

Charleston Cabinet-makers   67

Addenda   133

Cabinet-makers' Receipts   134

Notes   137

Works Consulted   143

Index   147

Illustrations

	FIGURES	AFTER PAGE
BED	17	22
BEDPOSTS—DETAILS	18–29, 142	38, 126
BOOKCASES	Frontispiece, 1–2	6
CABINETS	67–68	86
CANDLE STAND	131	126
CELLARETTES	72–74	86
CHAIRS:		
Chippendale Style	110–116, 118–121, 145	118, 126, 132
Corner	122, 124	126
French	108–109	118
Hepplewhite Style	123, 125–129	126
Transitional Style	117	126
CHESTS OF DRAWERS	7–14	22
CLOCKS	69–71	86
CLOTHESPRESS OR WARDROBE	15	22
COMMODE	136–137	126
DESK AND BOOKCASES	30–33, 147–148	38, 132
DOUBLE CHESTS OF DRAWERS	3–6, 36–37, 149	22, 45, 47, 132
FIRE SCREEN	140–141	126
HAT BOX	138	126
INLAYS AND BELLFLOWERS	53, 143–144, 146	62, 132
LABEL	139	126
PEDIMENTS	38–46	54
SECRETARY AND BOOKCASES	34–35	38
SECRETARY-WARDROBE	16	22
SIDEBOARDS	47–52, 54–66	54, 70
TABLES:		
Breakfast	85, 87–89	102
Card	86, 96–99	102
Dining	79–82	86
Dressing	90–93	102
Gaming	83–84	86
Gate-legged	77–78	86
Pembroke	100–103, 106, 143	102, 132
Sewing	104–105, 107	102
Side	75–76, 94–95	86, 102
Tea	130, 132–135	126

Part 1: EARLY CHARLESTON

Early Charleston

THE CULTURE OF ANY SOCIETY, WHETHER it be primitive or highly civilized, is unerringly revealed by the material things which the society needs and the degree of skill which it displays in producing or acquiring them. The converse is also true: the nature of the things themselves can be best understood if they can be judged by the known standards and requirements of the society which used them. Architecture is truly indigeneous to a region where it conforms to the climatic conditions, the building materials immediately available, and the way of life peculiar to that region. The same thing may be said of textiles, ceramics, furniture. Changes of form occur where influences from without begin to modify taste, and where affluence makes it possible for a people to import, imitate, or adopt, the products of other societies. It is desirable if not necessary, therefore, to understand as much as possible of the nature and history of a group and people if we are to understand the things they created or demanded for use in their daily lives.

From its very beginning the society of the Province of South Carolina, with its center at Charleston, was strikingly cosmopolitan. The Lords Proprietors had visualized it as a reproduction in America of the landed aristocracy of old England and actually provided, in the constitution drawn up by John Locke, for a nobility supported by the ownership of land to "avoid erecting a numerous democracy." [1] It is true that within half a century the nobility disappeared but the economic system with its traditions of gentility persisted for many generations.

While it is true that most of the early settlers came from England, it is equally true that numbers came from the Barbadoes. Even at that early date Barbadoes was becoming over-populated and the large land owners were looking for new lands to develop. Men of substantial wealth emigrated from the island to South Carolina shortly after the Province was established. After the Revocation of the Edict of Nantes in 1685 great numbers of Huguenots settled near Charleston. Many of these were artisans, who added considerably to the growing wealth of the colony. Irish, Jews, Germans, and Scots followed within the next few years. Still later came refugees from the French West Indies fleeing the uprisings and consequent massacres. And from time to time in the early history of Charleston one comes across a name of Dutch extraction. Before very long, then, the city was composed of people who variously traced their ancestors to England, France, Holland, Germany, Ireland, Scotland, and the West Indies; and nearly a century was required to bring about a merging of the different customs, traditions, religions, and languages of Charleston's population. [2] English culture predominated, but it was the fusing of many national elements that made Charleston a cosmopolitan city and created a unique civilization among the American colonies, the civilization of the Carolina Low Country.

During the first decade, from 1670 to 1680, the colony had a precarious existence. In addition to the menace of the Indians, there was always the threat from the Spaniards. South Carolina at that time was the southernmost colony, on land claimed by the Spanish. In their eyes the new colony was definitely an encroachment on

Spanish territory. In spite of this constant threat, the colony not only survived but prospered and in 1680 moved to the present location of Charleston. As early as 1700, John Lawson, the English traveler, was able to write of Charleston: * "The Town has very regular and fair streets, in which are good buildings of Brick and Wood, and since my coming thence has had great additions of beautiful, Large Brick Buildings, besides a Strong Fort and regular Fortifications made to defend the town. . . . This place is more plentiful in Money, than most, or indeed any of the Plantations on the Continent. . . . The Merchants of Carolina are Fair, Frank Traders. The Gentlemen seated in the country are very courteous, live very nobly in their Houses, and give very Genteel entertainments to all strangers and others that come to visit them." [3] The "fortifications" to which Lawson referred was the wall which was being built around the city by which Charleston enjoys the distinction of having been one of the few walled cities on the North American continent.

The early colonists were quick to see the profits that could be derived from the Indian trade. Daring explorers were soon pushing westward to make contact with the natives of the interior. The Indians already knew the white man; they had been carrying on trade with both the French and the Spanish for a long time. The economic rivalry between the old traders and the new sometimes delayed but never permanently stopped the westward march of the Charleston adventurers, and their pack trains penetrated farther and farther into the interior until they reached the Mississippi River, a thousand miles away. This lucrative trade brought the first great wealth to Charleston.

In the latter part of the seventeenth century rice was introduced into the Carolina Low Country. The one thing needed to make a landed gentry possible had happened. Rice culture flourished from the beginning and the plantation system thus firmly established brought tremendous wealth to the colony.

How quickly this new prosperity was manifested in the life of Charleston is reflected by the words of Peter Purry, who in 1731 wrote: "There are between 5 and 600 Houses in *Charles Town*, the most of which are very costly; . . . the People of *Carolina*, . . . are all rich, either in Slaves, Furniture, Cloaths, Plate, Jewels, or other Merchandizes. . . ." [4]

Just before the Revolution the exports from Charleston to Great Britain, during an eleven-year period (1763–1773) averaged £389,000 Sterling per annum. At this distance it is difficult to convert this amount into present-day monetary terms, but compared to the exports from some of the other colonies it was extremely large; for we find that during the same period the average exports from all of New England amounted to £132,000 per annum; New York, £71,000; and Pennsylvania, £34,000.[5] The exporting of any commodity means that the exporter received either cash or credit for his commodity. In view of Charleston's large export trade during this period, it is easily seen how the Carolina planters, merchants, shippers, and other investors amassed such large fortunes. There is no doubt that in per capita wealth and income, Low Country Carolinians led all Americans.[6]

* There is quite a variation in the spelling of the name *Charleston* before its incorporation in 1783. The general spelling appears to have been Charles Town with both words capitalized. Sometimes it was hyphenated; again spelled as one word; occasionally with an "e" on the end of it. After its incorporation in 1783, it became Charleston. In this work the spelling Charleston is invariably used.

A third source of wealth to the Province up to the time of the Revolution was indigo. It ceased to be a profitable crop when the British government discontinued the bounty that it had formerly paid for its production. By that time, however, cotton had been successfully introduced, and more than compensated for the loss of the Indian trade (caused by the extension of the frontier) [7] and the profits from indigo. In the end it was this white tide of cotton, augmenting that of rice, which made permanent the great plantation system, with its countless slaves and subsequent wealth.

Charleston had a gay social life. The rich planters and merchants vied with one another to see who could give the greatest dinners and balls. There were frequent concerts and plays at the local theatre. The social season culminated in Race Week, when every one of any means whatsoever appears to have entertained with a lavish hand.[8] If one can judge from old accounts, most business must have been suspended during that time. Many of the gentlemen maintained their own stables, frequently with imported blooded horses.[9] Some of them even had their own race tracks.

A description of Charleston appears in the *London Magazine* for June, 1762. It gives a rather detailed account of the city, describing some of the public buildings and having this to say about its inhabitants: "Here the rich people have handsome equipages; the merchants are opulent and well bred; the people are thriving and extensive, in dress and life; so that everything conspires to make this town the politest, as it is one of the richest in America." Lord Adam Gordon, who visited Charleston two years later, confirms the description of the *London Magazine;* in his journal he writes that "The Inhabitants are courteous, polite and affable, the most hospitable and attrac-

tive to Strangers, of any I have yet seen in America, very clever in business and almost all of them, first and last, have made a trip to the Mother-Country. It is the fashion to Send home [England] all their children for education. . . . It is in general believed, that they are more attached to the Mother-Country, than those Provinces which lie more to the Northward. . . ." [10]

Josiah Quincy, Jr., a young Boston patriot and lawyer, visited Charleston in the spring of 1773. He was so highly impressed by the city that he wrote to his wife that in "grandeur, splendour of buildings, decorations, equipages, number, commerce, shipping, and indeed in almost every thing," it surpassed all he had ever seen or expected to see in America. Quincy had only scorn and criticism for these gay pleasures, but he left no doubt that for fashion, elegance, gaiety, and wealth Charleston was without a parallel in Colonial America.[11]

Wealth brought not only luxury and a gay social life but leisure as well. And if one can judge from the inventories of their libraries the wealthy Charlestonians must have been proficient in more than one language and they must have had wide and varied interests. New cultural values brought to the Charlestonian the problem of educating his children. The boys were well grounded in Latin, Greek, and the classics. The girls were trained in music, drawing, needlework, dancing, and French. Feeling that the boys could not get the necessary education at home, many fathers sent their sons abroad, to attend Oxford, to be trained in the law at the Inns of Court, or to study medicine at Edinburgh or Leyden. The graduation present was usually a grand tour of the Continent, which must have cost their fathers a pretty penny. More Carolinians went abroad to receive their education than from any other colony.[12] Naturally the dominating influence upon these young travelers was that of England. Because of this influence, upon their return, they founded a library, a museum, and other societies and organizations, many of which have persisted until this day.

SOURCES OF FURNITURE
Charleston Cabinet-Makers

WITH ALL THIS ENORMOUS WEALTH, where did the Charlestonians get the furniture to go into their large and stately houses? Certainly it could not all have been imported; there would not have been sufficient shipping space for the furniture needed to fill the great town houses and the mansions on the country estates. The records reveal that from 1700 to 1825 nearly 250 bona fide cabinet-makers were plying their trade in Charleston, trying to fill their orders. This number does not include carvers, gilders, turners, or chair makers; many of these worked in conjunction with the cabinet-maker. Undoubtedly the early joiners made furniture, but with a few exceptions, in which their inventories or advertisements clearly indicate that they were actually making furniture and not building houses, their names have not been included in the list of cabinet-makers. The same applies to the chairmakers—of whom there were a great number—for fear of confusing them with the men who actually made riding chairs or chaises.

The first cabinet-makers (as distinguished from the joiners) had come to the Province by the early eighteenth century. At first there were only a few but as Charleston grew there was a gradual increase in their numbers. But with continued prosperity we find that in 1750 the number had doubled over that of the previous decade and it had again doubled by 1760. Thereafter the increase was more gradual. War and the enforced absence of many of the Charlestonians, especially at the time of the capture of the city by the British in 1780, brought a decline in their number. With the coming of peace and the gradual recovery from the economic chaos that followed the war, the number of cabinet-makers once more began to increase; thirty-five men were working in the city in 1790. Between 1790 and 1800 the increase was spectacular; there were sixty-three cabinet-makers in Charleston at the beginning of the nineteenth century. The all-high peak was reached ten years later, when the names of eighty-one men are listed. For a city as small as Charleston was at that time, eighty-one cabinet-makers is a prodigious number. Even when we make allowance for the fact that some of these cabinet-makers were employed by others, there still must have been one or two cabinet-makers' shops in every block. By 1820 the number had dropped to fifty-one, although as late as 1826 Mills in his *Statistics of South Carolina* lists sixty cabinet-makers working in Charleston at that time.[1]

The account book of Thomas Elfe reveals that during an eight-year period (1768–1775) he made approximately fifteen hundred pieces of furniture.[2] It is not to be supposed that all of the cabinet-makers equalled Elfe either in workmanship or in the quantity of furniture they produced. And no doubt Elfe received help from others. But if his output can be taken as any kind of criterion, it is interesting to speculate on the amount of furniture he made during the thirty years he worked in Charleston. If one man, with some outside

Fig. 1 BOOKCASE Height 8'11"; width 7'8"; depth—center 28½", end 25½"

Fig. 2 BOOKCASE Height 10'4"; width 8'3½"; depth 25"

help could make so large a number of pieces, what must have been the total number of pieces of furniture produced between 1700 and 1825 by the cabinet-makers (approximately 250) covered in this work? It must have been a fantastic figure.

English Importations

FURNITURE OF BOTH ENGLISH AND AMERican origin was imported into Charleston. All such importations were affected if not positively governed by two important considerations. The first is pure economics; the second shipping space. In the early period mahogany came from the West Indies. The logs had to be transported to London or some other English port where a duty was paid on them,[1] then sawed into lumber, made into furniture by cabinet-makers (who in all probability were paid a higher wage than the local craftsman), and then shipped back to America. There must certainly have been a great difference between the cost of a piece of locally-made furniture and one imported from London. The freight alone on the mahogany as well as on the finished work must have added tremendously to the cost of an imported piece.[2] And no doubt the Charleston cabinet-makers, many of whom had learned their trade in London, would have done everything possible to discourage importations. Something like proof of this fact seems to be contained in an advertisement of Josiah Claypool (q.v.), dated 1741: ". . . And whereas by a constant Hurry of Cabinet Work, it has so happened that I have disappoint'd several good Customers, this is further to give Notice, that in a short time I shall have two good Workmen from *London*, and shall then be in a Capacity to suit any Person who shall favor me with their Employ."[3]

Shipping space was at a premium. It is not to be forgotten that eighteenth century vessels were very small (as compared with modern ones). Again, because of the shallowness (15 feet)[4] of the bar at Charleston at that time, ships of over two hundred tons burden could not enter the harbor without lightening their cargo,[5] a precarious undertaking even in calm weather. Nevertheless, large quantities of materials were brought into the port of Charleston from abroad. The newspaper advertisements contain lengthy lists of these various articles. In fact, Governor Glen in 1749 was so worried about the expensive tastes of the Charlestonians that he wrote as follows: "I cannot help expressing my surprise and concern to find that there are annually imported into this Province considerable quantities of Fine Flanders Lace, the Finest Dutch Linens, and French Cambricks, Chintz, Hyson Tea and other East India Goods, Silks, Gold and Silver Laces, etc."[6] Such articles, of course, were easily stowed, but any large piece of furniture took up valuable shipping space. Certainly the merchants and ship masters of that day were fully cognizant of the fact.

It is not to be inferred, however, that no large pieces of furniture were imported. There are still some large pieces in Charleston that undoubtedly were made in England. This also is verified by inventories where, at rare intervals, one will find mention of a piece of either English or London-made furniture.[7] Probably chairs and bedsteads were the articles most frequently imported, for they could be most easily stowed.[8] If one may judge from the newspaper advertisements of the day—and they went into great detail as to the other articles that were being imported—a comparatively small amount of English furniture was brought into Charleston. The files of the Public Record Office in London confirm this.[9] In the years 1720–1728 chairs (not to be confused with riding chairs) to the value of £1232 were exported to all of the American Colonies. From 1740 to 1747 the recorded value of exported chairs amounted only to £377, showing that the American cabinet-makers were, with a few exceptions, taking care of the demands of their customers. During the earlier period there was no export of chests of drawers or cabinets; and escritoires amounted to only £5 which in all probability consisted of a single piece. In the latter period there was still no export of chests of drawers or cabinets and this time the escritoires were valued at £7. Strangely enough in an inventory dated March 1, 1744, there is an entry of "1 English Walnut Scrutore £8-0-0" [local currency].[10] If these periods can be taken as any kind of criteria, we have a complete explanation of so little mention of English furniture in the newspaper advertisements. This is further substantiated by the fact that only a small amount of early English furniture has come to light in Charleston and vicinity.

On August 17, 1801, the following advertisement was inserted in *The Times:* "The subscribers have imported from London a quantity of the most Elegant and Fashionable Furniture, perhaps ever seen in this city, which they offer for sale, on reasonable terms. . . . The articles are as follows: Satinwood and Pembroke Tables, Tambour Writing Desk, Secretary and Book Cases, Side Board, Ice Pails, Chairs, Sophas, Window curtains with Cornice complete, Fire Screen. The whole intended to furnish two drawing rooms." The same advertisement appears fairly regularly until December 31, 1801. What ultimately hap-

pened to the furniture is not known. The conclusion seems to be that either the Charleston people were not particularly impressed by the "Elegant and Fashionable Furniture" or that the price asked for it was too high. For it must not be overlooked that as early as 1790 the United States passed a 7½ ad valorem tax on all imported furniture.[11] This was one of our early protective tariffs.

By 1801, to further discourage foreign importation, the tariff was increased to 15%, and by 1807 it was again raised to 19¼% if the furniture was brought over in foreign bottoms. Such a tariff amounting to nearly 20% of the value must have cut foreign importation to a mere trickle. And by 1822 it had reached a high of 33% on all manufactured wood. [12]

American Importations

EARLY AMERICAN IMPORTATIONS INTO the port of Charleston were sporadic. The advertisements suggest that they were "venture" furniture, that is, furniture put on ships at their home ports, the selling being left to the discretion of the captain as he went from port to port. We find in 1769 that the Sloop "Sally" from New York had "a few low and high-backed Windsor Chairs." [1] The following year gives an advertisement which offers "Windsor Chairs from Philadelphia." An advertisement of 1774 reads: "Imported from Salem—Northward Rum, Desks, Riding Chairs, Potatoes, Mackeral and Herring in Barrels, Pears, Raisons. . . ." [2] Obviously this was a ship sailing from port to port and selling its cargo as best it could.

It is a matter of record that ships from New England sailed into Charleston with furniture as part of their cargoes.[3] Probably most of it was made of maple. If this furniture remained in Charleston, the fact is not revealed in the inventories. Nor is it reasonable to assume that the wealthy and sophisticated Charlestonian would have been particularly interested in maple furniture when mahogany was not only available but abundant and there were a sufficient number of excellent cabinet-makers to supply his needs. Frequently an advertisement appears in the newspaper stating that such and such a sloop from one of the Northern colonies was at one of the wharves and that she "had on board" some articles of furniture. Inasmuch as the furniture remained on board it is a clear indication that the captain or broker merely hoped to sell it to some prospective buyer. Therefore, it is not to be inferred that every ship that entered the Port of Charleston sold its entire consignment of furniture while there. If the captain or broker could not sell the "venture" furniture, as it was called, at a satisfactory price, it remained aboard and the captain sailed away, hoping for better success at his next port of call. On the other hand, there is a list (1789) which gives the names of the purchasers of some furniture brought in by a ship from Salem.[4] Not many of the names appear in the 1790 City Directory, and those that can be traced appear, with a few exceptions, to have been the names of people of small financial means. The explanation may lie in the fact that the furniture was on consignment and that the consignee, after holding it unsuccessfully for a time, sold it at reduced prices. In 1797 the Brig *Juno* arrived from Boston with a cargo consisting of gin, goods, and furniture.[5] It is not known how much of the cargo was sold while the ship was in port.

In 1789 there seems to have been a flurry of importation from New York and Philadelphia of Windsor chairs, with an occasional sideboard and card table. Frequently one finds an advertisement stating that there will be an auction of one hundred Windsor chairs, leading to the belief that possibly the chairs had not been sold as rapidly as anticipated. It is also reasonable to suppose that since there were about thirty-five cabinet-makers working in Charleston during this period (not to mention several chairmakers), they would regard importations with disfavor and would do everything possible to meet the competition. As early as 1784 Andrew Redmond (*q.v.*) was advertising that he made "Philadelphia Windsor Chairs, either armed or unarmed, as neat as any imported, and much better stuff." [6] And in 1798 we find Humiston & Stafford (*q.v.*) asserting that they made "Warranted Windsor Chairs and Green Settees, Of the newest fashion, and of an excellent quality superior to any ever imported into this city, . . ." [7]

By 1819 the advertisements show that a great deal of New York furniture was being shipped to Charleston. Much of it was made by J. L. Everett, and John Budd of 118 Fulton Street.[8] It became so common in the city that a furniture store was opened at 254 King Street under the name of "The New York Cabinet Furniture Warehouse." [9] In the same year we find another furniture store, located at No. 294 King Street, known as the Northern Warehouse, which was advertising that it had received from Philadelphia some Windsor chairs and settees of a handsome pattern.[10] It is also known that about this time quantities of Hitchcock chairs were brought into Charleston.[11]

It is not clear why the Charleston cabinet-makers—and there were fifty-one plying their trade at that time—could not compete with importations from the North though they were trying to meet it.[12] Probably mass production was the answer.[13] Even as late as 1832 the cabinet-makers were still endeavoring to meet this competition for we find the following advertisement: "CHARLESTON MADE FURNITURE. The subscriber has on hand a large assortment of FURNITURE, consisting of handsome Dressing and plain Bureaus; Sideboards of the latest fashion; Mahogany and plain bedsteads; Pillar and Claw Tea Tables . . . Wardrobes, Sofas of various pattern . . . Also, Windsor and Easy Chairs, . . ."[14] But it is clear that by the middle of the century, Charleston cabinet-making was on the decline, although many cabinet-makers have continued their trade down to the present.

Other Importations

ONLY RARELY DOES AN ADVERTISEMENT reveal that furniture was brought into Charleston from places other than England or the American seaport cities. A small advertisement in 1798 announces a shipment "From Scotland—Some elegant Furniture, & to be disposed of on Moderate Terms."[1] In the same year we learn that the ship *Eliza* has arrived from Bordeaux with some Bedsteads, Sofas and Chairs for Francis De Lorme (*q.v.*).[2]

Negro Cabinet-Makers

THERE CAN BE LITTLE DOUBT THAT DURING the period covered by this work an appreciable number of Negro cabinet-makers worked in Charleston. Presumably they were the slaves of white cabinet-makers, picked for special training in cabinet-making because they had shown some aptitude for it. Unfortunately, we have only a few records pertaining to these Negro craftsmen. It is probable that there were many more Negroes working as cabinet-makers than the records reveal.

As early as 1729 we find Thomas Holton, chair- and couch maker, putting up as collateral on a mortgage three of his Negro men "by name Sesar, Will, and Jack by trade Chairmakers."[1]

By 1755 so many Negroes were being trained in various trades, to the disadvantage of white workmen, that the provincial legislature framed an act intended to put some curb upon the increase of Negro artisans. The law reads in part: "And no master of any slave shall permit or suffer such slaves to carry on any handicraft trade in a shop by himself, in town, on pain of forfeiting *five pounds* every day. Nor to put any negro or slave apprentice to any mechanic trade of another in town, on forfeiture of *one hundred pounds*."

In the *South Carolina Gazette* for December 10–17, 1763, occurs the following advertisement: "Any person having a good negro ship-carpenter, cabinet-maker, or house-carpenter, whom he is willing to dispose of for no fault, and who can be recommended for sobriety and honesty, and is not old, may hear of a purchaser by inquiring of the Printer hereof." There seems to be nothing unusual in this advertisement, the indication being that the Negro cabinet-maker was a well established fact.

When John Fisher bought out the cabinet-making business of Stephen Townsend in 1771, he inserted the following advertisement: ". . . that he has purchased of Mr. Stephen Townsend his STOCK in TRADE and NEGROES brought up to the Business"; [2] and the account book of Thomas Elfe tells us how he would send his Negro cabinet-maker to various residences either to put or take down a four-poster bed or to do a minor repair job on a piece of furniture. Elfe's will reveals that he owned three Negro cabinet-makers.

A part of the City's revenue was derived from the sale of badges issued to the masters of slaves. In 1783 a City Ordinance provided in part that "no owner or other person having care and government of negroes or other slaves, shall permit any such slave to be employed or hired out of their respective houses or families, without a ticket or badge first had and obtained from the Corporation of this City, under the penalty of three pounds for every such offence; . . . And for each ticket or badge obtained from the Corporation the several sums following shall be respectively paid, . . . Cabinet-maker . . . 20 shillings . . ." [3]

In 1800 Joshua Eden emancipated a Negro by the name of William. In his will, probated two years later, Eden left "all his working tools and wearing apparel" to William. It is a fair assumption that William had been brought up in the trade and knew how to use its tools. The wills of many other cabinet-makers reveal that they owned slaves, and it can hardly be doubted that many of these slaves worked for their owners.

Thomas Charnock sold some property to Sarah Cooper in 1810. At that time he is spoken of as "a free man of color, and a carpenter and cabinet-maker." However, it is not until the middle of the nineteenth century that we begin to find free Negro cabinet-makers more frequently mentioned.

That there were Negro apprentices in cabinet-making is quite evident. For example, G. E. Barrite, a local cabinet-maker, advertised that "A colored Boy of proper age, will be taken as an Apprentice"; [4] and Joshua Neville & Son state that they want "three or four BOYS, to learn the Cabinet Making business, either white or colored." [5]

It is regrettable that there is no way of estimating the amount of furniture actually made by the Negro cabinet-maker.

Kinds of Furniture Used in Charleston

FEW OF THE INVENTORIES LIST THE ARTIcles contained in each room. In most of them the various articles are given in a long unbroken list. It is always interesting to note the amount and kind of furniture which normally would be found in the residence of a man of means. The inventory [1] of John Rattray (about whom nothing else is known) made in 1761, reveals that he had the following items in his dining room:

1 dozen Mahogany chairs with worked bottoms
1 dozen Mahogany chairs with leather bottoms
2 large square Mahogany Tables [Dining]
1 Marble Slab
1 Tea Table & Tea Board
1 Card Table
1 Pair Sconces Glass & Chimney Glass
1 Set Marriage a la mode [Hogarth]

In his "Front Chamber" are found the following articles:

1 Mahogany Bedstead with furniture
1 Chest
1 Half Chest of Drawers
1 Mahogany Desk & Bookcase
1 Close Stool Chair
1 Dressing Glass
1 Easy Chair

The other "chambers" of his residence contained furniture similar to the pieces in the foregoing list.

The inventory of Jacob Motte, a wealthy merchant, made on July 19, 1770,[2] shows that he had the following pieces of furniture in his residence:

27 Mahogany Chairs
2 Easy Chairs
53 other Chairs
2 Night Chairs
8 Mahogany Bedsteads
3 Dressing Tables
3 Marble Tables
3 Mahogany Clawfoot Tables
10 other Mahogany Tables
3 Double Chests of Drawers
2 Chests of Drawers
3 Desks
1 Couch
2 Presses
1 Cooler [Wine]
4 Knife Cases
1 Clock [grandfather]
4 Screens
3 Washhand Stands
1 Mahogany Stool
1 Glass door Cabinet
5 Looking Glasses
1 Tea Board
_____
Total—141 Items

The inventory of Mary Bull made on January 20, 1770,[3] lists the following articles:

55 Mahogany Chairs
2 Easy Chairs
2 Arm Chairs
8 Walnut Chairs
6 Windsor Chairs
1 Close Stool Chair
7 Mahogany Bedsteads
6 Dressing Tables

10 Mahogany Tables, Dining, Tea, etc.
1 Sopha
1 Couch
2 Chests of Drawers, Mahogany
7 Looking Glasses
1 Tall [grandfather] Clock
1 Bottle stand
3 Mahogany Cases containing silver-handled Knives, Forks, & Spoons
1 Desk & Bookcase
1 Desk
2 Rum Cases large
_____
106 articles of furniture

At this time Charleston was one of the larger cities, and certainly the richest, in the country. From the foregoing lists one can draw one's own conclusion as to the quality and quantity of furniture that was, at one time, to be found in Charleston.

Kinds of Furniture Not Made in Charleston

THERE ARE THREE PRIMARY SOURCES OF information concerning the types or styles of furniture manufactured and used in Charleston—inventories of personal property; advertisements by local cabinetmakers in the newspapers of the period; and surviving pieces of furniture now in Charleston homes. If a given type does not appear in at least one of these three places, the assumption is reasonably fair that the type was not produced in Charleston, though there is always the possibility that at almost any time a piece will turn up to contradict the generalization.

Thus far no records have appeared to indicate that furniture of the block front type of construction was either manufactured in Charleston or imported, though any number of Charlestonians must have been familiar with it. Before the Revolution it was customary for South Carolina planters to spend the summers, from May to autumn, in Newport, Rhode Island. Newport was so popular as a place of escape from the fevers of the Carolina Low Country that it was called the "Carolina Hospital." Newport also provided pleasures for the wealthy and in summer bore some resemblance to the city of Bath, England, a summer resort of the English aristocracy.

Carolinians at Newport could hardly have missed seeing the handiwork of the Northern cabinet-makers, but they were apparently not impressed by it.

The high chest of drawers, or as it is commonly called, the "high boy," seems not to have been made in Charleston. There are a few high boys now in the city, but their histories reveal that they are recent importations. The double chest of drawers took the place of high boys in the city residence or plantation home of coastal Carolina.

On the other hand, the dressing table was a common article of furniture in Charleston houses, as the inventories reveal. They were well executed. The Charleston dressing table usually had one long drawer or two small drawers. With one exception, nothing has yet been discovered that is comparable to the Philadelphia-style "low boy." Whether such a dressing table (the name "low boy" was not used in Colonial times)[1] was ever made in Charleston in any quantity only time and diligent research will determine.

Strangely enough, the bombé form has not been found in Charleston. Since it was used in England, it might be supposed that Charlestonians would have wanted it.

Future research may reveal that it was occasionally used here.

The "bonnet" top does not seem to have been used on the double chest of drawers. Some of the cabinet-makers advertised that they made double chests of drawers with "neat and light Pediment Heads, which take off and put on occasionally." Since, unfortunately, so few of these Pediment Heads have survived, they must have been removed more often than "occasionally."

Styles and Influences

ONE OF THE THINGS MOST STRESSED IN the advertisements of the Charleston cabinet-makers was that their furniture was made either in the latest style or the latest fashion. The first known advertisement of any cabinet-maker appeared in 1732 in the *South Carolina Gazette* offering furniture made in the "best manner."[1] Insistence on this kind of excellence persisted until the 1830's, when cabinet-making, as we now think of it, gradually declined.

Before the Revolution, Charlestonians, because of their wealth, had close ties with the mother country and were naturally partial to, if not actually governed by, its styles. With their balls and dancing assemblies, concerts and race meets, theatre and open-air gardens, cock-fights, billiards, and taverns, debating clubs and coffee clubs, Charleston was in many respects a miniature London—the London of wealth and fashion.[2] That the prevailing styles of London reached Charleston quickly is exemplified in an advertisement in the *South Carolina Gazette* of December 16, 1756: "James Reid proposes to sell his house and land contiguous to the rope walk . . . The said house is new built, strong, and modish,

[13]

after the CHINESE Taste, which spreads 60 feet square including the balconies . . ." Although the Chinese influence is shown in Chippendale's *Director*, published in 1754, Sir William Chambers did much to popularize the Chinese style in England by the publication in 1757 of his *Design of Chinese Building, Furniture, Dresses, Machines, and Utensils*. Yet we find a house in Charleston already built in the "CHINESE" taste a year before the publication of Chambers' work. Actually the house was probably chinoiserie in detail rather than truly Chinese.[3] This taste persisted in Charleston for several years; on December 12, 1761, the following advertisement appeared in the *South Carolina Gazette:* "PETER HALL, Cabinet-Maker, from London . . . where gentlemen and ladies of taste may have made, and be supplied with *Chinese* tables of all sorts, shelves, trays, chimney-pieces, baskets, &c. being at present the most elegant and admired fashion in London." And John Lord, a London trained carver, states in the *South Carolina Gazette; and Country Journal* for May 12, 1767, that he does furniture carving "in the Chinese, French and Gothic Tastes . . ." Some of the wealthy Charlestonians carried these prevailing styles to such an extent that they imported from London their carriages, horses, *and* coachmen.[4]

Crevecoeur, a Frenchman who visited Charleston just prior to the Revolution, was greatly impressed by the city and its inhabitants for he said that they "are the gayest in America; it is called the center of our beau monde . . . An (*sic*) European at his first arrival must be greatly surprised when he sees the elegance of their houses, their sumptuous furniture, as well as the magnificence of their table." [5] The Charlestonians appointed booksellers in London to send them regularly the latest current magazines and reviews. When the antiquarian craze swept London it was communicated to the Charlestonians soon afterward by such works as *Antique Paintings of Herculaneum* and *Baths of the Romans*.[6] In other words, Charlestonians thought of themselves as Englishmen who happened to be living in America, and naturally did everything possible to emulate the life of London society. Therefore Drayton in 1802 could write: "Before the American war [Revolution], the citizens of Carolina were too much prejudiced in favor of British manners, customs, and knowledge, to imagine that elsewhere, than in England, anything of advantage could be obtained." [7] Up to the time of the Revolution, therefore, all styles and influences came from London.

From 1775 to 1785 there is a hiatus. Charleston, like the other American seaport cities, was eventually captured and occupied by the British. During the occupation the city had a certain amount of communication with England, but it is doubtful whether the then prevailing styles of London had an appreciable effect even upon the people of Charleston who had sworn allegiance to the Crown. Conditions were too chaotic and in all probability there was not a sufficient amount of ready cash available to pay the cabinet-makers.

During the next five years local cabinet-makers did very little advertising. The financial condition of the country was still unstable and the average citizen was too busy making a living to spend money on new furniture. It is not to be inferred, however, that no new furniture was being made, for there were, in fact, many cabinet-makers working in Charleston at that time, though it is doubtful whether the production of furniture was comparable to that of the pre-Revolutionary period. This may explain in some degree why so little furniture of the so-called "Transition" period has been found in Charleston. The hiatus occurred during the time that the style was changing from the influence of Chippendale to that of Hepplewhite.

With the return of prosperity Charleston's foreign trade greatly expanded. Ships from Rotterdam, Hamburg, Bremen, and Bordeaux, and even from Sweden and Russia, brought into the port of Charleston innumerable articles, utilities as well as luxuries, that had formerly come from England. These new contacts must have had some effect on the tastes of the native Charlestonians. For the first few years of the last decade of the eighteenth century the French influence was probably the strongest.[8] In 1791, Delorme, a local upholsterer, stated that "he makes bed and window curtains, either after the French or English fashion." The Duke of Liancourt, who visited Charleston in 1796, had the following comments to make about the people: "Many of the inhabitants of South Carolina, having been in Europe, have in consequence acquired a greater knowledge of our manners, and a stronger partiality to them, than the people of the Northern States. Consequently, the European modes of life are here more prevalent." He went on to say the "hatred against England is almost universal." [9] Anything French was extremely popular everywhere in America and the people of Charleston were receiving the French refugees from Santo Domingo who were fleeing the native uprisings in that unhappy island.[10] It is thought that among these refugees were several cabinetmakers, who continued their trade when they eventually established themselves in Charleston. Though not numerous they would certainly have added a modicum of French influence to the style of Charleston cabinet-makers.

By the turn of the century the feeling against England was subsiding; trade with England was resumed in some degree and, in spite of this feeling, the influence of Adam, Hepplewhite, and Sheraton had already made itself felt. It is from this period that the influence of Adam manifests itself to quite a degree in Charleston architecture; while the influence of Hepplewhite is found in many sideboards of local origin. Styles based upon those of the French Empire and the English Regency were probably felt more quickly in Charleston that in other American seaport cities. Henry Adams, the New England historian, had this to say about the Charlestonians during the first administration of Jefferson: "with their cultivated tastes and hospitable habits, delighted in whatever reminded them of European civilization. They were travellers, readers, and scholars; the society of Charleston compared well in refinement with that of any city of its size in the world, and English visitors long thought it the most agreeable in America." [11] Wedged between the Ashley and Cooper Rivers, Charleston was the funnel of all import and export for the State and adjacent territory; it was the greatest exporting point on the American continent.[12]

It was not until after the War of 1812, with subsequent economic disruption, that the first influence of another American city appeared on the styles of Charleston furniture. That city was New York. There are several things which help to account for this influence. Charleston was making cotton its principal article of export. The New York merchants, anxious to participate in the lucrative cotton trade between Charleston, England, and France, created through keen business acumen a three-cornered trade often spoken of as the "cotton triangle." [13] The ships which took cotton to England or France instead of returning directly to Charleston would return by way of New York loaded with freight or immigrants, then turn southward loaded with a general cargo picked up at New York. By this arrangement New York articles could be delivered at Charleston or any of the Southern ports at very little cost. To control this trade by maintaining the "cotton triangle" many Northern merchants sent their representatives to live in Charleston. By 1819 so many of these men were living in the city that along with others they founded the New England Society. Undoubtedly they did everything possible to "popularize" Northern goods.

About this period also the New York cabinet-makers were beginning the mass production of furniture,[14] and in spite of freight rates they could probably undersell the work of the Charleston cabinet-maker.[15]

Finally there is that nebulous thing called style, for which there is no accounting. Articles from New York became stylish and for some reason Charlestonians developed a taste for New York products simply because such things were "stylish."

Schools

IT IS FREQUENTLY ASKED WHETHER THERE developed among the Charleston cabinet-makers a school of design and workmanship that was in any way comparable to the schools of Philadelphia or Rhode Island. At this time a categorical answer to such a question is impossible. Establishing a "school" of furniture is like proving a scientific fact. It cannot be based on one or even a dozen experiments or observations. To be valid, the conclusions require hundreds of such observations, and as yet not enough Charleston-made furniture has been identified to provide the required data.

The difficulty of positively identifying the work of Charleston cabinet-makers is greatly increased by the fact that their work bears no labels. Thus far (1955) there is actually only one known labeled piece of Charleston furniture. By contrast, many of the pieces produced by Northern craftsmen have retained their original labels. This makes it fairly easy to identify other pieces by the same craftsman, and as examples multiply the characteristic styles of individual artisans or groups of artisans begin to form a pattern in which the uniformity of detail helps make possible the definition of a school. It is clear, therefore, that the methods commonly employed for arriving at the characteristics of the Northern "schools" cannot be used in studying the work of the Charleston cabinet-makers.

From the pieces of furniture known to have been produced in Charleston as well as from the early history of Charleston, it now appears that the pre-Revolutionary cabinet-makers followed the English styles and methods probably more closely than did the cabinet-makers in the Northern colonies. This is especially noticeable in several double chests of drawers that are to be found in or near Charleston. Their dimensions appear to be very close to their English prototypes of the same period. The English method also appears in the cross brace, running from front to rear, in the bottom of the larger drawers. It is important to note that cypress was used as a secondary wood for these cross braces instead of oak which was so generally used by the English. The dust board extending almost to the rear and in some cases all the way to the rear appears to have been generally used by the pre-Revolutionary local cabinet-makers.

Because of the proximity of the West Indies it was easy to bring mahogany into Charleston at low cost. Consequently the cabinet-makers made lavish use of mahogany. Very frequently beautifully crotched mahogany was veneered on mahogany. This method was occasionally used in Philadelphia, and possibly elsewhere, but it was used often by Charleston cabinet-makers.

Fine chairs were imported from England to Charleston and copied by the cabinet-makers (*see* Richard Magrath) who had received their training in London. The locally made chairs probably differed only by having heavier mahogany rails and large mahogany corner blocks. Some chairs of local origin have solid brackets. This may eventually turn out to be another indication of Charleston workmanship. Doubtless there are in existence countless pieces of locally made furniture that, because of their similarity, are now regarded (erroneously) as being of English origin.

If a pre-Revolutionary Charleston school ever evolves (and it probably will), the preponderance of the present evidence leads us to believe that it will be very English in both its style and craftsmanship.

The post-Revolutionary period is another matter. After the Revolution when Charleston again became prosperous and building was resumed, the houses were usually of larger dimensions, the most notable difference being their higher ceilings. In order that their furniture might not look dwarfed in the high ceiling room, the local cabinet-makers, literally following the advice of Hepplewhite, made their furniture taller. The upper section of the secretary-book-

case of this period (1790–1820) is usually quite high, giving it a "long-waisted" appearance. Frequently the lower sections are of a higher proportion than those found elsewhere. The Charleston bed of this same period is to be identified by its great height (nine-foot bedposts are fairly common), movable headboards, mahogany rails, and mahogany headposts. Mahogany bedrails and headposts were used elsewhere, but they were common in Charleston. Some armchairs of this period, thought to be of local origin, have shorter arm-rests than those found elsewhere. However, until a large number of such chairs have been examined, it cannot be said with certainty that shorter arm-rests form another Charleston characteristic.

The bellflowers found in local pieces of furniture are usually "scratched" rather than scrolled or pieced and the edges are not scorched with hot sand. There are a few exceptions in furniture of local origin but the great majority of pieces have "scratched" bellflowers.

Again turning to history we find that during this period (1790–1820) Charleston was a highly cosmopolitan city. Historians and travelers both note this fact. In the last decade of the eighteenth century French styles prevailed. Taste in these styles was doubtless augmented by the French refugees from Santo Domingo. About this time also the records reveal that numbers of cabinet-makers from Scotland were working in Charleston and, judging by the inventories of their estates, they were highly successful. In addition there were cabinet-makers who had received their training in Germany, Sweden, Italy, London, and France. It is reasonable to assume that the Charlestonians as well as the cabinet-makers with this cosmopolitan background would not have followed anything but the then prevailing style. However, in the construction of their pieces they probably adhered to their early training. Several pieces of furniture are in existence that, because of their fine dovetailing (as well as other characteristics), have been ascribed to some of the Scot cabinet-makers.

If the characteristics thus far listed are of sufficient importance to individualize the Charleston-made furniture of the period, then it can be said that a post-Revolutionary Charleston school exists, although it must be admitted, however, that thus far the school is not as clearly defined as some of the other American schools of furniture. Anything like a final definition of a Charleston school still remains in the future.

Labels

IN THE FURNITURE PRODUCED BY NEARLY two hundred fifty cabinet-makers listed in this work only one labeled piece has come to light. The label is on a satinwood secretary-bookcase not now in Charleston, and it bears the name of Robert Walker, No. 53 Church Street, Charleston, S. C. There is one other possible exception. A secretary is known, on the side of a small drawer of which is written in ink, "made by Jacob Sass, Oct. 1794."

Whether pre-Revolutionary local craftsmen ever used labels is problematical. Labels were seldom used by their English contemporaries. Even if labels were attached to new work, it is not likely that they survived the first summer; for the hot, humid atmosphere of Charleston and the attacks of glue-eating insects would probably have caused the labels to disintegrate in a very short time.

Exports and Country Trade

THE EARLY RECORDS OF THE CHARLESTON Custom House were sent to Columbia for safekeeping and were destroyed when that city was wantonly burned in 1865. Therefore, there is no way of ascertaining the amount of furniture that was exported from Charleston. In 1768 Abraham Pearce, a local cabinet-maker, advertised that "Orders from the country, or any of the southern provinces, will be punctually complied with." [1] The interesting thing about this advertisement is that it reveals that the local cabinet-makers were then making more than enough furniture to take care of the needs of their customers and therefore had to look for other outlets for their products. The "southern provinces" probably included Georgia, East Florida, and the British possessions in the West Indies.

It is a matter of record that in the early part of the nineteenth century vessels from Charleston entered the port of Savannah with furniture as their cargo. [2] There were about eighty cabinet-makers working in Charleston at that time and they must have produced a tremendous amount of furniture, which more than sufficed for the local trade; hence the exportation of the surplus. While it is definitely known that furniture was exported from Charleston, it probably will never be known how much there was of it or where it was shipped.

With the development of the plantation system which produced such tremendous wealth the local cabinet-makers quickly saw the possibility of acquiring rich customers. In their advertisements they frequently stated that "orders from the country will be punctually complied with" indicating that the large and elegant plantation homes were filled with furniture of

Charleston origin. As early as 1773 Thomas Elfe was shipping furniture to Cheraw, South Carolina, a distance of about two hundred miles by water.

Each plantation owner had a factor who lived in Charleston. The relationship between the factor and the planter was usually a very close one. The factor sold the planter's crop, advanced him money, bought his supplies in the Charleston market, and attended to his many smaller needs. The accepted definition of a factor was one "who could, and in many cases did, do anything which the principal could do through an agent." [3] Frequently the planter's children were entrusted to the care of the factor on their visits to Charleston. Whenever the planter wanted any furniture he wrote to his factor telling him approximately what he wanted and the factor in turn would give the order to some competent cabinet-maker, and see that the furniture was shipped to the planter.

A Charleston factor who had been instructed by one of his clients, a rice planter, to make some purchases wrote as follows: "With respect to the Chairs, I am quite at a loss what to do, there is such a variety both in Pattern and Color that I wish you had mentioned the circumstance when you were in Charleston that you might have chosen the Pattern yourself." He also purchased for his client some "Carpeting," stockings, linens, and china. [4]

By the first decade of the nineteenth century cotton was bringing great wealth to the planter, not only along the coastal area with rice but in the interior of the State where rice could not be grown. In 1801 sea-island cotton was sold for forty-four cents a pound [5] and upland cotton brought twenty-five cents a pound. [6] Converted into terms of present-day purchasing power this was a fantastic price. With this new wealth the plantation owner in the interior of the State built his pretentious house and he naturally wanted furniture in keeping with his home. The logical place to get his furniture was in Charleston, through his factor.

In 1800 approximately sixty-two cabinet-makers were working in Charleston. A decade later the number had risen to eighty-one. Since the population of the City itself had not increased in the same proportion during that decade a question at once presents itself: why this spectacular increase in the number of cabinet-makers? The answer is not hard to find. These additional cabinet-makers were needed to take care of the "country trade" in the interior and upper part of the State. Another significant fact is that the cabinet-makers during this period did comparatively little advertising, an indication that they were so busy filling orders that they did not find it necessary to advertise their wares. Furniture from Charleston was shipped in flat boats as far inland as navigation permitted and from there overland to the plantation. [7] This explains why so many pieces of fine mahogany furniture of this period have been found in the interior of the State.

With the advent of the steamboat in the second decade of the nineteenth century the cabinet-makers in the interior could compete with the Charleston cabinet-makers because by this new method of transportation they could bring in mahogany either in boards or in logs. [8] In this manner they may have been able to undersell Charleston-made furniture, although the freight on the mahogany came to between $15 and $30 per ton, which would have added considerably to the cost of the finished product. [9] And it must not be overlooked that green mahogany is extremely heavy, weighing about $2\frac{1}{4}$ tons per thousand feet. It is reasonable to assume that the

Charleston cabinet-maker, disliking this competition, would have done everything possible to see that a cabinet-maker from the interior would have had to pay full market price for any mahogany that he purchased.

Within the memory of man many fine mahogany sideboards have been found in the upper part of the State.[10] Many were of the Hepplewhite style, indicating that they were made in the last decade of the eighteenth and the early years of the nineteenth century, which was the apex in the number of the Charleston cabinet-makers, and prior to the era of the steamboat.

Plantation-Made Furniture

IN RECENT YEARS MUCH HAS BEEN SAID about plantation-made furniture. Undoubtedly, some furniture was actually made on the plantation but the preponderance of evidence leads us to believe that little fine furniture was made there. In the first place, the inventories of many of the leading planters fail to list any of their slaves as cabinet-makers. On the larger plantations it was customary to have one or more slaves who had been trained as carpenters; some are listed as coopers; still others as blacksmiths; but no mention of one trained as a cabinet-maker has yet appeared. It is a matter of record that Negroes were trained as cabinet-makers (see Negro Cabinet-Makers) but they usually were the property of one of the local white cabinet-makers.

Again, any one with a knowledge of how fine furniture is made and who has ever been in the shop of a cabinet-maker will realize that it not only requires a large number of planes, gauges, chisels, and saws but also workbenches, clamps, a "glew pot," and innumerable other articles. Even applying a piece of veneer requires not only a skilled hand but many tools. It would have been economically unsound to have maintained a trained cabinet-maker to have made a comparatively small amount of furniture. If a slave belonging to one of the planters had shown a special aptitude and had been especially trained in this field, he undoubtedly would have been "hired out" to one of the white cabinet-makers in Charleston, thereby bringing his master some revenue. The "hiring out" of slaves skilled in trades was an accepted practice.

Though it is true that mahogany could have been purchased from some broker and transported to the plantation, it would have had to be sawed, after its arrival, into boards and cut to dimensions and air-dried, for at least two years, thereby necessitating another operation that was commonplace to the local cabinet-maker. Finally, the persistent advertisements of the Charleston cabinet-makers stating that "Country trade would be punctually complied with" indicates that the planters were their patrons.

Plantation-made furniture is generally of a simple kind. Close examination reveals that it does not have the sophistication nor does it show the trained hand of a master craftsman. Usually it was constructed of one of the native woods growing in the immediate vicinity of the plantation.

Prices of Furniture

AT THIS DISTANCE IT IS NOT EASY TO CONvert into present-day values the price paid for furniture by our forefathers. Generally speaking the pre-Revolutionary pound in South Carolina, frequently spoken of as "current money," had a ratio of approximately 7 to 1 to the English pound. In other words, if a cabinet-maker was paid £70 local currency for an article of furniture he was receiving the equivalent of £10 Sterling. The pre-Revolutionary pound Sterling, based on $5.00 for easy computation (not the devaluated English pound of today) probably had a purchasing power at least ten times * greater than today's pound or dollar. Therefore an article purchased for £70 current money actually cost £10 English Sterling. Multiplying the £10 Sterling by ten (today's purchasing power) would give £100. This multiplied by $5.00 (the then value of the English pound) would give us $500. Fine furniture in the old days definitely was not cheap.

In 1766 Thomas Chippendale made for Sir Rowland Winn, Bart., a set of twelve parlor chairs "horse hair and double brass nailed" for £19-10-0.[1] In 1774 Thomas Elfe (q.v.) made for General William Moultrie a set of twelve chairs "cov'd with hair & brass nailed" at a cost of £170 current money.[2] Converting the current money into the £ Sterling at a ratio of 7 to 1, we find that Elfe was paid the equivalent of slightly over £24 Sterling for his set of chairs or approximately £5 more than Chippendale. Of course, there is no way of comparing the chairs but it is reasonable to suppose that the set of parlor chairs made by Chippendale for Sir Rowland Winn were of high quality. Elfe's finest chairs

brought as much as £230 current money a dozen, or approximately £33 Sterling.

As near as can be ascertained the appraised value of mid-eighteenth century furniture fairly well approximated its true value. In the inventory of Thomas Elfe a desk and bookcase is appraised at £130 current money. Elfe's charge for a desk and bookcase with glass doors amounted to £140. A double chest of drawers with a desk is appraised at £100. This was practically the same price Elfe received for a similar article of furniture.

Occasionally pieces of furniture at public sale (although there are few records) brought considerably more than their appraised value. For instance, a marble slab with brackets was appraised at £15 and brought £24; eight mahogany chairs appraised at £50 brought £88; and a harpsichord appraised at £100 brought £160.[3]

During the last decade of the eighteenth century and especially during its closing years ready money became scarce. Many of the local cabinet-makers advertised that they would take either cash or "country produce." More than likely at that time the country produce would have been rice, which was always a staple commodity.

The receipt book of James Jervey reveals that in 1809 he paid McIntosh and Foulds (q.v.) "$65 for pair of mahogany sofas." The present whereabouts of the sofas is not known; hence there is no way of knowing how elaborate they were. And in 1817 a Charleston factor wrote to one of his clients (a rice planter) as follows: "I have enquired the price of those painted Green and Gilded [chairs] next to Mr. Highams they ask 75 dollars for 12 Chairs that is 10 Common and 2 arm, there are some in Setts of 10 without Arm Chairs that come [to] about 56 dollars, if you want them I will purchase them for you."[4]

* This is a purely arbitrary figure. Mrs. Edwin Williams, Baker Library, Harvard University, in a letter dated April 13, 1953, writes: "There is no simple formula for comparing the purchasing power of money in the 18th century and today for the question is often asked, and a survey of the literature does not show that a solution to the problem has been worked out. There are so many variable factors in attempting to measure the purchasing power of the dollar and such wide variations in prices in different parts of the country that an accurate comparison would be difficult if not impossible."

G. E. Barrite, a local cabinet-maker, advertised on November 16, 1824, in the *Courier* that he had the following articles of furniture for sale: "LaFayette Bedsteads, the most elegant pattern offered in this city, prices $55 a 65; Bureaus $16 a 25; . . . Ladies Work Tables, large size $18 a 20. . . ."

Based on the purchasing power of a dollar in 1824 against that of today (1955), which would have been approximately 10 to 1, a Lafayette bed would have cost at today's prices between $550. and $650.

Dearth of Local Furniture

IF THERE WAS SO MUCH ACTIVITY ON THE part of the Charleston cabinet-makers and so large a demand for their work, why is there today such a dearth of early, locally-made furniture? The question is often asked, and it is a very reasonable one. The following considerations give the answer: conflagrations, acts of God, migration of families, wars, the normal wearing out of furniture, and the sale of furniture.

Conflagrations: From its earliest history Charleston has been afflicted not only by many fires but by many conflagrations. Maps of areas destroyed by these various conflagrations, placed as an overlay on a map of the older part of Charleston, give an appalling picture; it becomes immediately apparent that at one time or another almost every part of the old city has been burned away.

One of the conflagrations that most certainly accounts for our lack of furniture of the earlier style occurred in 1740. The fire destroyed over three hundred houses in the oldest and most populated section of the

city. It was of such magnitude and caused so much destruction that the British Parliament voted twenty thousand pounds Sterling for the relief of the sufferers.

In 1778 another conflagration occurred which burned more than two hundred fifty dwellings besides stores and outbuildings. Much of the area destroyed had suffered similarly from the fire of 1740. Again in 1796 another large portion of the town was laid in ruins. "Five hundred chimnies were counted from which the buildings had been burnt." In 1810 some two hundred houses were burned. St. Philip's Church and many other buildings were destroyed by fire in 1835. Three years later fire wiped out the northern part of the city. Several people were killed when buildings were blown up in the effort to arrest the progress of the flames. It is said that the fire did major damage to over one thousand buildings, and that the light of the flames was visible eighty miles away. The banner heading which appeared in the newspaper: "One third of Charleston in Ruins," was literally true.

In 1861 the worst fire of all struck the city. It started in the eastern part of the city and, fanned by a stiff northeasterly wind, swept across the entire city in a south-westerly direction, destroying everything in its way—fine residences, churches, and public buildings. When the fire eventually burned itself out nothing was left but a charred area of over five hundred forty acres.[1] The amount of fine furniture lost in this conflagration is incalculable.

Similar disasters occurred in the country. Plantation house after plantation house was burned, usually as the result of someone's carelessness, and it is not difficult to imagine what great quantities of furniture must have been destroyed in these handsome, almost palatial residences.

Fig. 3 DOUBLE CHEST OF DRAWERS
Height 6′¾″; width 42½″; depth 23″

Fig. 4 DOUBLE CHEST OF DRAWERS
Height 6′4½″; width 43¼″; depth 23½″

Fig. 5 DOUBLE CHEST OF
DRAWERS WITH DESK
Height 6'4"; width 42"; depth 23⅞"

Fig. 6 DOUBLE CHEST OF
DRAWERS WITH SLIDE
Height 6'1½"; width 42½"; depth 22⅝"

Fig. 7 CHEST OF DRAWERS
WITH QUARTER COLUMNS
Height 31″; width 38″; depth 22⅛″

Fig. 8 CHEST OF DRAWERS
Height 30¼″; width 36″; depth 19¼″

Fig. 9 BOW FRONT CHEST OF
DRAWERS WITH QUARTER COLUMNS
Height 37¼″; width 41½″;
depth—center 23″, end 19¼″

Fig. 10 CHEST OF DRAWERS
WITH SLIDE
Height 33″; width 30⅝″; depth 17⅞″

Fig. 11
SERPENTINE CHEST OF DRAWERS
Height 38″; width 41″; depth 22¹⁵⁄₁₆″

Fig. 12
SERPENTINE CHEST OF DRAWERS
Height 38″; width 42½″; depth 23¼″

Fig. 13
SERPENTINE CHEST OF DRAWERS
Height 34½″; width 42⅞″; depth 23¾″

Fig. 14
DETAIL OF CHEST OF DRAWERS
(see Fig. 13)

Fig. 15
CLOTHESPRESS OR WARDROBE
Height 7'11"; width 48"; depth 24"

Fig. 16 SECRETARY-WARDROBE
Height 8'4"; width 46½"; depth 22⅝"

Fig. 17 BED Height 7′8¾″; width 49¼″; length 6′7″

Fire, then, has in all probability been the greatest destroyer of Charleston furniture.

Acts of God: After so many conflagrations one would think that Charleston had suffered its full share of catastrophes but there have been other disasters of almost equally devastating effect. From the earliest days hurricanes have visited the city with monotonous regularity, with an occasional tornado by way of variety. Some of these hurricanes and tornadoes have been of extreme severity, causing great damage not only to shipping but to houses as well. There is hardly an old house still standing that has not been unroofed at one time or another. The storms were almost always accompanied by torrential rains which caused inestimable ruin to the interior of the roofless building and to the fine furniture which it contained. In the early part of the nineteenth century a small tornado unroofed one of the largest and most pretentious houses in the city, causing over twenty thousand dollars' damage to the furniture and furnishings.[2] Even by today's scale of values, an enormous amount of handsome furniture must have been badly damaged if not totally destroyed.

Charleston was struck by a severe earthquake in 1886. The walls of almost every brick house in the city antedating that disaster are held together by earthquake rods and giant washers—visible evidence of the terrible force which wrecked and weakened the strongest buildings. Many houses and their furnishings were completely destroyed. In the lower section of the city stand some relatively modern houses which are referred to by the older inhabitants as "earthquake houses," signifying that they are built on the site of buildings that had been destroyed by the earthquake.

Finally Charleston's climate must be regarded as a potent if unspectacular force in the deterioration and ultimate destruction of furniture. Charleston stands on ground only a few feet above sea-level. Summer brings to the city a hot, humid, semitropical atmosphere which is ruinous to fine inlays and veneers, which can be preserved only by constant vigilance on the part of the owner.

Migration of Families: Charleston has possibly been less affected than most cities by the migration of families. Even so, throughout the history of the city, many young Charlestonians have moved to other parts of the country in search of greater opportunities for making a living. Consequently, over a period of years a great deal of Charleston made furniture has migrated to other parts of the country. There is a specific record, within the memory of the older inhabitants, of a will which provides that the furniture of one of the loveliest houses in the city must be distributed to the various heirs, wherever they might be. Some of it went to New Haven, Connecticut, some to San Francisco and Chicago, and some to Mobile. Charleston-made furniture should be looked for, and will probably be found, in every part of these United States.

Wars: Charleston has suffered the indignity of being occupied by two invading armies, the first time when the city was captured by the British in 1780, and the second when the Federal troops occupied it in 1865.

The British, when they evacuated the city in 1782, carried away with them innumerable slaves, the bells of St. Michael's Church, and quantities of silver. They probably did not take much furniture because it was too bulky, but they destroyed great quantities wantonly. The British soldier was adept at looting and he was especially violent in his attack upon any residence or plantation that belonged to a patriot.

During the War Between the States Charleston was subjected for many months to long-range bombardment from the Federal guns on Morris Island, a distance of about three and a half miles. The shells were fired indiscriminately into the city and caused a great deal of damage. Many houses were completely destroyed. The fire from the guns was so severe that the entire population living in the eastern part of the city had to be evacuated. And it is painful to think of the loss incurred by the wanton destruction of many plantation houses that were put to the torch by the troops of General Sherman.

The Normal Wearing Out of Furniture: Few pieces of Charleston-made furniture now exist that do not give evidence of having been repaired. It is usually the foot of the piece that has been damaged, the result of careless efforts to push or pull it to a new position in the room. Josiah Claypool (*q.v.*) as early as 1740, says that he "will warrant his work for 7 years, the ill usage of careless Servants only excepted." [3]

Opulent Charlestonians probably gave little thought to the repairing of furniture. When a piece was broken or damaged, the owner simply discarded it and bought something of a newer fashion to take its place.

Sale of Furniture: It has been written of Maryland furniture: "Much of our best old furniture has left the State permanently." [4] The same thing is true of furniture made in Charleston. For many years the average

Charlestonian took his antique furniture for granted. It had been there as long as he could remember and he didn't give it too much thought. But in time discriminating collectors and dealers discovered it, purchased it at bargain prices, and shipped it out of the State. Many families sold their antiques because they were in financial difficulties; others, because they had no particular interest in antiques and were glad to convert them into cash when high prices were offered. It is only in comparatively recent years that Charlestonians have awakened to the value of their antique furniture. During the past fifty years all of South Carolina has been periodically and systematically combed for antiques by dealers and collectors. The fact is lamentable but it is not reasonable to deplore it. Certainly the antique dealer is in a perfectly legitimate business. The only way in which he can keep up his stock is to visit various parts of the country for new material. And if he can buy antique furniture at bargain prices so much the better for him. And if the owner wishes to dispose of his furniture because of monetary need or because he prefers the cash, that is his own affair, however regrettable it may seem.

In view of the foregoing considerations one begins to wonder whether there is *any* Charleston-made furniture still in existence. As a matter of fact, Charleston still has some of its early furniture and there is certainly much of it scattered throughout the country. Whatever the amount still in existence it must be only a small fraction of that produced by the early Charleston cabinet-makers; and in comparison with extant furniture produced during the same period by other cities, comparatively few pieces of Charleston-made furniture have survived.

Conclusion

NO HISTORY OF CHARLESTON FURNITURE and furniture making can be regarded as definitive until all the surviving pieces have been located, identified, and completely described. In the face of so tremendous a task, the present work can be presented only as a beginning. Its purpose is to open the subject, not to close it. If the book in any degree stimulates interest in early Charleston furniture, or encourages present owners of antique furniture to examine their pieces more carefully for the sake of identifying them, or leads to the discovery of pieces which have been overlooked or under-valued—if it accomplishes any of these things—the labor that has gone into the preparation of the book will have been fully justified.

The study is limited to the cabinet-makers who produced furniture in Charleston from the end of the seventeenth century through the first quarter of the nineteenth century. The period actually covered is about one hundred twenty-five years—from the first joiner who made furniture [James Beamer, working 1687] to about 1825. The latter date is a natural stopping point, for it marks the end of an era. Thereafter furniture lost much of its eighteenth century delicacy and became heavy and cumbersome.

Yet it was during the first twenty-five years of the nineteenth century that the work of the Charleston cabinet-makers reached its peak. In 1810 there were about eighty cabinet-makers in the city. The number dropped to fifty by 1820 but rose to sixty by 1826, in spite of the fact that the years between 1810 and 1820 brought an increase in the amount of furniture imported to Charleston. It is not without significance also that in 1820 a mahogany saw-mill was established in Charleston. So large a volume of business reflects, of course, the general increase of wealth in the city and the surrounding areas in the years following the Revolution. Fine new houses were going up both in Charleston and on the plantations; they needed furniture to fill them; the owners were in a position to pay for good workmanship; and a relatively large number of cabinet-makers arose to supply the demand.

The present work has made use of many primary sources of information. Wills, newspaper advertisements, city directories, obituaries, deeds, and inventories have been searched diligently for names and dates. Not fewer than 1400 inventories have been studied, and the information they supplied has, after classification and comparison, yielded valuable data concerning trends in design and changes of fashion.

It may sometimes appear that undue emphasis has been placed on the account book of Thomas Elfe (1768–1775). It should be remembered, however, that the Elfe account book is one of the few such documents in existence. It is, in fact, something more than a record of accounts. It provides detailed descriptions of the kinds of furniture Elfe produced and the prices he charged; it shows the kinds of woods he purchased for his shop; it contains the inventories which he took; and it gives a list of his customers. From one point of view it is a unique picture of life and customs in Charleston during the last half of the eighteenth century.

Part 2: WOODS

In order to have a thorough understanding of antique furniture and fully to appreciate it, it is necessary to have a knowledge of the woods from which it is made.

Woods

FROM THE TIME OF THE FOUNDING OF THE Colony, the Lords Proprietors were interested in its natural resources. On May 23, 1674, they instructed Andrew Percivall, their representative, as follows: "You are to send . . . word what Trees fit for masts and to what bignesse and length you have any there and at what Distance from Water carriage and to send me Samples of the timber of your Mast Trees, and of any Dying Drugs or any sorte of Tymber or Wood that is finely grained or sented that you thinke may be fit for Cabinets and such other fine Workes." ¹ That there were many useful trees in Carolina is a matter of record. In 1682 T. A. [Thomas Ashe?] *"Clerk on Board his Majesties Ship the Richmond,* which was sent out in the year 1680, with particular Instructions to enquire into the State of that Country [Carolina] by his Majesties Special Command . . ." made the following report about its trees: "It's cloathd with odoriferous and fragrant Woods, flourishing in perpetual and constant Verdures, viz. the lofty Pine, the sweet smelling Cedar and Cyprus Trees, of both which are composed goodly Boxes, Chests, Tables, Scrittores, and Cabinets. . . . Wallnut Trees there are of two or three sorts: but the Black Wallnut for its Grain, is most esteem'd." ² The early colonists quickly found out the excellent properties of the local woods and used local woods in making their furniture.

In order to have a thorough understanding of antique furniture and fully to appreciate it, it is necessary to have a knowledge of the woods from which it is made. In this country the primary woods used were mahogany, walnut, maple, and cherry. Their use was determined to a large extent on the availability of the wood needed to make a piece of furniture. This was equally true of the secondary woods used in its construction. Overland transportation in the eighteenth and early nineteenth centuries was slow and laborious. On land the usual method was by cart. Only a few logs, even if squared, could be loaded upon a single cart and at best the cart was capable of traveling only a few miles a day. Even at low wages the cost of transportation must have been considerable. Therefore, the cabinet-maker used the wood that grew nearest to him and was most suited to his needs.

Due to Charleston's proximity to the West Indies, mahogany soon became the predominant wood used by the local cabinet-maker. In 1740 mahogany was being brought into the port of Charleston in such quantities that the duty on it was repealed. At that time the Commons House of Assembly stated that "it was not the Intention of this House to lay a Duty on Mahogany Plank . . . And that the Public Treasurer of the Province do not demand or take any Duty for the same." ³ The duty had been £20 per £100 value. It was cheaper to transport a mahogany log by water from some island in the West Indies than it was to haul a log of some native wood a few miles by cart.

One of the things strikingly revealed by the inventories is the amount of mahogany furniture owned by people of moderate means. It was definitely *not* a rich man's luxury. The inventory of a man who was a bricklayer, for example, reveals that he owned many pieces of mahogany.⁴

West Indian or St. Domingo Mahogany
(*Swietenia mahagoni*)

IT IS NOT KNOWN WHEN THE FIRST MA-
hogany was brought into Charleston from
the West Indies. As early as 1725, however,
mahogany was being transhipped to England.[1] It must have been known, of course,
to the local cabinet-makers, though at that
time they were using the native woods. After
so long a time there is no way of accurately
telling when the wood became fashionable.
It is to be noted that in 1732, Broomhead
and Blythe (*q.v.*) advertised: "Cabinet
Work, chests of Drawers, and Mahogany
Tables and Chairs made after the best manner; . . . Where all sorts of bespoke Work
is made . . . at the lowest price. . . ."[2]
There seems to be nothing unusual in this
advertisement. However, whether mahogany was in general use before this date
cannot be determined from advertisements
since the *South Carolina Gazette*, the only
medium of advertisement, was not founded
until 1732.

In an inventory dated April 21, 1724, is
listed a mahogany table valued at £11.[3]
This appears to be the first mention of any
piece of mahogany furniture, though it
must not be forgotten that inventories usually show a time lag of several years. From
1724 until about 1740 mahogany appears
sporadically in the inventories, but after
that time it became commonplace. And by
1750 the wood had become so common in
Charleston that it was listed in the newspaper along with the other commodities
such as rice, indigo, and naval stores. In
1749 the price quoted was 27s. 10d. per
hundred; in March of the following year
the price had dropped to 12s. 10d. per hundred,[4] a clear indication that a large amount
was being brought into the port. In 1786

the Charleston cabinet-makers were making
so many beds that mahogany was being
imported in "Bed Post" size.[5] It is frequently spoken of as Jamaican Mahogany
or occasionally as Hispaniola Mahogany.

Along with the change of style and with
the revival of the use of crotched woods,[6]
we find the following advertisement in one
of the local newspapers for March 27, 1819:
"for Sale—A cargo consisting of Prime St.
Domingo Mahogany. All Branch Wood.
The whole selected by a judge in St.
Domingo, and is considered superior to any
cargo imported into this port for many
years past."[7] The local cabinet-makers were
keeping abreast of the times. Much Charleston-made furniture has superbly matched
mahogany veneer.

There was such a demand for mahogany
among not only the local but the Southern
cabinet-makers that a mahogany sawmill
was established in Charleston in 1820. The
notice of its operation appeared on March
17, 1820, in the *City Gazette and Commercial Daily Advertiser:*

"TO CABINET MAKERS. The subscribers have the satisfaction to inform
all persons engaged in the above line,
that they have just put into operation,
in the City of Charleston, their SAW
MILL, (the only one at present in the
Southern States) erected for the sole
purpose of Sawing Mahogany into
Veneering, &c.

From the sample produced of its
cutting, and inspection of the Machin-
ery, it has been pronounced by the
most competent judges, to be equal to
any in the Northern States.

They now offer to supply such persons as may favor them with their custom, with any quantity and quality of
Mahogany Boards or Veneering,
agreeable to order and at the shortest
notice.

Having supplied themselves with a
large and choice assortment of the

above Wood, they will be able to supply their customers on as low, and perhaps lower terms than they ever had before.

All orders from abroad, directed to the Subscribers, post paid, and with due reference to some person in this place, will meet with the strictest attention by John Egleston and B. S. Ridgeway.

The Editors of the following papers, will publish the foregoing advertisement once a week for three months, and forward their bills to this Office—viz: Intelligencer, Petersburg, Virginia; Cape Fear Recorder, Wilmington, N. C.; Centinel, Newbern, N. C.; Observer, Fayettesville, N. C.; Register, Raleigh, N. C.; Chronicle and Herald, Augusta, Geo.; Republican, Museum, and Georgian, Savannah, Geo."

One very significant thing can be deduced from the request that certain Editors carry this advertisement in their respective newspapers: furniture in appreciable quantities was being made throughout the South at that time.

Honduras Mahogany
(Swietenia macrophylla)

HONDURAS MAHOGANY, A NEAR RELATIVE of the West Indian Mahogany, was brought into Charleston at what is thought to be a later date. Charleston had established trade relations with the Honduras coast as early as 1740,[1] but because the West Indian species was nearer and more abundant, it may be supposed that Honduras mahogany found little market in Charleston until the West Indian mahogany became more scarce. In the 1760's it became firmly established although it never commanded as high a price as the West Indian species. In the newspaper listings, Jamaica Mahogany (as

it was then called) was always quoted at a higher figure. Thus we find:

Jamaica Mahogany   5d 6d. per foot
Honduras Mahogany 4d. 5d. per foot [2]

The old newspaper files contain large numbers of advertisements stating that one of the local brokers has just received a shipment of St. Domingo or Honduras Mahogany, sometimes as much as a schooner load of logs at a time.[3]

The difference between the two species of mahogany is probably best told in Thomas Sheraton's own words. In 1803 he wrote:

"Hispaniola or Santo Domingo produces mahogany not much in use with us. From [Honduras] is imported the principal kind of mahogany in use amongst cabinet-makers, which generally bears the name of Honduras mahogany, and sometimes Baywood from the bay or arm of the sea which runs up to it. The grain of Honduras wood is of a different quality from that of Cuba, which is close and hard, without black speckles, and of a rosy hue, and sometimes strongly figured; but Honduras wood is of an open nature, with black or grey spots, and frequently of a more flashy figure than Spanish. The best quality of Honduras wood is known by its being free from chalky and black speckles, and when the colour is inclined to a dark gold hue. The common sort of it looks brisk at a distance, and of a lively pale red; but on close inspection is of an open and close grain, and of a spongy appearance." [4]

Southern Red Cedar
(Juniperus silicicola) [1]

FROM THE TIME OF THE SETTLEMENT OF Charleston until mahogany became commonplace, cedar was the dominant wood used in furniture. It was readily available, for it grows abundantly along the Carolina littoral; it is immune to worms, it keeps out vermin, and it is workable. In 1700 Lawson wrote: "Of this wood [cedar] Tables, Wainscots, and other necessaries are made, and esteemed for its sweet smell." [2]

The inventories of the end of the seventeenth century reveal that cedar was used not only for tables but for armchairs as well. Later on one finds records of a great number of cedar clothespresses, cedar chests of drawers, sideboards, writing desks, couches, dressing tables, scrutores and, occasionally a cedar bedstead. In fact, articles of cedar furniture are listed as late as the early part of the nineteenth century. But by the middle of the eighteenth century, if one is to judge by the inventories, the amount used had appreciably declined, cedar having been supplanted by mahogany.

Cedar was also used by the Charleston cabinet-makers as a secondary wood, that is, for drawer linings, etc., though this was not confined to the local artisans, cabinet-makers in the other colonies having been quick to see its advantages.

Cedar must have been held in high esteem in the early days. In 1722 we find the following items listed in the same inventory: [3]

1 large oval Cedar Table	£8-0-0
1 Walnut oval Table	4-0-0
1 small oval cedar Table	4-0-0

Again in 1733 we find: [4]

1 Cedar oval Table	10-0-0
1 Mahogany ditto	7-0-0

One of the most noticeable things in the early inventories is the large number of oval cedar tables, presumably of the gate-legged variety.

With one exception none of this early cedar furniture appears to have survived.

Walnut
(Juglans nigra)

WALNUT IS INDIGENOUS TO SOUTH CAROlina. It is not common in the coastal region, but it increases in abundance, size, and quality as one nears the foot-hills. This is the same species of walnut that is found in the northern part of America. It was never used to any great extent by the local cabinet-makers. Undoubtedly Elliott gives the correct explanation for the fact when he says in his Botany: ". . . were it not for the facility with which Mahogany is obtained, it [walnut] would form a great portion of the furniture of our houses." [1] It was infinitely cheaper to bring in shiploads of mahogany than to haul walnut in by cart from the foothills.

What is thought to be the first record of walnut furniture in Charleston is a black walnut chest of drawers, appraised at £10 and listed in an inventory dated 1722.[2] One gets the very definite impression from the later inventories that individual owners seldom possessed more than one or two large pieces of furniture in walnut, though walnut chairs were fairly common. The heavier pieces were "bureaus," settees, tables, chests of drawers, desk and bookcases, bedsteads, and clothespresses. Walnut occurs in the inventories well into the early part of the nineteenth century. Frequently it is called "Virginia Walnut," probably to differentiate it from its close relatives, the hickories.

The earliest records reveal that walnut

apparently had a higher value than the other woods with the possible exception of cedar. An instance occurs in an inventory dated 1735: [3]

1 large Mahogany oval Table £15-0-0
1 large Walnut ditto   25-0-0

After that date mahogany predominates.

Strangely enough, in spite of its comparative scarcity along the coast of South Carolina, walnut was exported to England from Charleston.[4]

Cypress
(Taxodium distichum)

THE EXCELLENT PROPERTIES OF CYPRESS, the "wood eternal," were well known to the early colonists, who used it for many purposes among which was that of furniture, but not to the same extent as cedar. It was used for bedsteads, presses, cupboards, desks, tables (both square and oval), bookcases, and even buffets, but at no time did cypress ever command the same price as cedar. It appears in inventories throughout the eighteenth century.

Because of its excellent properties and availability—cypress grows in the immediate vicinity of Charleston—cypress was used by the local cabinet-makers as a secondary wood, chiefly for the sides and bottoms of drawers. Thomas Elfe (q.v.) continually purchased cypress, at one time in the amount of 8870 feet. At another time he specified that it must be ¼ inch in thickness, which is the thickness of the cypress frequently found in the drawer bottoms of pieces attributed to him.[1] Cypress is mentioned in the inventories of Josiah Murphy (q.v.) and of Thomas Lining (q.v.), so undoubtedly it was very generally used as a secondary wood in the eighteenth and

early nineteenth centuries by the local cabinet-makers. D. J. Browne in *The Sylva America* (1832) states that "cabinet-makers also choose it for the inside of mahogany furniture."[2] One cabinet-maker, William Luyten (q.v.), knowing the indestructibility of cypress, used a cypress bedstead in place of a tombstone on his wife's grave, which can be seen to this day in St. Michael's churchyard.

Red Bay
(Persea borbonia)

RED BAY, AN INTERESTING BUT VERY little known wood, was used by the eighteenth century cabinet-makers of Charleston. The wood takes on a lovely polish, and has beautiful wood rays. Mark Catesby in his *Natural History of Carolina* (1732) writes that "The Wood is fine grain'd, and of excellent use for cabinets etc."[1] The inventory of William Hammet, a local chairmaker, made on January 8, 1738, shows that he had about 150 feet of Red Bay valued at £7. Its use was probably limited because of the fact that trees of sufficient size for furniture-making were rare. And in 1819 Andrew Michaux in his *Sylva of North America*[2] remarks that although red bay is used by cabinet-makers one must go to the uninhabited portions of Georgia and Florida to find large trees, a clear indication that by that time the large trees in the vicinity of Charleston had already been cut. The general range of the red bay is in the coastal region extending as far north as Southeastern Virginia. Small specimens are common throughout the littoral.

Red bay seems to have been used principally for tables, though occasionally there is mention of a desk or bedstead. At no time does it appear to be common. Judging from inventory values, it compared favorably with mahogany in the eyes of the Charlestonians.[3]

If a red bay piece of furniture ever comes to light and can be recognized as red bay, there is an excellent probability that it is of local origin.

Poplar
(Liriodendron tulipifera)

IT SEEMS STRANGE THAT CHARLESTONIANS should not have discovered the use of poplar before the time of Thomas Elfe (1747–1775). The inventories prove conclusively that very little poplar was used for furniture in the early days. Elfe seems to have employed it for bedsteads, of which he made fifty-five during an eight year period (1768–1775). In addition, his account book reveals that he made frequent purchases of "poplar Plank." The inventory of Robert Liston (q.v.) shows that he had "a parcel of Poplar Plank" valued at £5. It appears to have been used for the most part as a secondary wood in the last decade of the eighteenth and the first quarter of the nineteenth century.

Long-leaf Pine
(Pinus palustris)

IN THE EARLY DAYS LONG-LEAF PINE WAS the most used of the several pines that grow in the vicinity of Charleston, though not to any great extent for furniture. From time to time inventories make mention of a pine table or a pine bedstead. Long-leaf pine

was most certainly used as a secondary wood and is frequently found in sideboards as well as in other pieces of furniture. Any piece of furniture containing long-leaf pine as a secondary wood is probably of Southern origin, for this species of pine does not grow farther North than the area of Norfolk, Virginia.

White Pine
(Pinus Strobus)

WHITE PINE, ALTHOUGH NOT INDIGENOUS to South Carolina, was an important factor in Charleston-made furniture. If one is to judge from the newspaper advertisements, great quantities of white pine were shipped to the port of Charleston after the Revolution. In fact, white pine became so common that in 1788 it was quoted in the newspapers along with other commodities, the quotation price at that time being 6 shillings per 100 feet.[1] Some of the pine came from Philadelphia.[2] Often it is spoken of merely as "Northern Pine Boards,"[3] or "Albany Pine." Occasionally a sloop from Maine or New Hampshire came in loaded with lumber and spars of white pine.[4]

The reason for these large importations of white pine was the fact that the post-Revolutionary houses in Charleston contained many more mouldings than did the pre-Revolutionary ones. The house-joiner and carpenter quickly learned the superiority of white pine over cypress for the carving of mouldings. Cypress usually leaves a slightly fuzzy edge, but white pine is clean cut and very easily worked.

Misapprehension concerning these facts has led to certain errors in the identification of Charleston-made furniture. Until recently any piece of furniture found locally containing white pine was summarily judged to be of Northern origin. This is no longer true. A secretary made for James Jervey by James Hefferman, a local cabinet-maker, is owned by his descendants. They still retain the receipt from Hefferman which is dated May 9, 1809. The secondary wood used in the construction of the secretary is white pine. There is also in existence a satinwood secretary which bears the label of R. Walker, 53 Church St., Charleston, S.C. Walker, a Scotsman, was working in Charleston by 1799. He too used white pine for the bottoms of the larger drawers that are in the secretary. William W. Purse, another local cabinet-maker, made a bookcase for James Jervey. It is owned by one of his descendants who also retains the receipt. It is signed by Purse and dated November 8, 1822. White pine is used as a secondary wood in its construction. In still another piece, a lovely serpentine chest of drawers, the drawer sides are of long-leaf pine, and the bottoms are made out of magnificent heart cypress, clear proof of local manufacture. Nevertheless, the dustboards which extend to the rear are made out of white pine. Another case in point is provided by the secondary woods used in the construction of a large secretary-wardrobe. The bottom, sides, and backs of the large drawers as well as the bottoms of the sliding shelves are made of cypress. The dustboards, the entire rectangular top supporting the pediment, and a three-inch vertical supporting strip for the back are made out of white pine. Roughly, the secondary wood used in this piece consists of about 60% cypress and 40% white pine.

Such examples make it clear that the late eighteenth and early nineteenth century Charleston cabinet-makers commonly used white pine as a secondary wood.

Since an appreciable amount of furniture in Charleston contains white pine as a secondary wood, under no circumstances should any piece of furniture that has white pine used in its construction be dismissed as an importation until it has been thoroughly examined. Single pieces of Charleston-made furniture are in existence that have as many as four secondary woods—cypress, poplar, white pine, and ash.

Southern Red Maple
(*Acer rubrum*)

WHAT IS THOUGHT TO BE THE FIRST MENtion of maple appears in an inventory made in 1733, when 6 maple mated (*sic*) chairs were appraised at £6 and 6 Maple Cain Chairs were valued at £10.[1] From then on only an occasional piece of maple furniture is listed, clearly indicating that maple was not used to any extent in furniture-making in Charleston. It is quite possible that the pieces so rarely listed were importations from New England. Occasionally, maple was used as a secondary wood.

The Southern red maple, which grows abundantly along the coast, is a much softer wood and should not be confused with the hard maples of the Northern states.

White Oak
(*Quercus alba*)

WHITE OAK, WHICH IS COMMON IN THE vicinity of Charleston, was little used by the local makers of furniture. Rarely is a piece of oak furniture listed in the early inventories. It was probably used to some extent, however, as a secondary wood. There are in existence certain pieces of furniture, apparently of Charleston manufacture, that have oak as their secondary wood. No doubt white oak was used by some of the London-trained cabinet-makers who later worked in Charleston. During their apprenticeship they had used oak and when they found a very similar wood in Carolina they continued using it. It was also used as a secondary wood by the Baltimore cabinet-makers.[1] Recently a letter has been received from the United States Forest Laboratory at Madison, Wisconsin, stating that they know of no way of telling the English oak from its American cousin.[2]

Satinwood
(*Zanthoxylum flavum*)

APART FROM INLAY, SATINWOOD DOES NOT appear to have been generally used by the eighteenth century Charleston cabinet-makers. This is not true for the nineteenth century. Robert Walker, a local craftsman, advertised in the *City Gazette* on January 31, 1810, that he had for sale some "Mahogany Boards, Plank Veneers, Sattin Wood, Holly . . ." also the "best Dublin Glue." Because of Charleston's proximity to the West Indies, the satinwood probably was the variety that grows there and therefore was easily imported. Walker appears to have been one of the few who used satinwood as a primary wood although time may reveal that other local craftsmen used it in a similar manner.

Other Woods

HICKORY (*Hicoria* SP.): SEVERAL species of hickory indigenous to coastal Carolina were used occasionally for chairs.

SWEET GUM (*Liquidamber styraciflua*): As early as 1700 Lawson wrote of the sweet gum treet: "No wood has scarce a better grain; whereof fine Tables, Drawers, and other Furniture might be made. Some of it curiously curled."[1] Apparently the early colonists did not use this wood; in over fourteen hundred inventories gum furniture is mentioned only twice. Once in 1752 a large oval gum table is appraised at £8 and in the following year another is listed.[2] It does not appear that the local cabinet-makers ever used gum as a secondary wood, although it is extremely abundant in the Charleston area. Unless properly dried, sweet gum has a tendency to warp and for that reason does not recommend itself for furniture making or fine cabinet work.

WHITE ASH (*Fraxinus americana*): Ash is rarely mentioned as being used for furniture, and then only for bedsteads; but it was frequently used as a secondary wood, especially in the gates of Pembroke tables. Occasionally the inventories of cabinet-makers list it; for example, the account book of Thomas Elfe (*q.v.*) reveals that he frequently purchased ash planks.[1] Ash can easily be confused with oak but, unlike oak, it has no wood ray.*

PALMETTO (*Sabal Palmetto*): The very early inventories frequently mention Palmetto chairs or Palmetto-bottom chairs. On the face of it this is puzzling, but the

---

* The woods of the oaks feature prominent ribbons of tissue, which, on the cross sections of logs, appear to radiate outward from the center of the log to the bark. These ribbons are known as wood rays and serve as storage tissues in the living stem. On the faces of flat sawn boards the ends of the rays appear as long, spindle-shaped bodies often ½" to 3" high along the grain. On the quarter, they appear as splashes or spangles and lend to the attractiveness of the figure. Rift cut or quarter-sawn oak is a term applied to lumber sawn at an angle of 45° to these rays and results in an unusual figure which is largely traceable to the ray tissue.

inventories seem to mean that the seats were woven out of palmetto leaves which, when properly braided, make a very strong material, while the chair frames were made out of one of the local woods.

MULBERRY (*Morus* sp.): Mulberry was sometimes used for tables in the first half of the eighteenth century.[1]

HOLLY (*Ilex opaca*): John Drayton (c. 1807) says that the wood of the holly "is very white; as such used by Cabinet Makers, for inlaying Mahogany."[1]

Fig. 18 *Fig. 19* *Fig. 20* *Fig. 21*

DETAILS OF BEDPOSTS

Fig. 22   *Fig. 23*   *Fig. 24*   *Fig. 25*

DETAILS OF BEDPOSTS

Fig. 27 DETAILS OF TOP
OF BEDPOST (see Fig. 17)

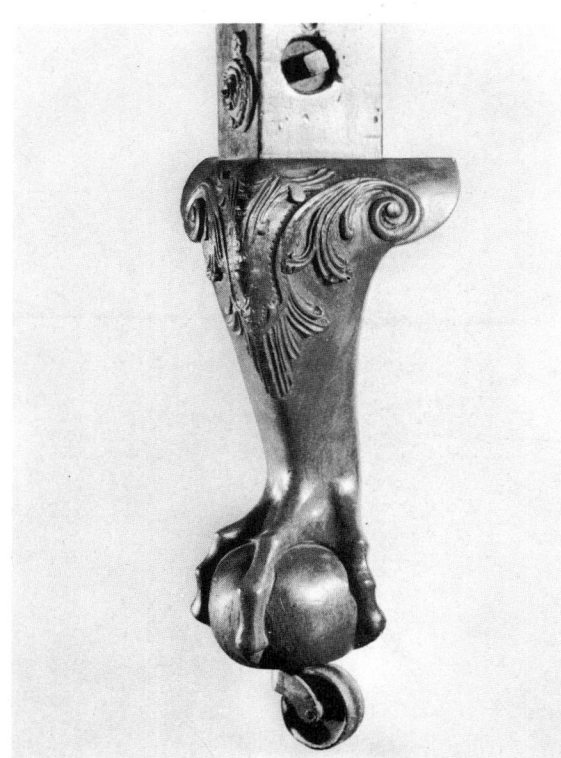

Fig. 28 FOOT OF BEDPOST (see Fig. 17)

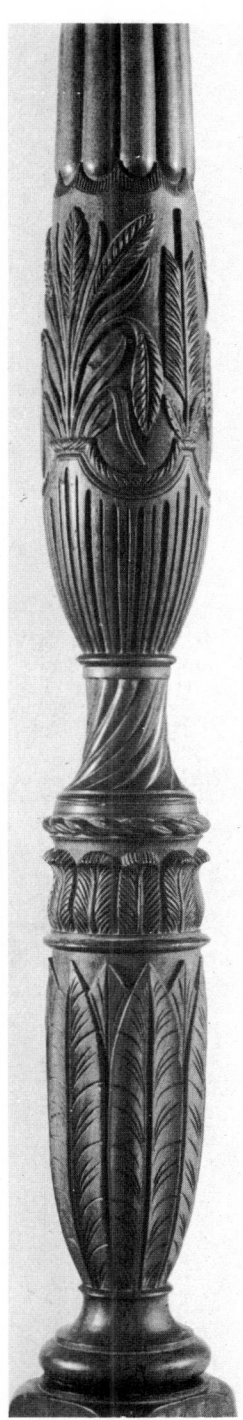

Fig. 29 DETAILS
OF BEDPOST

Fig. 26 DETAILS OF BEDPOST

Fig. 30 DESK AND BOOKCASE
Height 7′6½″; width 39¼″; depth 22½″

Fig. 31 DESK AND BOOKCASE
Height 7′6½″; width 39″; depth 23½″

Fig. 32 DESK AND BOOKCASE
WITH GLASS [MIRROR] DOORS
Height 7'10¾"; width 40¼"; depth 22½"

Fig. 33 DESK AND BOOKCASE
Height 8'5"; width 44"; depth 23⅜"

Fig. 34 SECRETARY AND BOOKCASE
Height 8'5½"; width 48¼"; depth 22½"

Fig. 35 SECRETARY AND BOOKCASE
Height 8'9½"; width 47¾"; depth 24¼"

Part 3: CHARLESTON-MADE FURNITURE

Beds

THE EARLY INVENTORIES DO NOT, UNFOR-tunately, give any clear indication of the kinds of woods used in beds of the late seventeenth and early eighteenth centuries. In all probability both cedar and cypress were used. Beds are commonly spoken of as a "bed and furniture" or as a "feather bed and furniture" or occasionaly as a "standing bedstead." In the last decade of the seventeenth century there is frequent mention of cabin beds. The middle of the eighteenth century brought in field bed-steads and camp bedsteads. By that time also the mahogany bedstead was common.

In spite of the amount of material used in beds for the pavilion, curtains, valances, and testers, there must have been a con-siderable difference in the value of the beds themselves; the point is illustrated in an inventory dated January 26, 1725: [1]

> One bed and furniture in lower room £50.
> One bed and furniture in an upper room £100.
> One bed and furniture in another upper room £60.
> One bed and furniture in another upper room £40.

In 1745 the estate of James Mathews listed "one Blue Chintz bed and furniture with pavilion" appraised at £200. John Mc-Kenzie (1771) had a "Mahogany Bedstead with Bedding, Curtains & complete" valued at £600—a remarkable price even if it was in local currency. Thomas Elfe (*q.v.*) at that time (1768–1775) was charging only £50 for his finest mahogany bedsteads with carved knees and ball and claw feet.

Though mahogany appears to have been the wood generally used, the inventories reveal that other woods were also used for bedsteads. Very occasionally an ash bed-stead is listed; and from time to time one encounters the mention of a pine bedstead, usually in the inventory of a person of very small means. Only once is an oak bed-stead listed. [2] Cedar and cypress bedsteads persisted until the end of the eighteenth century. But mahogany bedsteads were the kinds most common by 1750, even in the homes of people of moderate means.

A noteworthy exception to the popu-larity of the mahogany bedstead appears in the number of poplar bedsteads produced by Thomas Elfe during his working period in Charleston (1747–1775). His account book (1768–1775) shows that during that time he made fifty-five poplar bedsteads. Sometimes he made one with poplar head-posts and mahogany footposts.

Only one of these earlier beds has come to our attention. It is now in the Heyward-Washington House, a branch of the Charleston Museum, and is attributed to Elfe. The posts are of mahogany, the rails of poplar. The footposts have claw and ball feet with carved knees, the headposts are plain with a stump foot, and the head-board is movable. The rails have knobs to which ropes were originally attached to support the sacking upon which the bed-ding rested (Fig. 17). The other beds pro-duced in Charleston are either late eight-eenth century or early nineteenth century. These beds are generally distinguished by their large size, in width, overall height, and height of rail. An exception appears in an inventory made on April 2, 1795, which lists "5 Small Mahogany Bedsteads." [3] Be-fore antiques came to be fully appreciated, many of these large beds had the bottom of their posts cut off in order to lower them so that the owners would not need steps to get into bed or bruise various parts of their anatomy if they fell out. Most have mahogany rails with a small beading on the upper and outside edge.

The headboard, which was usually made of one of the less valuable woods, was movable. It was held in place by two strips attached to each headpost, usually of the same kind of wood, and was easily removed. Presumably the purpose of removing the headboard was to get a freer circulation of air. It is not to be inferred, however, that all Charleston-made beds have movable headboards. Many that are thought to be of local origin have the customary tenoned headboard. What appears to be another Charleston innovation, due again to climatic conditions, was the method used to support the bedding [mattress]. Slats approximately five inches wide, laid from side to side at intervals of about five inches, were used to support the bedding instead of the customary rope or canvas sacking. Travelers from other parts of the country noted this fact. Ebenezer Kellog, a New England school teacher who visited Charleston, commented on the hardness of the beds and said that the use of slats "is the common way of fitting bedsteads here." Sheraton in his *Dictionary* [1803] advocated the use of laths for this purpose but the Charleston cabinet-makers had adopted this method prior to this time. There is evidence that this type of construction spread from Charleston northward at least as far as Philadelphia.

Other characteristics of the Charleston bed of this period are mahogany headposts which are usually plain; the carved rope motif on the footposts; the double-leaf carving on the top to compensate for its height, each reed ending in a half-circle with incised lines below on a splayed surface (Fig. 142); and finally the unusually heavy spike, presumably to take care of the wooden cornice.

Many of these characteristics, of course, may be found on beds made in other parts of the country, but when several occur in one bed there is an excellent chance that it is of Charleston origin.

Tester-tops (or cornices, as we now know them) were probably first used before the middle of the eighteenth century when mahogany beds became established. If Elfe's account book can be taken as good evidence, tester-tops were very common by the third quarter of that century. Elfe made large numbers of them of cypress or mahogany. It is unlikely that any of these early cornices have survived; even those of a later date are rare. Presumably, as the years brought changes in style the cornices were removed, stored in the attic, and eventually thrown away.

Elfe usually equipped his beds with casters, and doubtless his contemporaries also used them. Since none of their account books has come to light the fact must remain inferential. Elfe was careful to make an extra charge of £2 for a set of bed casters.

Double Chests of Drawers

DOUBLE CHESTS OR, AS THEY ARE NOW commonly called, chest-on-chests, were numerous in Charleston during the last half of the eighteenth century. Inventories sometimes show that as many as three such chests were to be found in a single residence of a person of means.[1] While it is a well-known fact that double chests were made in other parts of the country, they are very definitely associated with Charleston; and any double chest, wherever found, should be carefully scrutinized to see whether it has any characteristics that identify it as a Charleston-made piece.

In his account book, which covers an eight year period (1768–1775), Thomas Elfe reveals that during that time he made twenty-eight double chests of drawers. The prices varied according to the wishes of his customers. A plain one was priced at £75 or £80; one with a desk made out of the top drawer of the lower section cost £95; a "pediment head cut through" cost £5 extra and the same amount was charged for a fret. These prices were in local currency.

It is not to be supposed, however, that Elfe was the only cabinet-maker who made double chests of drawers, for at that time about thirty-four other cabinet-makers were working in Charleston, several of whom advertised that they would make such articles of furniture. One cabinet-maker, Richard Magrath, advertised in 1772 that he made "Double chests of Drawers, with neat and light Pediment Heads, which take off and put on occasionally. . . ." [2] Though the double chest did not become common until the last half of the eighteenth century, an inventory dated 1734 lists a double chest of drawers valued at £15. [3]

All double chests that have come to our attention were made of mahogany with the drawer sides and bottoms constructed of heart cypress. The drawer fronts of many of these double chests are made of figured mahogany, veneered on mahogany, although one has been found that is veneered on soft maple. Others have solid mahogany drawer fronts. In the construction of the back, two types have been discovered: in one type the rear of the side panel has been rabbeted and the back fitted into it; in the other, the side panel is grooved, the back

being fitted into the groove and inserted from the top. The latter mode of construction can be easily ascertained by feeling the outside edges of the back panel. Those that are fitted into the groove are slightly tapered toward the edge. Most of the double chests have dustboards (made out of cypress) that extend almost to the rear; a few extend all the way to the back. The mahogany edging is made from 1½ to 2 inches in width. The foot is usually a well-proportioned ogee bracket foot; occasionally one is found with a plain bracket foot.

Some of these chests are very plain; those that do not have a fret usually have a plain cornice, frequently with a dentil. Close examination reveals that in some the dentil is not applied but is an integral part of the pediment, being cut out of the solid mahogany. The lower section usually has square corners. However, one chest has been found with the corners of the lower part forming a quarter-column, fluted and stopped-fluted. The upper section of most double chests has the corner chamfered, usually fluted and stopped-fluted. The upper part of the flute ends in an inverted "U" or with a crescent superimposed by a large dot. With one exception all have five flutes, the exception being one with four. Those that are fluted have a lamb's tongue block at the base which varies somewhat both in design and size. One is known that has a rather unusual chamfered stile.

The lower section of these double chests has three large drawers extending across the piece. The usual sequence of the drawers of the upper part is to be seen in the line drawings. A few have a different drawer sequence. Sometimes the upper drawer of the lower section is made into a desk. Chests having desks made out of the drawer are remarkably alike. The entire drawer pulls out a few inches and the front, which is on quadrants, drops down and makes part of the writing desk. On each side of the center door there are usually two horizontal drawers with three superimposed pigeon holes. The door of the center compartment is plain and is flanked by two letter-drawers which have a fluted pilaster. The top of the flute usually ends in an inverted "U" or with a crescent superimposed by a large dot.

Measurements of several of these double chests reveal that they are remarkably alike in size although they vary considerably in detail.

Chests of Drawers

THE INVENTORIES GIVE EVIDENCE THAT chests of drawers or, as they were frequently spoken of, half drawers or dressing drawers, were commonly used in Charleston. In 1732 Broomhead and Blythe advertised "Chest of Drawers"; many of the articles made by this firm at that time were constructed of mahogany. In the same year James McClellan, another cabinet-maker, advertised "New-fashioned chest of drawers" and Josiah Claypool informed the public, in 1740, that he would make "Chest of Drawers of all fashion fluted or plain." Obviously there must have been a heavy demand for this article by the early Charlestonians. Whether any of these pre-mid-eighteenth century drawers has survived is problematical. Inasmuch as none of these early pieces has been examined there is no way of knowing what secondary woods were used in their construction. Presumably it was cypress.

During the third quarter of the eighteenth century many of the cabinet-makers advertised chests of drawers along with in-

numerable other articles of furniture. The account book of Thomas Elfe indicates that he made several different kinds of drawers. His most expensive kind were "Lady's Dressg. Drawers with columns," for which he charged £45. A "half drawers" cost anywhere from £28 to £35; and a plain "dressing drawers" cost from £20 to £26. The price range suggests that there must have been a large variation between the plain drawers and the ladies' dressing drawers which Elfe produced. According to one entry he made a "Mahogany commode dress'g drawers" at a cost of £65. Several chests of Charleston origin were made with a mahogany slide (Fig. 10).

The pieces of this period that have been examined use cypress as a secondary wood. Some have the drawer bottoms made with the cross bracing running from front to rear (see Elfe) with the grain of the drawer bottom running lengthwise with the piece; others have been found that have their drawer bottoms inserted from rear to front with no cross brace. In such pieces the grain of the wood usually runs from front to rear instead of lengthwise.

After the Revolution and particularly during the last decade of the eighteenth century, the local cabinet-makers advertised that they made "Ladies dressing Chests of different patterns" or "Ladies commode chest of drawers of different forms" or the same article "plain straight," an indication that the customers were keeping up with the latest styles and were not wedded to any one form or design.

The serpentine ladies' dressing drawers shown on figure 13 has nicely proportioned lines and the drawer fronts are made of beautiful crotch mahogany veneered on white pine. The top drawer has compartments with a mahogany sliding shelf. The drawer bottoms are made from magnificent

Fig. 36. **DOUBLE CHEST OF DRAWERS AND DETAILS**
Height 7' 2"; width 42"; depth 23"

heart cypress; the sides are constructed of long-leaf pine and the dust boards of white pine. The chamfered corners are inlaid with crotch mahogany running crosswise, edged on either side by a thin strip of satinwood.

Some serpentine chests, instead of having the drawer fronts veneered on a secondary wood, have the fronts made of a solid piece of mahogany. In this type of construction it was necessary for the local cabinet-maker to use a piece of mahogany at least four inches thick.

Clothespresses or Wardrobes

THE CLOTHESPRESS OR WARDROBE IS AN article of furniture that seems to be associated with the South and especially with Charleston. Today such presses are ordinarily used for the storage of linens; in former times they were meant for clothes. Clothes were not then hung but were laid away [1] and for this purpose several large movable trays, running lengthwise, were usually placed in the upper part of the piece. Very often the trays, with the exception of the outer strip, were made of a single piece of heart cypress, long-leaf or white pine, the narrow outer strip being made of mahogany to match the rest of the piece. The lower part of most presses consists of two long drawers with two smaller upper ones, although some early ones have only the two long drawers. The doors are solid. Frequently a piece is found that has a lovely pediment, clearly indicating that in addition to being utilitarian the press was also intended to be ornamental. Even without the pediment, locally made presses were tall in order that they might not look dwarfed in the large Charleston rooms with their high ceilings.

The early clothes presses were made entirely out of cypress, cedar, red bay, or walnut. It is doubtful whether any of the presses constructed of these woods have survived. When mahogany became common it generally superseded the former woods. As late as 1774 Thomas Elfe was making "Close press." [2] His charge for a mahogany press was £75; however, if "pediment head and casters" were wanted the cost was £5 extra. His cypress presses usually cost about half that amount.

Secretary-Wardrobes

IT IS NOT KNOWN WHETHER THE SECRE-tary-wardrobe is indigenous only to Charleston. In the advertisements of some of the cabinet-makers who worked in the last decade of the eighteenth century one frequently finds listed a secretary-wardrobe. Several such pieces of furniture are in existence that are of Charleston origin.

As its name implies it is a combination of desk and clothes-closet. The lower section has a pull-out secretary with the front on quadrants and usually with drawers beneath; some have paneled doors instead of drawers. The upper section is a wardrobe with solid-paneled doors, the interior being equipped with several sliding shelves to hold clothes. Most secretary-wardrobes have a well-executed pediment.

The piece was probably used in the bedroom where it added to the convenience of a clothes storage space and a desk for the owner's correspondence.

Fig. 37. DOUBLE CHEST OF DRAWERS AND DETAILS
Height 6′ 4″; width 42¾″; depth 22¾″

Tables

EARLY TABLES: THE EARLIEST TABLES were made out of the native woods, which were cedar, cypress, red bay, and walnut. What is believed to be the earliest piece of Charleston-made furniture extant is a gate-legged table in the Charleston Museum. It is made of cedar and cypress (Fig. 77). Presumably many of the early tables, made out of the native woods, were constructed in a similar manner but, unfortunately, few have survived. With the advent of mahogany these tables were probably relegated to the kitchen or outhouse and ultimately disappeared.

Dining Tables: Until the time that the end table was designed to go with the dining table, the inventories, as well as the Elfe account book, speak of dining tables as being "square." Most inventories reveal that they usually came in pairs. Probably one sufficed for the family (although these were usually very large at that time); if guests arrived the other table could be added to it and, if necessary, still a third. Elfe's favorite size for a dining table was "3½ feet." He usually made them in pairs, for which he charged £32. However, he also made dining tables in the following sizes: 3 feet, 3 feet 3 inches, 3 feet 9 inches, 4 feet, and one 5½ feet wide. Occasionally, he made one that was 3 feet by 4 feet. His prices varied according to the size of the table.

On October 3, 1771, Thomas Chippendale billed David Garrick, the celebrated English actor, for "a set of mahogany Dining Tables with circular Ends to Joyn together complete."[1] Garrick, a leader of London's fashion, probably did much to popularize this style of dining table. In January, 1773, John Stewart, Commissioner of Indian Affairs for the Southern Colonies, bought from Thomas Elfe "1 large Square Table with 2 leaves & side Boards d° Rounded off to match d°" at a cost of £58. These tables and leaves were probably needed for the formal dinners given by the Commissioner. The following month Elfe made a similar set of tables for Alexander Wright. Inasmuch as the leaves were not included, Elfe's charges were £48. From then on the rounded ends to go with the main table became common. All told, during an eight-year period, Elfe made 132 dining tables. Several of the dining tables of this period that have been examined have square legs, slightly tapered with a thumbnail groove on the sides. By the end of the century practically every cabinet-maker who did any advertising informed his readers that he had "Sets of Dining Tables," indicating that the rounded ends always accompanied the center table.

Tea Tables: From the earliest days tea drinking appears to have been fashionable with the Charlestonians. This is verified by the records of large importations of tea. On January 27, 1732, James McClellan (*q.v.*) advertised in the *South Carolina Gazette* that he made "Tea-boxes." By 1740, Josiah Claypool, the "expatriated" cabinet-maker from Philadelphia, was advertising that he made "all sorts of Tea Tables." The inventories reveal that this kind of table was commonly found in the average household.

It has been said of tripod tea tables that they "are treasured above all others by collectors."[2] They are rare in Charleston. Fine examples are no longer to be found in the city. Those that remain are usually quite plain, with snake feet of excellent proportions but with no bird cage. Round tea tables are frequently found in the inventories, and judging from their appraised values they must have been elaborate. As early as 1740 "one round Mahogany Claw-foot table" is listed in an inventory.[3]

The Elfe account book reveals that he made "a Scallop tea table with Eagle Claws" at a cost of £25, and for some of his "Scollop" tea tables he received as much as £35.

So many round tea tables having once been produced in Charleston it is difficult to believe that at least a few have not survived. But until they are located and recognized as being of local origin there is no way of knowing what type foot was used, whether they had bird cages, or what design was used for the scalloped edge. It has been said that the "Pie-crust tables bought out of the South . . . have shorter scallops in the rim than the Philadelphia type";[4] this may be correct. Because English styles were so dominant in the pre-Revolutionary period, it is not at all unlikely that many locally made tables of this kind followed closely the English type of construction and design and may be regarded by their present owners as having been made in England.

Card Tables: Card playing, like tea drinking, was a popular diversion with the eighteenth century Charlestonians and there is hardly an inventory of a person of means that does not contain at least two card tables. Judging from Elfe's charges, card tables must have varied greatly in design and carving. Elfe usually made them in pairs and his prices range from £30 to £40 for a pair. However, for a pair of "commode" card tables he charged £70. Such a difference in prices leads us to believe that the "commode" table must have been elaborately carved. Others were made with legs fluted. Some of the tables must have been quite plain, but all appear to have been lined with green cloth. The "commode" style card table must have been extremely popular just before the Revolution for we find other cabinet-makers advertising that they also made similar tables.[5]

Card tables made toward the end of the eighteenth century are frequently circular in design; several are what might be called "long oval." When the leaf of such a table is raised at right angles it gives the appearance of being elliptical in shape, but when extended the table is nearly circular. There is usually less than an inch of variation between the width and the depth.

Breakfast Tables: Breakfast tables were popular. Elfe made several different styles of breakfast tables and it is reasonable to suppose that the other cabinet-makers working in Charleston during the same period did likewise. There is such a variation in the prices charged by Elfe for tables of this kind as to suggest considerable variation in his designs. Probably not all of them contained drawers. He did, however, make many such tables "with Draw & Stretcher" at a cost of £18. For other breakfast tables (possibly the drawer-less ones), he charged only £16. A commode breakfast table usually cost £30; and one with the "ends carved," £28 (Fig. 88). On occasion Elfe made a "square" breakfast table or one with "fluted legs & Chinese brackets." Richard Magrath, one of Elfe's competitors, advertised in the *South Carolina Gazette* on July 9, 1772, that he made "Breakfast tables with stretchers."

The cabinet-makers during the last decade of the eighteenth and the first decade of the nineteenth century frequently advertised "Breakfast Tables." These were probably pembroke tables of various styles and shapes.

China Tables: The china table illustrated in Chippendale's *Director* shows it as having a raised edge to protect the china against damage.[6] It is mentioned by the local cabinet-makers working in the third quarter of the eighteenth century, and is often called a "Chinese" table. One case in point is the advertisement of Peter Hall (q.v.) which appeared in the *South Carolina Gazette* on December 19, 1761. Among other kinds of furniture he mentions "Chinese tables of all sorts."

Elfe made a number of china tables, and judging from the price of some of them they must have been very elaborate. A "China frett tea table" could be purchased for as little as £20. One with a stretcher was priced at £26. For one with a "Carved Acorn" the price was £30. The acorn was probably on the finial in the raised center portions of the stretcher. Elfe was continually repairing rims of "China Tables." We also find that he made "commode fret China Tables with castors" for £46 and at least on one occasion he charged £70 for a "large China Table." The latter must have been very ornate, for one could have purchased from Elfe one of his plain double chests of drawers for a like amount. No doubt a large number of china tables were made in Charleston but if any have survived, their present whereabouts is not known.

Pembroke Tables: What appears to be the earliest use in print of the word "pembroke," in reference to tables, is given in the *New English Dictionary* which appeared in 1778.[7] Yet five years prior to that time we find that Elfe made "a Pembroke tea table" for Peter Stevenson at a cost of £16. Towards the end of the eighteenth century the pembroke table became extremely popular and practically every cabinet-maker advertised it. Pembroke card tables occur frequently in the in-

ventories. Tables of this period are inlaid and many are elliptical in shape when their leaves are extended; a few have enamel escutcheons.

Slab Tables: "Slate Tables" are occasionally mentioned in the inventories of the 1730's,[8] but by the next decade the marble slab table, or "Marble Slab and frame" as they were generally called, came into vogue. In 1740 Josiah Claypool, formerly of Philadelphia, was advertising that he made "frames for Marble Tables . . . after the newest and best Fashions . . ."[9] If one may judge from the inventories, they were very common by the end of the century. The mahogany frames were made by the local cabinet-makers. During the eighteenth century the marble was imported from abroad,[10] but in the early nineteenth century marble was also being brought in from Philadelphia.[11] The probable reason for importing American marble was a $19\frac{1}{4}\%$ tariff on foreign marble by 1807.[12] Therefore a piece of furniture containing "Chester County" marble, (the kind quarried in the vicinity of Philadelphia) should not be arbitrarily assigned as being of Philadelphia origin until it has been carefully examined.

Mahogany slab tables were also common, a thick mahogany board taking the place of the marble slab. Thomas Elfe (q.v.) made a number of these tables. His charges for them varied from £12 to £30. Doubtless the wide differences in price were determined by the relative amount of carving on the frame.

Dressing Tables: Many early Charleston dressing tables have a single narrow drawer. This, combined with their long legs, gives them a light and delicate appearance (Fig. 93). The top is usually moulded on three sides and the outer edges of the stiles have a delicate beading. The legs are tapered, slender, with a well-executed ankle usually ending with a padded Queen Anne foot. However, one has been discovered that has a ball and claw foot (Fig. 90). The secondary wood of all known examples is cypress.

So far there has come to light only one locally made dressing table that can be called a "low boy" (Fig. 92). (The name "low boy" was not used in Colonial times.) [13] This piece has an unusual Spanish foot; the top is moulded on three sides and the secondary wood throughout is cypress.

Almost all of these tables have large, handsome brasses, even a large escutcheon for the keyhole.

Side Chairs

THE INVENTORIES REVEAL THAT LARGE numbers of chairs were used in normal Charleston households. It is not unusual to find thirty or forty chairs in a single residence; occasionally, in the larger ones, as many as fifty or sixty. Only rarely are more than a hundred listed in a single inventory.

The early side chairs were probably made from the local woods. By 1725 there is frequent mention in the inventories of White Chairs and Black Chairs, the latter being sometimes called "Carolina made," a type which persisted until the 1750's.[1] Many chairs were spoken of merely as "Cain Chairs"; there were also "Walnut Tree matted Chairs."[2] By 1732 the local cabinet-makers were advertising that they would make mahogany chairs "after the best manner."[3] Today there is no way of knowing when mahogany chairs became

common, but in all probability they were in general use by the 1740's, along with other articles made of mahogany.

That invaluable document, the Elfe account book, gives us a pretty clear indication not only of the number but of the types of chairs made just before the Revolution. In the eight-year period covered by the account book, Elfe made six hundred forty-three side chairs. This in itself is an exceedingly large number, but it must not be forgotten that more than thirty other cabinet-makers were working in Charleston during the same period. It is impossible even to approximate the number of chairs that must have been made in the city during the time.

Elfe seems to have made three distinct types of side chairs: scroll backs, splat backs, and carved backs. The scroll-back type was the cheapest and Elfe charged £90 or £95 a dozen for them. If a customer wished chairs with splat backs he paid £160 for his dozen, and if a particularly fine set of chairs with carved backs was ordered the purchaser paid as much as £230 for them. Occasionally Elfe made a set of chairs with "Compass seats"; he made other sets with the "fronts fluted"; and one entry shows that he made six chairs with "Commode fronts."

Richard Magrath, one of Elfe's competitors, advertised in 1771 that he would sell "Half a dozen Carved Chairs, . . . with Commode fronts, and Pincushion seats, of the newest fashion, and the first of that construction ever made in the province."[4] Apparently it was Magrath who introduced this style of chair, for it is not until some time later that we find Elfe meeting this competition. The following year Magrath published another interesting advertisement stating that he made "Chairs of the newest fashion, splat Backs, with hollow slats and commode fronts, of the same Pattern as those imported by Peter Manigault, Esq.— He is now making some Hollow-seated Chairs, the seats to take in and out, and nearly the pattern of another set of Chairs imported by the same gentleman, which have a light, airy Look, and make the sitting easy beyond expression." [5] It would appear that Peter Manigault, who was one of the richest men in the colony, had just imported a set of chairs of the newest fashion. Magrath's advertisement suggests that before that time locally made chairs did not have "seats to take in and out."

Elfe must have made quantities of chairs that did not have movable or "slip" seats. In his inventory of stock taken on January 1, 1768, are listed "40 thousand brass chair nails" and "10 thousand Princess metal chair nails." [6] Therefore, all pre-Revolutionary chairs that do not have movable or "slip" seats should be carefully scrutinized to see if they are of local origin and not arbitrarily assigned as English or as coming from some other American city.

Many of the chairs made in the third quarter of the eighteenth century closely followed their English prototypes. In the making of a side chair practically none of the secondary woods was used which, in other kinds of furniture, often serve to identify the piece as being of local origin. The most noticeable difference between a Charleston-made chair and one of English origin of this period is the amount of mahogany used in its construction. The rails of the locally made chair are frequently thicker and most chairs have heavy mahogany corner blocks (Fig. 120) with the grain horizontal. There is in existence a so-called State chair which is thought to have been made about 1765 by Elfe and Hutchinson (q.v.). In spite of the fact that the seat covering covers the rails and is

nailed, the front rail is made out of mahogany with a thickness of $3\frac{5}{8}$ inches. Such lavish use of mahogany would probably have been made only by a local craftsman.

Because of the cutting off of all trade with England during the Revolutionary period and the economic confusion that followed, it seems unlikely that very many chairs of the so-called "Transition" period were made by Charleston cabinet-makers. The supposition is further substantiated by the fact that few chairs of this type are to be found in and around Charleston.

With the return of prosperity and the resumption of trade with England and the continent, Charlestonians were influenced, as they had formerly been, by the latest styles from abroad. John Marshall, one of the local cabinet-makers, advertised in 1795 that "He Has On Hand . . . Several dozen Mahogany Chairs of the newest fashion." [7] The advertisements from that date to the gradual decline of Charleston cabinet-making indicate that whenever any change of style occurred, the local cabinet-maker quickly adjusted himself to the wishes of his customer.

Easy Chairs

JUDGING FROM THE INVENTORIES AND THE advertisements, easy or wing chairs were very common during the last half of the eighteenth century. They must have been in common use by 1741, for in that year Walter Rowland, Upholsterer from London, advertised that he will "stuff . . . easy Chairs." Strangely enough, the account book of Thomas Elfe reveals that he made comparatively few easy chairs. Most of those which he produced had "Eagle Claws," and his usual charge was around

£30. He repaired easy chairs by putting new stretchers and casters in them, but it is not known whether such chairs were made by him or by some other cabinet-maker. The most important fact here, of course, is that some of the easy chairs had stretchers.

An extant easy chair made in the last quarter of the eighteenth century reveals the following characteristics: the rails are of oak which, judging by its annular rings,* was probably of local growth; some of the supporting members are of cypress; and the chair contains still a third wood which appears to be cherry. As yet, however, the number of easy chairs available for examination is not great enough to permit any conclusions regarding the difference between those that were made in Charleston and in other places. It may be predicted that when such conclusions become possible, they will be derived from an examination of the secondary woods which the chairs contain.

French Chairs or Armchairs

FRENCH CHAIRS OR, AS THEY ARE NOW generally known, Martha Washington chairs, were fairly common during the last half of the eighteenth century. Chippendale, in the first edition (1754) of his *Director* gives several designs for the French Chair. It is not known when this design was first used by the Charleston cabinet-makers, but by 1765 these chairs were in such general use that John Mason, an upholsterer, advertised in the *South Carolina Gazette* on February 2 of that year that he would furnish a "French chair cover" for "one

---

* Oak growing along the Southern littoral averages from four to eight annular growth rings to the inch. Oak grown in the mountains and in the North usually has from eight to twelve such rings.

pound." The inventories reveal that such chairs usually occurred in pairs, although some inventories list as many as eight in a single household.[1] The cabinet-makers working during the third quarter of the eighteenth century frequently advertised that they made "French Chairs." Thomas Elfe made comparatively few French chairs during the eight years covered by his account book. His charges for a pair of such chairs came to £60. Such a price, compared to what he received for some of his other furniture, indicates that the chairs must have been very handsome.

The one shown on figure 109 has yellow pine and ash as its secondary wood. The carving on the end of the arm is very well executed. This chair is no longer in Charleston; but recently a companion chair has been found in the possession of a Charleston family, which acquired it by inheritance.

Windsor Chairs

THE WINDSOR CHAIR WAS PROBABLY THE most important single item of furniture imported into Charleston. What is thought to be the earliest mention of a Windsor chair in the Colony is found in the inventory of John Lloyd, dated May 28, 1736, listing "3 open Windser (*sic*) chairs. £3."[1]

Thereafter Windsor chairs are occasionally mentioned in the inventories, though usually only a few such chairs are listed at any one time. The majority of the Windsor chairs were imported sporadically from England, Philadelphia, and New York. In January, 1759, the vessel "Prince of Orange, Capt. White from London" arrived with a shipment of Windsor chairs.[2] On June 23, 1766, an advertisement in the

South Carolina Gazette announced that some Windsor chairs had just arrived from Philadelphia. Later advertisements reveal that throughout the closing years of the eighteenth century and the first quarter of the nineteenth Windsor chairs arrived by ship with some regularity.

If one were to judge solely from the advertisements he would conclude that all Windsor chairs in Charleston during that period were imported. The local cabinet- and chairmakers, however, very definitely made efforts to meet the competition from importations. John Biggard inserted the following advertisement in the *South Carolina Gazette* for March 24, 1767: "The subscriber, who is lately arrived from Philadelphia, has opened a Turner's shop on the Bay, the Corner of Queen-Street, where Gentlemen may be supplied with Windsor and Garden Chairs. . . ." Biggard, working in Philadelphia and seeing the demand for such chairs in Charleston, must have decided that it was a good place in which to establish his shop. At once the problem arises of distinguishing between a Biggard chair made in Charleston and one imported from Philadelphia, for it can hardly be doubted that Biggard would have made his Charleston chairs in exactly the same manner as he had made them in Philadelphia. Furthermore, there is a very good chance that he would have used some of the same woods in both places.

After the Revolution when Windsor chairs were again being imported, we find Andrew Redmond advertising in the *South Carolina Gazette and General Advertiser* on January 13, 1784, that he "still carries on Turnery in all its Branches . . . Likewise Philadelphia Windsor chairs, either armed or unarmed, as neat as any imported, and much better stuff." The question again arises how to differentiate between the two.

Humiston and Stafford, Chair Makers, stated in the *City Gazette and Daily Advertiser* for November 28, 1798, that they made "Warranted Windsor Chairs and Green Settees, Of the newest fashion, and of an excellent quality, superior to any ever imported into this city . . . A few Journeymen and one or two Apprentices are wanted for the Chair making Business." The latter statement suggests that Humiston and Stafford had a shop of considerable size.

From time to time the city directories list the names of Windsor chairmakers. As late as 1832 we learn that J. J. Sheridan, the strong advocate of Charleston-made furniture, was producing this type of chair.[3]

People living in the interior of the State wanted Windsor chairs and the Charleston chairmakers must have endeavored to supply the demand. About 1813 Charles Martin Grey was "bound out" to Mr. Pugh of Augusta, Georgia, maker of Fancy and Windsor chairs.[4] Pugh probably supplied the wealthy planters in the Aiken and Edgefield region who had formerly been getting their chairs from Charleston. On March 15, 1805, the following advertisement appeared in the *City Gazette:* "Wanted immediately—Two Journeymen, one that understands the Riding Chair business, the other the Windsor Chair making business. . . . apply to my shop in Camden [S. C.]. Joseph H. Hoell."

It is noteworthy that, despite the large number of Windsor chairs imported to Charleston and produced by local cabinetmakers, no definite type can be traced. A type or style may have evolved, but so few chairs have survived that there can be little hope of discovering anything resembling a local style. It is not difficult to understand why the Windsor chair did not survive in Charleston. First, it probably was regarded as piazza or garden furniture[5]

Fig. 38 PEDIMENT OF DESK AND BOOKCASE *(see Fig. 31)*

Fig. 39 PEDIMENT OF DESK AND BOOKCASE

Fig. 40 PEDIMENT OF DESK AND BOOKCASE *(see Fig. 32)*

Fig. 41 PEDIMENT OF DESK AND BOOKCASE

Fig. 42 PEDIMENT OF DESK AND BOOKCASE *(see Fig. 33)*

Fig. 43 PEDIMENT OF SECRETARY AND BOOKCASE *(see Fig. 34)*

Fig. 44 PEDIMENT OF CLOTHESPRESS *(see Fig. 15)*

Fig. 45 PEDIMENT OF CLOTHESPRESS

Fig. 46 PEDIMENT OF SECRETARY AND BOOKCASE *(see Fig. 35)*

Fig. 47 SIDEBOARD Height 39″; width 61¾″; depth—center 27½″, end 20½″

Fig. 48 SIDEBOARD Height 39″; width 67½″; depth—center 29³⁄₁₆″, end 19¾″

Fig. 49 SIDEBOARD Height 39½″; width 66¼″; depth—center 28¾″, end 21¾″

Fig. 50 SIDEBOARD Height 37½″; width 61¾″; depth—center 27″, end 24″

Fig. 51 DOUBLE-TIERED SIDEBOARD dimensions not available

Fig. 52 DOUBLE-TIERED SIDEBOARD Height—back 45¼″, front 38⅞″; width 68″

and was therefore not highly valued; again, it was fairly fragile and when once broken was relegated to the woodshed; finally, some of the woods used in its construction may have been subject to borers. Whatever the explanation, Windsor chairs in and around Charleston, other than recent importations, are rare.

Sofas, Couches, and Settees

IT IS INCREDIBLE THAT NOT A SINGLE SOFA locally made during the third quarter of the eighteenth century has been found in Charleston. The local cabinet-makers advertised them; the inventories reveal that they were in Charleston homes of that period; and the account book of Thomas Elfe shows that he actually produced sofas. No doubt some have survived, but they are still to be discovered. Richard Magrath, a local cabinet-maker, advertised in the *South Carolina Gazette* on July 9, 1772, that he made ". . . Sophas, with Commode fronts divided into three sweeps, which give them a noble look . . ." The following year he again advertised that he had some "Sophas, . . . of the newest fashion and neatest construction, such as were never offered for sale in this Province before . . ." Elfe's charge (1774) for a "sopha" was £90 current money. For casters he made an additional charge.

During the last decade of the eighteenth century the local cabinet-makers frequently advertised that they made sofas "of the newest fashion." Even sofas of this period are practically non-existent in Charleston.

The couch (or daybed) appears fairly regularly in the inventories. In 1739 the inventory of Maurice Lewis lists "1 Leathern Bottom Couch £4." [1] By the 1740's

they are usually spoken of as "Mahogany Couches" showing that by this time couches, like practically all other pieces of furniture, were being made of mahogany. Couches continued to be produced in Charleston until the time of the Revolution.[2] During the last decade of the eighteenth and the first decade of the nineteenth century the couch may have gone out of style, for the cabinet-makers, judging from their advertisements, made only sofas.

Because the settee appears only rarely in the inventories and is not mentioned in the advertisements of the local cabinet-makers, it is reasonable to assume that it was not in common use in Charleston.

Sideboards

THOMAS SHEARER IS GENERALLY ACCREDited with designing the sideboard in its present form.[1] In his *Cabinet Maker's London Book of Prices* published in 1788 is illustrated a "bow-fronted" sideboard showing a sideboard as we now think of it.[2] It is not known how long it took for this new design to reach Charleston, but Andrew Gifford, a local cabinet-maker, advertised in the *City Gazette and Advertiser* of March 16, 1790, that he had "Side boards plain and inlaid"; and the inventory of Dr. Andrew Turnbull made in April, 1792, lists "1 Mahogany Sidboard." [3] Thereafter the inventories reveal that the sideboard was a common article of furniture in the Charleston residence.

In 1795 John Marshall, a local cabinet-maker, stated that he had some "Elegant commode sideboards." [4] The following year both Alexander Calder (*q.v.*) and Charles Watts (*q.v.*) advertised that they had "Elegant Sideboards of different forms and kinds." [5] The inventory of John Douglas (*q.v.*) made on December 31, 1805, includes "5 Sideboards $250.00." It is obvious that the Charlestonians were not partial to any one style or shape.

It is interesting to note that all these cabinet-makers with the exception of Gifford, were Scottish. It was their aptitude for fine workmanship which explains why so many handsome sideboards have come out of the South. During the past quarter of a century many fine mahogany sideboards have been found in the upper part of South Carolina. The preponderance of evidence leads us to believe that these sideboards are of Charleston origin. The reasons for this conclusion are given under the section on "Exports and Country Trade."

There appears to be no hard and fast rule for the dimensions of a Charleston sideboard. Some are very large, obviously made to fit a particular place in the dining room; others are quite small. The locally made sideboard does not have the slenderness of body and length of leg found in the Baltimore pieces.[6]

It is noteworthy that the Charleston makers of sideboards were conservative in their use of inlay. Although they commonly employed the bellflowers and fan they avoided such gaudy designs as those found in pieces made elsewhere.

The serpentine sideboard of the Hepplewhite style has the center only moderately bowed. In other words, the depth of the center is only a few inches greater than the depth of the ends. Another distinctive feature in some of the broken serpentine sideboards is in the construction of the two center front legs. Instead of the customary four-sided legs, which are frequently slightly canted, the two center legs are five-sided (Fig. 64). Other types of locally made sideboards are known that have a

sweeping curve in the back of the center leg just before it enters the carcass. Looking at it in profile it shows a comparatively slender leg below the piece, but the part extending into the carcass is approximately twice as thick as the exposed part. In some sideboards the uppermost cross member is dovetailed into the corner stile, as is customary, but in addition it is dovetailed into the side panel. This not only gives it added strength but keeps the side panel from bulging.

With but few exceptions all sideboards attributed to Charleston cabinet-makers are of the six-legged design. One of the exceptions is an eight-legged Sheraton-style sideboard of large dimensions with two large inlaid panels showing the cotton plant in bloom as well as the cotton boll (Fig. 65). This piece was made for one of the wealthiest planters in the State. The other piece is of similar design and was undoubtedly made by the same cabinet-maker (Fig. 62).

The secondary woods used in the construction of the local sideboards vary greatly. Most pieces contain a combination of woods. Some make use of cypress and white pine; others, white pine and cedar; still others have a preponderance of longleaf pine; many have poplar usually in combination with one of the other woods.

The double-tiered or so-called Scotch type sideboard [7] was probably introduced into Charleston by the many Scottish cabinet-makers who were working there during the last decade of the eighteenth and the first decade of the nineteenth centuries. Possibly they may have been made elsewhere in this country. Uncertainty on this point arises from the fact that only a few such pieces have survived and that although some of them can be identified as having been made in Charleston, others can be traced only as having "come out of the South."

Before the age of Shearer, the sideboard was primarily a table, and as its name implies was a long board. In the inventory of John Smith made April 17, 1725, is listed "a side Board Cedar Table." By the middle of the eighteenth century, however, the Charlestonian wanted drawers in his mahogany sideboard table, presumably for convenience' sake. From then on until the last decade of the eighteenth century—with the advent of the new design—the inventories frequently mention a "Side board Table with Drawers." The account book of Thomas Elfe shows that he made sideboards with drawers, usually at a cost of between £25 and £30.[8] Any sideboard table with drawers of this period should be carefully examined for drawer linings made of cypress or for some other evidence of local workmanship.

Knife Cases and Urns

BECAUSE OF HIS GREAT WEALTH, THE Charlestonian acquired, among other things, quantities of silver. Even at an early date frequent mention is found in the inventories of silver spoons and silver-handled knives and forks. A place in which to keep such articles was necessary, and the knife box was the logical receptacle.

The first such boxes were usually spoken of as "Shagreen Cases." Such cases were often covered with sharkskin. The wooden knife case came into common use during the last half of the eighteenth century. The inventory of one man reveals that as many as six such boxes were needed to take care of his silver.[1] This was probably an exception, but in any event a pair of boxes was usually to be found in the home of any person of means.

Unless the primary wood in the knife case is a native American wood it is difficult and sometimes impossible to distinguish between an American-made box and one of English origin, for it appears to have been the custom of the English craftsman to use pine (deal) as a secondary wood,[2] and no doubt the American craftsman followed the same practice.

Thomas Sheraton (1802), in speaking of the knife case, makes the following statement: "As these cases are not made in regular cabinet shops, it may be of service to mention where they are executed in the best taste, by one who makes it his main business; i.e., John Lane, No. 44, St. Martin's-le-Grand, London." Whether the eighteenth century Charleston cabinetmaker made knife boxes is still a matter of conjecture. Because it was small the box could easily have been imported. The inventory of Michael Muckenfuss, a local cabinet-maker, made in 1808, lists a knife case and the inventory of William Walker (q.v.) made in 1811 shows that he had "a pair of Knife Cases." It is reaosnable to suppose than a highly skilled cabinet-maker would have made his own knife boxes rather than purchase imported ones, if for no other reason than pride of craftsmanship.

There is a knife box that is thought to be of Charleston origin. This assumption is based on the secondary wood used in its construction and the inlay on its top. A somewhat similar inlay has been found in several pieces of furniture of local origin that were probably made in the last decade of the eighteenth century.

The knife urn was contemporaneous with the knife box, although the more slender form was of a later period.[3] What has been said about the box will in all likelihood apply to the urn.

Wine Coolers and Cellarettes

BY THE TIME OF THE REVOLUTION the "wine cooler" or "butler" was usually found in the home of every man of means. Occasionally the inventories reveal that as many as three coolers were owned by a single person.[1] The possession of several coolers does not necessarily indicate that the owner was a heavy drinker; more than likely he kept his various wines in separate coolers for convenience. Occasionally a "copper Japanned cooler" appears in an inventory.[2] The wine cooler of this period was usually either octagonal or elliptical in shape, brass-bound, and mounted on a stand. Almost all had lead or metal linings, so that either water or ice could be placed in them to cool the wine. Some of these coolers still have the drain cock in the bottom.

It is probable that the word "cellarette" was not generally applied to such pieces until the time of Hepplewhite. In the third edition (1794) of his *Guide* Hepplewhite shows "cellarettes" both in octagonal and elliptical shapes with compartments to hold the bottles. In 1803 Thomas Sheraton wrote the following description: "Cellaret, amongst cabinet makers, denotes a convenience for wine, or wine cistern." Occasionally it was spoken of as a "Mahogany Butler for liquors."[3]

Thomas Elfe made several "Mahogany Cases for bottles with brass handles" at a cost of £12. The price indicates that they were semi-portable cases, each holding about six bottles. In 1796 John Marshall, a local cabinet-maker, advertised that he had "Handsome Cellerettes of the newest fashion" and the following year Jacob Sass (*q.v.*) announced that he too had Sellerets (*sic*).

The inventory of Nicholas Silberg (*q.v.*) made in 1802 lists three "commode" cellarettes; the inventory of Michael Muckenfuss (*q.v.*), taken in 1808, reveals that he also had three such articles. The largest, which had a "raised top," was appraised at $50. Such a price suggests that the cellarette must have been a very elaborate one, for by this time the appraised value of articles nowhere represents their true worth.

It seems rather strange that cellarettes were still popular at this time, for the sideboard had become common and usually had one drawer fitted out to take care of bottles, thereby outmoding the cellarette.

One reason for the present rarity of cellarettes in Charleston is probably best explained in *Reminiscences of Old Charleston*.[4] The author in describing his grandfather's house (*c.* 1840) states that "In the corner as you enter the door in the dining-room stood the 'wine cooler' of polished mahogany, inlaid with wreaths of satin wood, octagon in shape, about three feet high, on six spindling square legs, divided inside with compartments, each to hold a bottle of wine. The centre lined with lead to hold ice or water. Being on rollers it was wheeled up to the side of the host at the head of the table and the cooled bottle handed out as needed. 'The fashions of the world change,' and those who have been accustomed to partake of its contents, now that it was all gone and never refilled, have failed to return, and for years it was debased to the humble purpose of a scrap box, its glory had departed, and like its owner seemed to be growing larger in body, and more spindling in the legs."

Corner Cupboards

UP TO THE MIDDLE OF THE EIGHTEENTH century the corner cupboard appears to have been a fairly common article of furniture in the Charleston house. The earliest pieces were probably made of cedar, cypress, or possibly red bay. Very rarely is a cupboard of walnut mentioned in the inventories.[1] Cupboards were made of mahogany as soon as that wood became common. By the time of the Revolution (our only source of information being the inventories) corner cupboards appear to have gone out of style and they are rarely mentioned in the inventories of the later periods.

A handsome mahogany cupboard is illustrated on Plate xii in Burroughs, *Southern Antiques* (1931) with the notation that it is from South Carolina. It has a rather unusual medallion inlay in the pediment. Inasmuch as this motif has been found in other pieces of furniture that are thought to be of local origin, it is reasonable to suppose that this cupboard is also of Charleston workmanship.

Desk and Bookcases; and Secretary and Bookcases

THE DESK AND BOOKCASE, BETTER KNOWN today as a secretary, was a favorite article of furniture with the Charlestonians. The term *desk and bookcase* signified that the lower section consisted of a slope front desk with drawers underneath with a superimposed section to hold books. By 1732 the local cabinet-makers were advertising that they made such articles of furniture;[1] in 1740 Josiah Claypoole (*q.v.*) stated that he made "Desk and Book Cases, with Arch'd, Pediment and O. G. Heads."[2]

From the early 1740's[3] the mahogany "desk and bookcase" begins to make its appearance with great regularity in the inventories and by the next decade the desk and bookcases are listed as having glass doors, from which it may be inferred that the earlier ones had solid-paneled doors (Fig. 30). Probably, due to climatic conditions, the wire mesh in place of the solid or glass door was apparently never used by the local cabinet-makers. The later form is occasionally spoken of as a "Scrutore and Book case [with] glass doors."[4] The term Scrutore was usually applied only to a desk.

Thomas Elfe made "Mahogany Desk and Book Case[s] with Chinese Doors" at a price ranging from £130 to £150. The desk and boockcase shown (Fig. 32) is ascribed to Elfe. It has the so-called Elfe fret; secondary wood of cypress; the same rabbeting on the edges of the drawers; and the cross brace in the center of the drawers. It is a matter of record also that Elfe made "Mahogany Desk and Book Cases with Glass Doors" at a cost of £140. The "Glass Doors" here meant "Mirror" doors. Another desk and bookcase (Fig. 31) has a different fret on the pediment and has the same motif incised on the foot. Again we find that the desk and bookcase has cypress as a secondary wood with the cross brace in the drawers, but whether it was made by Elfe or by one of the thirty-four local cabinet-makers working at that time is still a matter of conjecture. Several desk and book cases of this period have solid doors. Presumably the original owners did not wish to pay the extra charges for "Glass" or "Chinese" doors. All the desk and book cases of the pre-Revolutionary period attributed to Charleston cabinet-makers employ cypress as a secondary wood.

The secretary and bookcase differs from the desk and bookcase in that the entire writing section pulls out a few inches, and the front, which is on quadrants, falls and makes part of the writing desk. Some secretary and bookcases have the usual drawers beneath, others have paneled doors. The pull-out secretary is attributed by some to the Sheraton school [5] though both styles can be seen in Hepplewhite's *Guide*.

The Charleston cabinet-makers were quick to adopt the new style. In 1795 John Marshall (*q.v.*) advertised "Desk and book-cases of different patterns" and "Secretaries and book-cases of different patterns." Other local cabinet-makers quickly followed suit. Some even advertised that they made "Ladies writing Tables and Book Cases."

Some of the post-Revolutionary Charleston secretaries contain cypress as the secondary wood; others have been found that have white pine, ash, and cedar. Although mahogany was the wood generally used in locally made secretary and bookcases, a labeled piece by Robert Walker (*q.v.*) is made of satinwood edged with mahogany. The satinwood is veneered on mahogany.

Hepplewhite, in comments on the desk and bookcase (which would have also applied to the secretary and bookcase) writes, "The dimensions of this article, will in general, be regulated by the height of the room, the place where it must stand, or the particular use to which it is destined. . . ." [6] The post-Revolutionary Charleston cabinet-makers appear to have taken Hepplewhite literally, for we find that Charleston-made desk and bookcases, as well as secretary and bookcases, are usually "longer waisted" than those made in other parts of the country. In other words, the upper section and, in many cases, the lower part are higher than those generally found elsewhere. This is understandable for otherwise the pieces would

have looked dwarfed in the high-ceiling post-Revolutionary Charleston rooms.

The secretary and bookcase was such a popular article of furniture that the local brokers, upon receiving a shipment of hardware from abroad, would advertise among other things "hinges for cabinet-work, bed furniture, and quadrants" [7] the last being, of course, for the secretary and bookcases.

Bookcases

MANY CHARLESTONIANS OF WEALTH HAD equipped their libraries with handsome bookcases; some owned as many as "three large Mahogany Book Cases. . . ." [1] The inventory of John Morton made on January 9, 1752, lists a mahogany bookcase valued at £100. Another inventory made in 1761 reveals a bookcase and books appraised at £400. [2] Of course there is today no way of knowing the value of the books that it contained. Just before the Revolution we find another entry of a "Mahogany Book Case sash'd £150." [3] Elfe's charges for a bookcase varied from £100 to £140. The appraisal value of these bookcases found in Charleston homes, compared with other articles of furniture, indicates that the bookcases must have been very handsome. There apparently were so many bookcases in Charleston that William Wayne felt justified in inserting the following advertisement in the *South Carolina Gazette; And Country Journal* for January 5, 1773: "Glass cut to all dimensions; Chinese Book Cases, glazed in the neatest Manner . . ."

The design for the bookcase shown on figure 1 has obviously been taken, with some slight variations, from Chippendale's *Director*. It is attributed to Thomas Elfe.

This assumption is based on the fact that it has the so-called Elfe fret; cypress is the secondary wood; and the Elfe account book reveals that he made several large bookcases, some with frets.

The bookcase shown as the frontispiece is now in the Heyward-Washington House, a branch of the Charleston Museum. It was bequeathed by Mrs. Nellie Hotchkiss Holmes, who inherited it from her husband, George S. Holmes. It is an unusually large piece, being 10 feet 9 inches high, 8 feet 3¾ inches wide. The pediment has a fine flower inlay of many kinds of woods and the little bellflowers are of ivory. The texture and matching of the mahogany is superb. The secondary wood used for the drawer linings is beautiful heart cypress. The back, however, is made out of white pine.

Another bookcase (Fig. 2) is now in the Yale Museum of Fine Arts. This piece came from one of the Alston plantations near Georgetown, South Carolina. There are sufficient similarities in its construction to lead to the belief that the piece probably came from the same workshop that produced the Holmes bookcase. It differs, however, in having its drawer linings made out of cedar.

An interesting item appeared on July 27, 1786, in the *Charleston Morning Post and Daily Advertiser*: "[Auction] A very compleat Book-Case, Eight feet wide, and nine feet high, the upper part in three pieces, kept together by a beautiful cornice. For taste, elegance and workmanship, this piece is not exceeded by any in the State."

The Heyward-Washington House contains another large bookcase. From its style it was probably made in the first decade of the nineteenth century. Its dimensions are as follows: height 9 feet 11 inches, length 12 feet 1¾ inches. Its size indicates that it must have been designed for a certain part of the house. The large panels are made of beautiful crotch mahogany, veneered on mahogany. It is attributed to Robert Walker. This assumption is based on the fact that there is a certain similarity, both in design and construction, to a secretary and bookcase that bears Walker's label.

Clocks

As early as 1733 William Carwithen, a local cabinet-maker, advertised in the *South Carolina Gazette* that he was a maker of clock-cases. Since the *Gazette*, the only medium of advertising in the Province, was not founded until 1732, there is no way of knowing how long he or his contemporaries had been making clock-cases. The inventories indicate that wealthy Charlestonians had clocks, and the appraised values indicate that they were in all probability tall, or as they are now commonly called, grandfather clocks.

During the eighteenth century there were fifty clock-and watch-makers working in Charleston. Because tall clocks needed a large case to house the works, it is highly probable that the local clock-makers employed the local cabinet-makers to make the cases for them. Thomas Elfe charged £40 for making such a case.[1]

The works of the clock shown on figure 69 were made by Joshua Lockwood, one of the best known of the local clock-makers.

The works of the desk clock (Fig. 70) were made by John James Himely of Charleston. It is quite possible that the case of this small clock was made by a local cabinet-maker.

Fig. 53. INLAYS AND BELLFLOWERS

[62]

Inlays and Bellflowers

CONTRARY TO GENERAL BELIEF, IT HAS been found that the amount of inlay usually employed by the Charleston cabinet-makers was conservative. This will doubtless come as a surprise, for heretofore it has been believed that the farther South one went the more gaudy the inlay and the more ornate the furniture.

What appears to be the earliest mention of any inlay work is found in the inventory of Thomas Gadsden made on April 7, 1740: "1 old Fashion Case of Drawers Inlaid with Ivory £1." An early date for inlay work of the later period is that of an advertisement printed April 13, 1773, in the *South Carolina Gazette:* "Cabinet-Making, in all its branches, Also, Inlaid-work in any Taste, by Martin Pfeninger." It is not known when inlay was generally used by local cabinet-makers, but in 1780 an "Inlaid Mahogany Pembroke Table" valued at £4 is listed in the inventory of William Wragg.[1] There appears to be a complete hiatus during the war years, but with the return of prosperity, along with the change of style which had taken place during the interim, practically all locally made furniture during the next decade appears to have some sort of inlay.

A favorite style with the local cabinet-makers was the use of the narrow three-line inlay. The center strip is usually made out of some light-colored wood stained black; occasionally it is made out of ebony. The two outer strips are made of a light-colored wood to give a contrasting effect. Holly and satinwood were used for this purpose but the greatest amount of such inlay appears to be hard maple. Card tables, pembroke tables, and some sideboards are known that have inlaid panels made out of satinwood. Other woods used for this purpose were amboyna, rosewood, and tulipwood.

The bellflower was commonly employed by the local cabinet-makers. Considerable variation has been noticed in both its size and shape, yet most of the designs fall somewhat into a general pattern (*see* line drawing). Many are blunt with the center petal only a little elongated and they are usually "scratched" rather than scrolled or pieced and the edges are not scorched in hot sand. The "scratches" were rubbed with lamp black to accentuate the lines. Occasionally some bellflowers had scorched edges.

Some extant pieces of local furniture are inlaid with ivory bellflowers. These too are scratched but their shape is much more pagoda-like. To what extent the ivory bellflower was used by the local cabinet-maker is not known. Ivory was imported from Africa directly into Charleston.[2]

The fan inlay was commonly employed but it seldom reached gaudy proportions and was used rather sparingly on individual pieces of furniture. The segmented wooden rosettes, frequently found on the swan-necked pediments, generally have a small wooden core in the center where the segments come together.

In some cases the decoration is not limited to one side of the leg but has been found on two or even three sides. Line inlay has been noted on both the top and underside of the leaves of card tables; sometimes on the edge. How general this practice was has not yet been determined. The light-colored cuff is fairly common on the sideboard, pembroke, and card tables. It appears to vary both in height from the floor and in the height of the actual cuff.

[63]

Ball and Claw Foot

THE EIGHTEENTH CENTURY INVENTORIES reveal that quantities of ball and claw (or as it was frequently called "clawfoot") furniture was in the homes of the Charlestonians. Locally made pieces, however, are now so rare in Charleston that no adequate description of the style can be given. Only after a large number of such pieces have been located and carefully studied will a definitive description be possible of the kind of foot generally used by the local cabinet-makers. The few pieces of local origin that have been found in Charleston have a virile clean-cut foot with the rear toe fully accentuated.

For many years collectors have assiduously sought ball and claw foot furniture and this is probably the greatest single factor accounting for its local scarcity. Certainly an appreciable amount of such furniture must have survived, but, as with almost every kind of Charleston-made furniture, there is still the question of where it is and under what origin it is masquerading.

Japanned Furniture

IT IS A MATTER OF RECORD THAT THE Charlestonians owned japanned furniture. The early inventories occasionally, though rarely, mention a piece of japanned ware among the household effects of opulent planters or merchants. In an inventory dated July 27, 1724, is listed a "Japan Chest-of-Drawers" valued at £40.[1] The following year appears a "Jappand Scriptore" value at £20;[2] a little later there is mention of a "Japanned Corner Cupboard." Until about the middle of the eighteenth century, a piece of japanned furniture is rarely listed in the inventories; after that time there is practically no mention of it.

The rare occurrence of japanned furniture can be readily explained by the fact that it deteriorated rapidly in the moist climate and the humid summer heat of South Carolina unless it were the true oriental lacquer. Moreover, most japanned furniture is made out of an inferior wood which would be subject to borers. Finally Charlestonians quickly recognized the superiority of mahogany for its enduring qualities, and the early cabinet-makers produced mahogany furniture to meet that preference. Nevertheless, some japanned furniture must have been produced.

Records prior to 1732, the date of the founding of the *South Carolina Gazette*, fail to reveal the name of any japanners, but on April 7, 1757, John Davison advertised in the *Gazette* that "Having undertaken to follow the business of House and Ship Painting, Plumbing, Glazing, and Japanning, takes this method to acquaint the public therefore . . ." Wayne and Ruger, Painters and Glaziers, advertised in the *South Carolina Gazette; And Country Journal* on May 10, 1768, that "they carry on the House and Ship-Painting Business, in all its Branches; Signs and Floor Cloths, painted as neat as any in London, Gilding, Japanning, Glazing, etc. etc." So far it is only in these advertisements that any reference to japanning has been found.

Among the articles in the sale of Mrs. Loocock's furniture which took place on April 12, 1800, is found "an elegant set of JAPANNED Chairs and two SOFAS."[3] Presumably this furniture was done in the prevailing style of japanning of that time, and is not to be confused with the japanning of the earlier period.[4]

Brasses

TECHNICALLY SPEAKING, BRASSES SHOULD not be included in a study of furniture, but furniture requiring brasses would indeed look strange without them. From the mid-eighteenth century "brasses for furniture" is often listed by the various merchants in their advertisements noting the arrival of a shipment of goods from London.[1] In fact, furniture brasses appear so frequently in the advertisements during this period that even if one did not know the number of cabinet-makers working in Charleston, one could not help but draw the conclusion that a large amount of furniture was being made there.

Feeling that he could compete with the importation, John Robertson started his own brass foundry, as is indicated by his advertisement in the *South Carolina Gazette* of December 16, 1760: "John Robertson, Brass-Founder, in King-Street. Begs leave to return thanks to those gentlemen and others who have been pleased to favor him with their custom, and at the same time informs them that he continues to make, in the neatest manner, all sorts of brass candlesticks and church-lusters or branches; also cabinet, desk, drawer, coach, chair and chaise mountings; brass tongs, shovels and fenders; bells, brass weights, . . . READY MONEY will be given for old brass, copper, pewter, bell mettal (*sic*) or lead, by said *Robertson*." No doubt many of the local cabinet-makers availed themselves of the brasses from Robertson's foundry. While it would be gratifying to the owner of a Charleston-made piece to surmise that he was also the owner of Charleston-made brasses, there probably will never be a way of telling a locally-made brass from an imported one.

Throughout the last decade of the eighteenth century and well into the nineteenth century one finds advertisements telling of brasses imported from abroad.[2] One of the most attractive features of Charleston furniture is its lovely brasses.

Polishes

AT SO REMOTE A PERIOD IT IS EXTREMELY difficult to know how the local cabinet-makers finished their furniture. Records are fragmentary; therefore any statement will have to be based a great deal on assumption. Because of the strong influence of London and the large number of London-trained cabinet-makers working in Charleston, it is reasonable to assume that furniture made in the pre-Revolutionary period was finished in the then prevailing London style. That invaluable document, the account book of Thomas Elfe, reveals that from time to time he purchased linseed oil and varnish,[1] undoubtedly to use on his furniture. He and his contemporary cabinet-makers possibly used beeswax dissolved in turpentine to give their furniture its final polishing.[2]

When it became stylish to have furniture more highly polished, we get a hint of the method from the following advertisement in the *City Gazette* for March 15, 1805: "G. Graham, Student from the Royal Academy, London, Portrait Painting, in oil or water . . . Furniture varnished." Undoubtedly the Charlestonians were keeping abreast of the prevailing style. However, the following letter from Joel R. Poinsett [after whom the Poinsettia was named] throws a rather interesting sidelight on what he thought about new-looking furniture. The letter is dated October 5, 1833, and is addressed to J. B. Campbell. It reads in part: "I just recollect to have forgotten to call and tell Mr. May the Cabinet maker on Qn. [Queen] St. what is to be done with my Card Tables—tell him they are to be levelled, nothing more and especially let him abstain from cleaning them up and making them look new—a thing I abhor—I like old looking furniture and as they will probably go to the Cottage newness must be avoided." [3]

During the last quarter of the nineteenth century it appears to have been the custom among many Charleston families to have their furniture varnished. This was probably done at irregular intervals or whenever the furniture became dingy. Many pieces of furniture have come to light that show many layers of varnish. With the passage of time these many coats have become so deeply cracked that the surface gives the appearance of being "gator" backed.

Tools

IN ORDER TO MAKE FINE FURNITURE IT IS necessary to have fine tools. While it is true that the local cabinet-makers were undoubtedly ingenious in devising certain types of tools needed in their trade, the vast majority came from abroad. An advertisement in the *Gazette* of May 13, 1769, states that a shipment of carpenters' and cabinet-makers' tools had just arrived from London. Such an advertisement would lead us to believe, if we were not already aware of the fact, that a considerable number of cabinet-makers were plying their trade in Charleston. It seems to have been the custom to import cabinet-makers' tools, for a similar advertisement appeared in the *Times* on November 2, 1801. It was during this decade that we find the greatest number of cabinet-makers working in Charleston.

Part 4: CHARLESTON CABINET-MAKERS

These are the men who made the furniture. It is hoped that eventually their work will be identified and belated recognition be accorded their craftsmanship.

Josiah Allen
WORKING 1809–1813

We know very little about Josiah Allen. His name appears for the first time in the 1809 directory. The following year he assigned a lot in Bottle Alley to Silvia Manwill;[1] and on Christmas Day, 1811, his son Josiah Smith was baptized.[2] His name is again listed in the 1813 directory, but after that time there appear to be no extant records of him.

Robert Archbald
WORKING ?

In taking out his citizenship papers in Charleston in 1799, Robert Archbald stated that he was a cabinet-maker by profession and a native of Dalyshire, Scotland.[1] Nothing is known of his activities as a craftsman or of what became of him.

John Artman
WORKING 1803

John Artman's name appears in only one directory, that for 1803, where he is listed as a cabinet-maker at No. 28 Meeting Street. It is reasonable to suppose that he gave up cabinet-making and became a planter; on December 5, 1817, letters were granted to Peter Artman, coachmaker, to administer the estate of John Artman, planter of James Island.[1]

Charles August
WORKING 1809

Charles August appears in but one directory, that of 1809, at which time he is listed as a cabinet-maker at No. 99 Queen Street.

William Axson, Jr.
1739–1800   WORKING 1768–1800

It is not known under whom William Axson learned his trade, but by 1763 he was in business with Stephen Townsend (*q.v.*) on the northeast corner of Tradd and Church Streets.[1] Two years later most of their shop was destroyed by a fire which occurred in the early morning hours. They were held in such respect by the citizens that a subscription was started to help reimburse them for this loss, and the money was raised by the end of the day.[2] Axson's association with Townsend came to an end by 1768, for at that time Townsend is advertising that he is moving his shop to Meeting Street,[3] while Axson states that his shop is on White Point.[4]

The interior woodwork in Pompion Hill Chapel on the Cooper River and in St. Stephen's Church, in the Parish of that name, was done by Axson. He seems to have formed some sort of partnership with Villepontoux but it is thought that Villepontoux probably furnished the brick and did the actual brick work for both churches. Axson was paid £300 for doing the woodwork of the gallery of St. Stephen's, under contract terms providing that if it was not finished within a period of four months there was to be a penalty of £50.[5] Axson's name, together with a masonic emblem, can be seen to this day incised on both Pompion Hill Chapel and St. Stephen's Church.[6] The churches were built in 1763 and 1767.

Axson, the son of William Axson, was probably born in Charleston. In 1761 he married Elizabeth Mouzon[7] and two years later his twin sons, Jehu and John, were born.[8] In 1773 he was elected a member of the South Carolina Society.[9] During the Revolution he is shown as being on the Muster Roll of Capt. James Bentham's Company of Militia (1778).[10] When Charleston was captured by the British, Axson was sent aboard one of the terrible prison ships anchored in the harbor.[11] Presumably for not taking the oath of allegience to the Crown, Axson, his wife, and two children were banished to Philadelphia.[12]

After his return from banishment we hear little about him, but in 1788 he marched in the Federal Procession as a cabinet-maker.[13] Axson died on September 2, 1800, in his 61st year. In his will he mentions his wife Mary and four sons.

Jonathan Badger
WORKING 1746–c.1755

Either Jonathan Badger was very versatile or there were two men of the same name living in Charleston during the same period. The cabinet-maker is first made known to us in 1746 when he purchased ½ part of a lot on the south side of Tradd Street from Ann Waight.[1] Two years later he sold a Negro girl to Joseph Vanderhorst for £125.[2]

However, on November 13, 1752, the following advertisement appeared in the *South Carolina Gazette:* "Just Published (neatly engraved on a fine Copper-Plate) a collection of the best Psalm and Hymn tunes, to be sold by the Subscriber at his house . . . As this is the first collection of the kind ever made in this Province, and all the choicest tunes are inserted therein, tis hoped, all Lovers of Vocal Musick, will be disposed to encourage the Compiler, the price of the book is no more than 20 Shillings. Jonathan Badger." It is rather remarkable for a cabinet-maker to be selling such an item. Three years later we find that he leased a lot on Tradd Street from Alexander Garden and at that time he is spoken of as a joiner.[3] But two years later when he purchased a lot in Ansonborough he speaks of himself as "Gentleman," [4] the inference being that if there was only one man by that name in Charleston, he had by that time made enough money to retire from the cabinet-making business. In the same year his daughter Mary was born.[5]

In 1763 and for the next three years we find that Jonathan Badger was keeper of the Assembly, and that in 1765 he received, from that body, the sum of £100 for the "Valuation of a house pulled down in the late fire." [6] Frequently houses were pulled down or blown up to prevent fires from becoming conflagrations and apparently the owners were reimbursed for their loss. Badger was appointed attorney for Mary Scottowe to administer on the estate of Joshua Scottowe in 1768.[7] In April 1770 he was a member of the Grand Jury [8] but in the next month he appointed Joseph Badger, Painter and Glazier, to be his true and lawful attorney; at that time Jonathan Badger and his wife Mary were living at Newport, Rhode Island. In this instrument he again speaks of himself as "Gentleman." [9] Badger must have remained at Newport, for we find that four years later Mary Scottowe had to revoke his appointment as her attorney because "the said Jonathan Badger hath since removed from Charles Town and it becomes necessary for me to appoint some other person in his stead." [10]

It is not known whether he returned to Charleston. However, on March 20, 1793, a Jonathan Badger was admitted to Orange Lodge No. 14 (Masonic). The late date makes it unlikely that this was the cabinet-maker; more probably it was his son or some near relative bearing the same name.

Thomas Barker
WORKING 1694

The date of Thomas Barker's arrival in Charleston is unknown but it must have been early. On February 14, 1694, Thomas Barker, Joyner, administered the estate of John Parker, mariner of Jamaica.[1] In the following year Mrs. Barker entered a caveat to the estate of June Futthy and prayed for letters of administration.[2] The fact that Mrs. Barker was acting in behalf of her husband leads to the suggestion that either he was not in the colony, or that he had died. The latter supposition, however, is doubtful, for on April 22, 1706, Mr. Louis Pasquereau and Company entered their caveat to the estate of Thomas Barker, deceased, as principal creditors,[3] and it seems hardly likely that Pasquereau and Company would have waited a decade before entering their caveat. It is much more likely that Barker died shortly before the date of the caveat.

These legal instruments refer to Barker as a "joyner." Had he been a carpenter he would have been spoken of as a "house joyner." Hence, it may be assumed that he was actually a maker of furniture.

Charles Barksdale
–1757   WORKING 1741–

An advantageous marriage probably explains why Charles Barksdale was able to

Fig. 54 SIDEBOARD Height 40″; width 6′1″; depth—center 27½″, end 19½″

Fig. 55 SIDEBOARD Height 39″; width 70″; depth—center 27¾″, end 23″

Fig. 56 SIDEBOARD Height 42″; width 6′11½″; depth 32″

Fig. 57 SIDEBOARD Height 39¼″; width 65″; depth—center 29″, end 22½″

Fig. 58 SIDEBOARD Height 35⅛″; width 49⅞″; depth—center 22″, end 20½″

Fig. 59 SIDEBOARD Height 38½″; width 66″; depth—center 27³⁄₁₆″, end 24″

Fig. 60 SIDEBOARD Height 36½″; width 57¼″; depth 23¾″

Fig. 61 SIDEBOARD Height—back 49½″, front 42″; width 6′7⅞″;
depth—center 26½″, end 22⁹⁄₁₆″

Fig. 62 EIGHT-LEGGED SIDEBOARD
Height 39½″; width 7′2″; depth—center 23½″, end 16⅛″

Fig. 63 SIDEBOARD Height 36¾″; width 54⅛″; depth—center 23⅞″, end 20⅞″

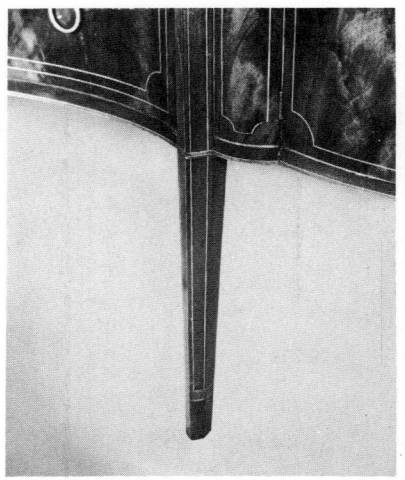

Fig. 64 DETAIL OF FIVE-SIDED LEG *(see Fig. 57)*

Fig. 65 COTTON BOLL INLAY IN SIDEBOARD

Fig. 66 FOUR-LEGGED SIDEBOARD dimensions not available

amass a substantial amount of worldly goods by the time of his death. On the fifth of May, 1741, Mary Wingood, widow of Charles Wingood, and her daughter, conveyed some property to John Sauseau with the consent of Charles Barksdale, cabinet-maker.[1] Two days later Barksdale married the widow Wingood.[2] He seems to have continued his trade for a few years in Christ Church Parish, for we find that in 1745 he bought some Negroes and at that time he speaks of himself as a joiner.[3] When we next hear of him, several years later, he is spoken of as a "planter," [4] and he appears to have continued as a planter from that time on. There is nothing to indicate when he gave up the trade of cabinet-making.

In 1755, when he purchased 482 acres of land in Christ Church Parish, he is spoken of as being a large land owner.[5] His will shows that he had three sons and two daughters.[6] It is possible that one of the girls mentioned in it as his daughter was actually his step-daughter. His inventory reveals that he had among other things a large number of Negroes, cattle, oxen, and sheep. The total value amounted to £15,758, a sizeable amount even if it was in local currency.[7]

James Barnes
WORKING 1801

The 1801 directory shows that James Barnes, a cabinet-maker, resided at No. 132 Church Street Continued. His name is not listed in the directory for the following year, nor is it known what happened to him. Probably he was one of those cabinet-makers who kept moving from place to place.

Gerred E. Barrite
WORKING 1824

Barrite's name does not appear in the 1822 directory. We first hear of him on April 1, 1824, when he purchased a piece of property on Church Street from Charles B. Mease.[1] On November 16 of that year the following rather pretentious advertisement appeared in the *Courier* reading: "G. E. Barrite, Cabinet-Maker. Gratefully acknowledges the goodness

and liberality of the citizens of Charleston and its vicinity, and begs leave to inform them that he has re-commenced his business at No. 107 *Church street* in front of Concert Hall . . . LaFayette Bedsteads, the most elegant pattern offered in this city, price $55 a 65: Bureaus $16 a 25; Ladies Work Tables, large size $18 a 20 . . . Mahogany half Blinds, $6 a piece . . . Sofas and Chairs re-stuffed and covered at short notice . . . Two Journeymen will find steady employment. N. B. A colored Boy of Proper age, will be taken as an Apprentice."

Several interesting facts may be deduced from this advertisement: first, Barrite must have been working before this time if he "re-commenced" his business; second, Lafayette Bedsteads were in vogue, and their price is also given; third, Barrite must have been successful at this time if he could offer employment to two journeymen cabinet-makers; and finally, his taking a colored boy as an apprentice indicates that such apprenticing was a normal custom of the time.

In spite of this advertisement, apparently Barrite did not prosper. The 1829 directory lists a G. E. Barit (*sic*) as a grocer. His name does not appear in the directory for 1831. Two years later the property that Barrite had purchased in 1824 was sold at public auction to Mrs. Harriette Sollee for a foreclosure of a mortgage,[2] and with that date the records end.

Mitchell Barville
WORKING 1807–1816

Although he is listed in the directories as living on Society Street nothing further can be ascertained about Mitchell Barville. In all probability he was employed by some other cabinet-maker. The records of the Register of Mesne Conveyance provide no evidence that he owned any property nor is his will filed in the Probate Court.

William Baylis
WORKING 1796

All that is known about William Baylis comes from an advertisement inserted in the

City Gazette and Daily Advertiser on July 1, 1796: "Lost, on the night of the Fire, Two Cabinet Maker's Benches; two Brass Backed Saws; one Dining Table; Two Breakfast Tables; one shell of a Bureau. Whoever will be so generous as to deliver any of the above Articles at William Baylis, opposite the Scotch Meeting, will receive a reward, if required." The fire referred to was the great conflagration of 1796 which destroyed a large part of the city.

It is quite possible that Baylis was associated with, or worked for, Alexander Calder (*q.v.*), for we find that Calder, a few months later, advertised that he was opposite the Scots Church. Nothing further is known of the activities of Baylis except for a deed recorded on May 17, 1797, from Henry Geddes to William Baylis, carpenter, for 640 acres of land in the Orangeburg District.[1] If this was the same Baylis, he probably moved to his new holdings.

James Beamer
–1693/4   WORKING C. 1687–1693/4

While James Beamer is spoken of only as a joiner, his inventory clearly reveals that he made furniture. The inventory lists "rings for drawers," "a parcel of bed Scrues," a large number of "gouges" and "chissells," "200 foote of cedar boards," and a parcel of cedar.[1] The mention of this last item helps to substantiate the theory that cedar was the wood most used in the seventeenth century.

It is not known when Beamer came to this country, but in 1687 he devised to his stepson, Joseph Tattnall, certain properties that were to be delivered to him at the age of twenty-one.[2] In Beamer's will, recorded on March 19, 1693/4, he mentions his two sons, John and Jacob, his wife Margaret and his son-in-law [step-son] Joseph Tattnall.[3]

Claude Becaise [*Becaisse*]
1763–   WORKING 1806–1816

As his name indicates Charles Becaise was a Frenchman. The date of his arrival in Charleston is unknown but his name is listed for the first time in the 1806 directory. It was not until 1815 that he took out his citizenship papers. At that time he stated that he was fifty-two years old and late of Provence in France.[1] Undoubtedly he learned his trade in that country, and it is quite reasonable to suppose that he would have added a distinctive French touch to his furniture. It is not known what eventually happened to him.

Lewis Besseleu
WORKING 1806–1807

A Lewis Besseleu (probably the cabinet-maker) was born on March 26, 1779.[1] Besseleu appears in two directories, those of 1806 and 1807. He is listed as a cabinet-maker at No. 29 Beaufain Street. It is not known what happened to him after 1807. Letters of Administration were granted to Elizabeth Besselleu (*sic*), widow, on November 2, 1827, to administer on the estate of John Lewis Besselleu, coach-maker.[2] Possibly this is the same man, who had given up cabinet-making to become a coach-maker.

John Biggard
WORKING 1767

John Biggard, "lately arrived from Philadelphia," was primarily a turner but in the advertisement which he inserted on March 23, 1767, in the *South Carolina Gazette; And Country Journal* he states that he has opened his shop on Queen Street "where gentlemen may be supplied with windsor and garden chairs, walking sticks and many other kinds of turnery ware, as neatly finished and cheaper than can be imported." At the time, Windsor chairs were being imported from both England and Philadelphia. Biggard no doubt made his Windsor chairs in the same manner as he had been taught to do in Philadelphia. Which brings up the interesting question of how one is to distinguish between a locally made Windsor chair turned by Biggard and an imported Philadelphia-made Windsor chair.

The records fail to reveal how long Biggard maintained his turner's shop on Queen Street or what eventually happened to him.

Martin Binsky
−1758   c. 1748–1750

Martin Binsky or Bensky is preserved for us not because of the furniture he made but because he lost his wife. The following item appears in *The South Carolina Gazette* for September 13–16, 1751: "MARY ANN BINSKY, the Wife of *Martin Binsky*, having eloped from her husband, with most part of his effects. This is therefore to *forwarn* all persons, from trusting the same *Mary Binsky*, in the name of her husband, for he will not be accountable for any debts by her contracted, after publication hereof. MARTIN BINSKY." The name of Mary's paramour is unknown. Binsky and Mary Stongeon had married on February 9, 1748.[1]

Apparently Binsky continued in business and ultimately found himself a new wife, for in his will which was probated on April 15, 1758, he names his wife Christina executrix and leaves £300 "lawful money to his son Johannes to purchase a negro boy not exceeding 13 or 14 years of age to be bound out to a Cabinet Maker."[2] The largest single item in Binsky's inventory is fifty gallons of rum valued at £50.[3]

Jonathan Bird
1777–1807   WORKING C. 1807

All that is known about Bird is contained in an article in the *City Gazette* for September 22, 1807: "Died, on Sullivan's Island, on Saturday morning last, Mr. Jonathan Bird, Cabinet-maker, aged 30 years, a native of Yorkshire, England. The pleasing manners and disposition of this young man, had endeared him to his friends and acquaintances who will long deplore the loss of so valuable a friend and member of society." His inventory shows that Bird was a man of small means.[1] It is not known when he came to Charleston or for whom he worked.

Nathaniel Block
WORKING 1809

Block is another cabinet-maker of whom practically nothing is known. Doubtless, he worked for some one else and then moved to another locality. He is listed only in the directory of 1809, and is shown as living on Wentworth Street.

John Bonner
WORKING 1822–1855

For a man who worked in Charleston as a cabinet-maker for over thirty years, remarkably little is known about John Bonner's activities. His name appears for the first time in the 1822 directory; the last in the directory of 1855. The only other record that we have of him comes from the Records of the Stewards of the Orphan House. "Sept. 11, 1828 Francis Payne an Orphan House Boy was bound out to John Bonner, cabinet-maker." Two years later Payne was transferred from Bonner to William Meeker, though the reason for the transfer is not given.

Bonner's will is not in the files of the Probate Court nor is any notice of his death to be found in the records of the Health Department.

Thomas Bradford
−1799   WORKING 1792–1799

Were it not for the fact that the Probate Court, when granting letters of administration to Mrs. Lydia Ann Bradford, widow, speaks of the late Thomas Bradford as a cabinet-maker, he would not be included in this work,[1] for it is thought that he was primarily an upholsterer. In 1792, when he formed a copartnership with Henry Clements, a cabinet- and chairmaker, he speaks of himself as an upholsterer.[2] It is not known how long the copartnership lasted.

In 1794 Bradford purchased from Edward Rutledge a lot on King Street for £550 Sterling money.[3] Two years later he purchased, at a Sheriff's sale, a lot on the east side of Church Street for £924.[4] In neither deed is his occupation given. The inventory of his estate makes no mention of any cabinet-maker's tools but lists a great deal of material that would normally be found in a dry goods store.[5] This material was probably used by Bradford in his upholstery business.

Charles Brewer
WORKING PRIOR TO 1729

Nowhere can a mention of Charles Brewer's occupation be found. However, in the inventory of his estate taken on September 29, 1729, is listed a large number of planes, gauges, and chisels; of even greater significance is the entry of "a parcel of Turning tools" and "1 glew pott and brushes."[1] Such articles give strong indication that Brewer must have made furniture.

Richard Brickles
WORKING PRIOR TO 1738

In his will, dated August 13, 1737, and probated a year later, Richard Brickles speaks of himself as a joiner. He also mentions owning part of lot No. 136 "bounded to the northward on my Dwelling House commonly known by the name of the Crown Inn in which I now dwell." He appoints his wife Sarah and Archibald Young, carpenter, as executors. Brickles speaks of his son Thomas and desires that "he go to school until 14 and then apprenticed to a carpenter."[1]

Brickles and Sarah Warmingham were married in January, 1732. The date of his marriage and the date of his will, considered together, suggest that Brickles died when he was a comparatively young man.

The following January their son Richard was born,[2] but the child must have died in infancy, for he was not mentioned in his father's will. Brickles' son Thomas must have been very young at the time of his father's death; in September, 1747, John Nelson was granted letters of guardianship to Thomas Brickles until he should reach the age of fourteen.[3]

Broomhead & Blythe
WORKING 1732

It is not known when the partnership of Broomhead and Blythe was formed. Their only advertisement appeared in the *South Carolina Gazette* for August 12–19, 1732: "At New-Market Plantation, about a mile from Charleston, will continue to be sold all sorts of Cabinet Work, chests of Drawers, and Mahogany Tables and Chairs made after the best manner; as also all sorts of peer Glasses, Sconces, and dressing Glasses. Where all sorts of bespoke Work is made and mended at the lowest Price, by Mess. Broomhead and Blythe."

One very significant thing in this advertisement is the early mention of mahogany. There seems to be nothing new or unusual about it and one can infer that it was already in common use in Charleston by that time.

After this advertisement Broomhead disappears completely. It is thought that Blythe moved to Georgetown, S. C., for in 1733 a "Thomas Blythe of Winyaw, Joyner," sold lot No. 116 in Georgetown to Isaac Chardon and Thomas Laroche.[1]

Daniel Brown
WORKING 1801

Daniel Brown is listed in the 1801 directory as a cabinet-maker living on King Street. There appear to have been other Daniel Browns living in Charleston during the same period. In 1806 a Daniel Brown applied for a license to sell "Spiritous Liquors."[1] Whether Daniel the cabinet-maker moved away or changed his profession is not known.

Hugh Brown
WORKING 1772

Were it not for the fact that Hugh Brown conveyed some property to John Kelly it would not be known that he worked as a cabinet-maker in Charleston. In the deed dated December 30, 1772, Hugh Brown, cabinet-maker, and his wife Mary conveyed some property on the west side of King Street to Kelly.[1]

On February 4, 1774, a Hugh Brown of Granville County, planter, and Mary his wife conveyed to James Henry Butler a lot of land in Charles Town.[2] The following year a citation was granted to Mary Brown of St.

Mark's Parish to administer on the estate and effects of Hugh Brown, late of the said parish, planter.[3] The similarity of the names gives some basis for the presumption that Hugh Brown, the cabinet-maker, ultimately became a planter.

Michael Brown
WORKING 1809

In all probability Michael Brown was another peripatetic cabinet-maker. His name appears in but one directory, that of 1809, where he is named a cabinet-maker at No. 99 Queen Street. It is not known for whom he worked or where he went.

Bulkley & Co.
WORKING? 1819

The name of this firm is listed in one directory, that of 1819, which states that they are "cabinet makers" at No. 254 King Street. Since this was the same location as that of the New York Cabinet Furniture Warehouse, it seems likely that Bulkley & Co. were only importers of furniture. At that particular time a good deal of furniture made in New York was being imported into Charleston. The firm must have been in existence only a short time for no further information has been discovered concerning them.

Patrick Burke
WORKING 1801–1803

The name of Patrick Burke suggests that he must have been of Irish extraction. He is listed for the first time in the 1801 directory as being at No. 43 Queen Street. The next year he is shown as being at No. 40 Queen Street, which was the former location of the shop of Jacob Sass (q.v.). By the following year he had either moved a third time or the street numbers had been changed. The records of the Register of Mesne Conveyance provide no evidence that he owned any property nor is his will filed in the Probate Court.

James Burn
WORKING c. 1790–c. 1802

James Burn is another very little known cabinet-maker. He is listed in the city directory of 1790 as being at No. 285 King Street. In the 1802 directory he is listed as being at No. 39 Church-street-continued, but after that time there appears to be no extant record of him. Doubtless, he worked for some other cabinet-maker.

Isaac Caine
WORKING PRIOR TO 1786

The only record concerning Isaac Caine is contained in his will, dated March 28, 1786, and probated ten days later. In the will Caine, who speaks of himself as a cabinet-maker, leaves his estate to his mother; after her death it is to go to his brother John. Caine also mentions another brother by the name of Daniel.[1]

The fact that Caine was a post-Revolutionary cabinet-maker may explain why so little is known about his activities, for at the time of his death Charleston was just beginning to recover from the economic disruption caused by the Revolution.

Alexander Calder
1773–1849   WORKING 1796–c. 1807

It is not known when Alexander Calder came to Charleston, but by 1796 he was so well established that on December 10 he inserted the following advertisement in the *City Gazette and Advertiser*: "Alexander Calder, Cabinet-maker, opposite to the Scots Church, Meeting-Street, Begs to inform the Public in general, that he has on hand a Variety of elegant and useful Cabinet Work, consisting of Secretaries and Wardrobes—Secretaries and Book Cases of different patterns—Ladies dressing Chests of different forms, Card and Breakfast Tables, do, do. Elegant Sideboards, do, Sets of Dressing Tables, A variety of handsome Chairs and Sofas of the newest fashion."

Calder and a Mrs. Scott were married on February 15, 1797.[1] In taking out his citizenship papers in 1803, Calder stated that he was thirty years of age, a cabinet-maker by profession and a native of Edinburgh, Scotland.[2]

During the month of January, 1801, Calder inserted several long advertisements in the *South Carolina State Gazette, and Timothy's Daily Advertiser* stating that he had on hand "Sideboards of different patterns, Card Tables, Tea Tables and Chests of Drawers of various patterns. Also many other articles including Sofas." He ended his advertisements with "All of which will be sold low for cash or produce." It would appear that ready money was scarce and that Calder was perfectly willing to take rice or some other commodity in payment.

About 1807 Calder seems to have given up cabinet-making and gone into the hotel business. In 1809 an Alexander Calder, presumably the same man, purchased from John Ward for $16,000 the lot on the southwest corner of Queen and Church Streets "whereon a theatre formerly stood." [3] This was the site of the Planters Hotel, now the site of the Dock Street Theatre. A decade later Calder opened the Planters Hotel on Sullivans Island, S. C., for the summer.[4]

Calder became a member of Orange Lodge No. 14 (Masonic) on December 4, 1807, and was admitted to the St. Andrews Society in 1819. Calder appears to have died childless; in his will, probated March 17, 1849, he mentions Alexander Calder, son of his nephew James Calder, and several other nephews and nieces.[5] Calder died of "old age" at the age of seventy-eight and is buried in the churchyard of the First Presbyterian Church,[6] opposite his old shop.

James Calder
1790–1855   WORKING 1809–1855

James Calder, a nephew of Alexander Calder, came to Charleston as a very young man. In 1809 his shop was situated at No. 38 Meeting Street, probably at the same location as that of his uncle. By that time, however, his uncle seems to have abandoned the cabinet-making business and to be devoting his time to running a hotel.

In taking out his citizenship papers in 1813,

James Calder stated that he was twenty-three years of age, a cabinet-maker by profession, and a native of Glasgow, Scotland.

In 1813 his son Alexander, undoubtedly named for his uncle, was baptized. His wife Marion (*sic*), daughter of Thomas Wallace, another Scotchman and cabinet-maker, died on November 14, 1816, at the age of twenty-two.

Like all good Scotchmen, Calder became a member of the St. Andrews Society, to which he was admitted in 1816. He continued in the cabinet-making business, moving to different locations in the city, until the time of his death, which occurred on November 21, 1855. Strangely enough, Calder is interred in the "Lutheran Burying Ground."

It is not known when he remarried or to whom, but in his will Calder mentions his wife Sarah and seven children.

Another James Calder, a merchant, lived in Charleston at the same time as the cabinet-maker.

Benjamin Canter
WORKING 1813

Canter appears in only one directory, that of 1813, where he is shown as living at 64 Broad Street. Elzas, in his *Jews of South Carolina*, lists a Benjamin Canter as being in Charleston in 1802. This is probably the same man, though it is strange that his name does not appear in any of the previous directories.

Andrew Carman
1785–1806   WORKING 1806

The only information that can be found about Carman is contained in his obituary notice, which appeared in the *Courier* on November 7, 1806: "Departed this life, on Friday last, the 31st ult., after a lingering illness, in the 22d year of his age, Mr. Andrew Carman, cabinet-maker." It is not known under whom he learned his trade.

John Carne
WORKING C. 1765

The name of John Carne occurs in an indenture, dated May 12, 1765, by which

Mary Hutchinson transferred three slaves to Thomas and Mathias Hutchinson. Carne is there spoken of as a cabinet-maker. The marriage of John Carne and Mary Hutchinson took place a short time later.

Little is known of Carne. In 1764 Edward Weyman, an upholsterer and plate glass polisher and grinder formed a copartnership with Carne. On March 31, 1764, they advertised in the *South Carolina Gazette* under the name of Weyman and Carne. In addition to saying that they would quicksilver and frame old glass, they stated that they were also engaged in the "several Branches of Cabinet-making." It is reasonable to suppose that Carne was the new partner. The copartnership was of short duration for on December 2, 1766, Edward Weyman was advertising by himself. What subsequently happened to Carne is not known.

William Carwithen
1704–1770   WORKING 1730–c. 1750

William Carwithen married Mary Bisset on January 1, 1730.[1] That is the earliest fact that we have concerning him. In 1732 Mary Carwithen, the wife of William Carwithen, purchased from Jane Bissett, widow of Elias Bissett, a lot on Middle Street (Elliott Street).[2] Jane was probably the mother of Mary.

When Carwithen was well established, some one (possibly a competitor) started a rumor that he was going out of business. Carwithen answered the rumor with the following advertisement in the *South Carolina Gazette* on April 21, 1733: "Whereas I have been informed by People thro' several Parts of the Country, that there has been a Malicious Report, persuading my Customers that I have left off Trade: These are to satisfy all People as shall want Desk and Book-Cases, Chests of Drawers, Clock Cases, Tables of all Sorts, Peer-Glass Frames, Swinging Frames, and all other sorts of Cabinet Ware, made as neat as ever, and Cheap."

On August 7, 1735, Carwithen was granted 450 acres on the Edisto River by "His said Majesty by his Letters Patent under the great seal of the Province." Two years later he sold this property to Samuel Fley.[3] In 1746 Carwithen and his wife Mary sold a piece of property on Middle Street to Isaac Holmes. This may have been the same piece of property that Mary bought in 1732. In the deed Carwithen is spoken of as a cabinet-maker.[4]

Nothing more can be found about Carwithen the cabinet-maker. However, on November 20, 1756, Governor Lyttleton appointed William Carwithen, Gentleman, to be messenger to the Commons House of Assembly.[5] In April, 1770, William Carwithen was a member of the Grand Jury.[6]

On September 3, 1770, the following obituary notice appeared in the *South Carolina & American General Gazette*: "Last Sunday died, aged 66 (41 of which he had resided in the province) Mr. William Carwithen, Librarian of the Charles Town Library Society." On October 5, 1770, a citation was granted to Mary Carwithen to administer "the Estate and Effects of William Carwithen late of St. Michael's parish Gentleman as nearest of kin."[7]

It is not known when Carwithen gave up cabinet-making nor when he became Librarian of the Charles Town Library Society.

Thomas Charnock
WORKING c. 1810–c. 1822

Charnock was a free Negro. In 1810 he sold a lot and building on the north side of Parsonage Alley to Sara Cooper for $600.[1] His name appears in the 1819 directory as a cabinet-maker at No. 16 Magazine Street. Three years later he moved to 37 Anson Street.[2]

By 1819 there were probably many Negro cabinet-makers working in Charleston. No doubt most of them were slaves owned by white cabinet-makers. Since the free Negro cabinet-maker does not make his appearance until many years later, Charnock appears as an exceptional figure. He may have been, as a matter of fact, the first free Negro cabinet-maker to work in Charleston.

John Clarke
WORKING 1809

Clarke's name appears only in the directory of 1809, where he is listed as a cabinet-maker at No. 29 King Street. Nothing further can be discovered concerning him.

George Claypoole
WORKING C. 1728

The Claypoole family appear to have been cabinet-makers in Philadelphia. The only information that we have about George comes from a single deed made "Between George Claypoole late of Philadelphia but now of Charles Town, Joyner and Thomas Kimberly, chairmaker," for six acres of land near Charleston for £400 current money. "Whereas the sd Rebecca Weekley formerly Rebecca Rouse Died intestate leaving issue one Daughter named Rebecca then married to one Joseph Claypoole of the city of Philadelphia . . . Joiner which sd Rebecca Claypoole is since Deceased leaving Issue behind her the above named George Claypoole the eldest son and heir." [1]

It is not known when George Claypoole came to Charleston or how long he worked there. Except for the deed just quoted, his name does not appear in the records of the Register of Mesne Conveyance nor in the Records of the Probate Court.

Josiah Claypoole
WORKING 1740–1757

Josiah Claypoole was the son of Joseph Claypoole. No doubt he learned his trade from his father in Philadelphia. In 1738 Joseph gave to his son "his Stock and Implements of Trade" and apparently retired from business. [1] Within two years Josiah had moved to Charleston, for the following item appeared in the *South Carolina Gazette* on March 22, 1740: "Notice is hereby given, that all Persons may be supplied with all sorts of Joyner's and Cabinet-Maker's Work, as Desk and Book Cases, with arch'd, Pediment or O G Heads, common Desks of all sorts, Chests of Drawers of all Fashions fluited or plain; all sorts of Tea Tables, Side-Boards and Waiters, Rule joint Skeleton Tables, Frames for Marble Tables, all after the newest and best Fashions, and with the greatest Neatness

and Accuracy by *Josiah Claypoole* from *Philadelphia,* who may be spoke with at Capt. *Crosthwaite's* in *King-*street, or at his Shop next Door to Mr. Lormier's near the Market Square, he has Coffin Furniture of all sorts, either flour'd, silver'd or plain. NB He will warrant his Work for 7 years, the ill Usage of careless Servants only excepted."

Claypoole prospered to such an extent that he was unable to supply the demands of his customers, for he advertised in the *South Carolina Gazette* on April 9, 1741, that ". . . whereas by a constant Hurry of Cabinet Work, it has so happened that I have disappointed several good Customers, this is further to give Notice, that in a short Time I shall have two good workmen from *London,* and shall then be in a Capacity to suit any Person who shall favor me with their Employ."

The next year Claypoole advertised for "an indented Servant from *London,* named Robert Allen, by Trade a Carpenter, but can work at the Cabinet makers Business . . ." Allen had run away. The advertisement continues with a description of Allen and warns all Masters of vessels to be careful not to give him passage. Claypoole then offers a reward of £25 and all reasonable expenses. [2] Allen may have been one of the two workmen Claypoole expected from London. It is not known whether he was apprehended.

In 1745 Claypoole requested that all persons indebted to him make payment by the first of April "in order to receive Twenty Shillings in the Pound." [3] Three years later Claypoole was in financial difficulties and he was taken into custody by the Provost Marshal for a debt he owed William Greenland (*q.v.*). [4]

Claypoole's wife was named Sarah. Their son John was buried on October 16, 1756. Another son, Thomas, was buried on October 23, 1757. The records reveal that Thomas was the son of Josiah Claypoole deceased, [5] indicating that Josiah, the cabinet-maker, must have died between October 1756 and October 1757.

Henry Clements
WORKING 1792

In March 1792 Clements formed a copartnership with Thomas Bradford (*q.v.*).

On June 28, 1792, they advertised in the *City Gazette and Advertiser* that they were moving their shop from King Street opposite Price's Alley to No. 30 Broad Street and that they would "carry on the above branches in the compleatest manner, having the newest patterns, a good assortment of wood, also a sufficient number of good workmen, which enable them to execute any quantity of furniture with dispatch and punctuality, and on the most reasonable terms for cash or produce. . . . All orders in the above branches will be well and neatly executed, such as cabriole sofas, and Chairs of various patterns, cabinet furniture of any kinds; bedsteads of all kinds and prices, Venetian blinds . . ."

They did no more advertising and it is not known how long the copartnership lasted.

William Cocks

WORKING 1798

Cocks, a Philadelphia cabinet-maker, was probably in Charleston only for a very short time. He advertised in the [Philadelphia] *Federal Gazette* on July 14, 1798. On September 14, 1798, he inserted the following advertisement in the *City Gazette and Advertiser* "At the store in Broad street . . . has for sale, for Cash or Produce only, as he intends to return immediately to the Northward. A Most elegant Assortment of Furniture just imported from Philadelphia, which he intends to sell for cost and charges." It is certain that whoever availed himself of such an offer secured a bargain.

It is not known why Cocks did not stay in Charleston. The advertisement of the "Estate of Wm Cocks, deceased" appeared in the [Philadelphia] *Federal Gazette* of November 28, 1799.

Thomas Coker

WORKING c. 1772–c. 1775

We are first introduced to Coker by an entry in the account book of Thomas Elfe (*q.v.*). In April 1772 Elfe paid Coker £30 for making a dozen chairs.[1] Whether Coker worked for Elfe on a piece basis or as an independent cabinet-maker is not clear. Coker's name appears from time to time in Elfe's account book, the last entry being in June, 1775, (a few months before the death of Elfe) when Elfe paid Coker £38 "in full."[2] Nothing more is known about him. In 1793 a Thomas Coker was living in the Georgetown District.[3] Possibly this was the same man.

Thomas Cook (e)

WORKING 1774–1792

Cook, like Coker (*q.v.*) worked for Thomas Elfe (*q.v.*). In September 1774 Elfe paid Cook £30.[1] Possibly this was also for making a dozen chairs. Nothing more is heard of him until 1781 when a Thomas Cooke (*sic*) was sent aboard one of the British prison ships lying in Charleston Harbor.[2] At the end of that year Cook and many others were banished to Philadelphia,[3] presumably for not taking the oath of allegiance to the Crown.

It is not known when Cook returned to Charleston but on May 10, 1784, he qualified as an executor of the estate of Benjamin Wheeler, another cabinet-maker.[4] The following year Cook executed a mortgage to Aaron Loocock for £476 "at the rate of 21 shilling and nine pence Sterling to the Guinea and four shillings and eight pence Sterling to the dollar, payable in gold or silver . . ." Cook gave as collateral Lot No. 6 in Romney on Charleston Neck.[5] In 1786 he was one of the sureties for the estate of Jane Massey.[6]

Cook did no advertising and he is not heard of again until 1790 when his name appears in the directory for that year as being a cabinet-maker at No. 12 Meeting Street.[7] The mortgage that he had given to Aaron Loocock was satisfied on February 3, 1792. After that time no further record can be found about him.

William Cooley

WORKING 1819

The 1819 directory lists William Cooley as a cabinet-maker residing on the King Street Road. This meant that Cooley was living outside the then city limits. It is not known what happened to him. Neither his will nor his inventory appears in the records of the Probate Court.

Charles Coquereau
WORKING 1798–1816

Charles Coquereau, "about five feet high," late of Rochelle in the French Republic, took out his first citizenship papers on April 2, 1798.[1] It is not known what happened to him for the next few years. In 1814 John Henry Schoup, an orphan house boy, was apprenticed to Coquereau and the following year another orphan house boy by the name of John Bross was also apprenticed to him.[2] The directory for 1816 lists Coquereau as a cabinet-maker at No. 196 King Street. Coquereau was one of the founders of the Societe Francaise of Charleston.[3]

His name appears in none of the later directories nor is his will recorded in the Probate Court. It is not known what eventually happened to him.

John Cowan
1790–1850   WORKING 1819–1850

John Cowan was a native of Scotland. The date of his arrival in Charleston is nowhere recorded. His name appears for the first time in the 1819 directory, where he is listed as a cabinet-maker at No. 68 Meeting Street. Subsequent directories continue to list him as a cabinet-maker. The last time his name appears is in the 1849 directory where he is shown as living at No. 5 Philadelphia Alley.

Unlike most Scotsmen who came to Charleston, Cowan apparently did not prosper, for no record can be found where he purchased any property. He died intestate at the age of sixty on November 24, 1850, of heart disease.[1]

Adam Culliatt
–1768   WORKING 1757–1768

In 1733 an Adam Culliatt was one of the petitioners requesting a new minister for Purysburg.[1] This was a settlement consisting mostly of Huguenots on the South Carolina side of the Savannah River. Whether this was the cabinet-maker or his father is not clear. The first record of the cabinet-maker appears in an advertisement in *The South Carolina Gazette* for April 14, 1757: "Being removed [from Charleston] to Jacksonborough, Pon-pon, gives notice to all gentlemen and ladies who may want any kind of Cabinet, Joiners or Carpenter's work done that they be served by him to their satisfaction . . ." Jacksonboro, situated on the Edisto River, is about twenty-five miles south of Charleston and is surrounded by many large plantations. In making this move Culliatt must have thought that there was a sufficient number of people living on these plantations to keep him occupied.

Just before his move, Culliatt purchased from Charles Lowndes, Provost Marshal, Lot No. 48 in the Village of Jacksonboro, along with three acres of land in Pon Pon for £361 currency.[2] After his establishment there Culliatt purchased additional property from time to time.

His will, which was probated on September 13, 1768, leaves land and buildings at Jacksonboro to his wife and his five children, Mary, John, James, Margaret, and William.[3] Adam Culliatt and Mary Campbell were married on July 16, 1751.[4]

Richard Cyrus
WORKING 1809

Richard Cyrus appears only in the directory of 1809, where he is named as a cabinet-maker at No. 29 King Street. This one item constitutes all that is known of him.

Robert Deans
WORKING 1750

Robert Deans, joiner from Scotland, advertised for the first time in the *South Carolina Gazette* for January 22, 1750, stating that "all kinds of cabinet and joiners work are done after the best manner, and at as low rates as any where in town . . . for ready money or country produce." It is thought that Deans gave up cabinet-making for house building, for in 1756 when he was admitted to Union Kilwinning Lodge (Masonic) he was spoken of as an architect. Three years later Deans became a member of the St. Andrews Society.

About 1758 Deans along with Benjamin Baker submitted, unsuccessfully, a bid to the Commissioners "for undertaking & furnishing the whole inside and the west front" of St. Michael's Church, which was then being built. It was specified that the inside of the Church was "to be of Cedar and we finding Timber turning & carving." [1] The next year Deans gave a mortgage to John Remington, at which time Deans was spoken of as a carpenter. [2]

We hear nothing further of Dean's activities until 1764 when he sold parts of lots Nos. 119 and 120 to James Skirving. [3] Here again Deans is spoken of as a carpenter. In the same year Deans gave Alexander Petrie, a silversmith, his power of attorney, because he was "about to depart from the Province of South Carolina for some time." [4]

With the return of peace after the Revolution, the heirs of Robert Dean (sic) submitted a claim to regain some "Confiscated Estates belonging to British Subjects lying and being in the State of So. Carolina." [5] It is not known whether Deans ever returned to Charleston nor is it known when he died.

John Francis Delorme
WORKING 1791–c.1819

Were it not for the fact that John Francis Delorme states specifically that he has for sale, "some furniture, made by himself in the newest taste," [1] he would not be included in this work, for he was primarily an upholsterer.

Before he came to Charleston Delorme lived in Philadelphia. [2] His first advertisement in Charleston appeared in the *City Gazette and Daily Advertiser* of October 19, 1791; he there speaks of himself as an upholsterer from Paris and "Informs the public in general, that he makes bed and window curtains, either after the French or English fashion," at a time when the prevailing style was French.

In 1793, when Delorme took out his citizen-ship papers he declared that he was a native of France. [3] During the years which followed he seems to have prospered, for he made frequent purchases of real estate.

Delorme occasionally imported furniture from Paris and at one time in his career "engaged several of the best hands in the Cabinet-Makers Line: any orders for any kind of Furniture, shall be neatly and punctually executed." [4] As late as 1819 Delorme was still advertising as an upholsterer. [5]

Charles Desel
1749–1807   WORKING c. 1777–1807

Charles Desel, who was of German descent, must have come to Charleston before the Revolution, for on April 11, 1777, he purchased from John Fyfe, another cabinet-maker, a house and lot on Colleton Square. [1] There is no further record of him until October 14, 1783, when he bought a lot on Church Street from Godfrey Pringle for £110 Sterling "now the lawful money of South Carolina." [2]

Desel seems to have done no advertising in the newspapers. Either he was so well established that he did not think it necessary or he worked for some one else. His name appears twice in the directory for 1790, once at No. 15 Maiden Lane, the other at No. 44 Church Street. Presumably, the latter location was his shop, in all probability located on the lot he had purchased from Pringle.

His name appears in the 1801 directory through the 1807 directory as being a cabinet-maker at No. 50 Broad Street. During the period Desel purchased several pieces of property, indicating that he must have been a success as a cabinet-maker.

Desel died on October 24, 1807, at the age of fifty-eight and was buried in the St. John's Lutheran graveyard. [3] He bequeathed his house and lot on the corner of King and Broad Streets to his wife Mary Barbara, together with eight slaves and other property. His will mentions his five children, Ann Mary, Samuel, Eliza, Mary Barbara, and Charles Lewis. [4] In his inventory is listed "a lot of Cedar and Mahogany Boards in the Cellar." The total amount of his estate was appraised at nearly fifteen thousand dollars.[5]

Desel worked in Charleston during a period when styles in furniture were undergoing a great change. In all probability the Hepplewhite style did not manifest itself in any great degree in Charleston until after the Revolution. It is interesting to conjecture how Desel, with his German background, adapted his probably heavy style of workmanship to requirements of the lighter and more delicate Hepplewhite.

Samuel Desel
−1814   WORKING −1813

Samuel Desel, the son of Charles Desel, followed in his father's footsteps. In the 1813 directory (six years after the death of Charles Desel) a Charles Desel is listed as a cabinet-maker at No. 53 Broad Street. Presumably this is an error; the name should have been Samuel. In the same year Samuel Desel, Executor of Charles Desel, sold to Charles L. Desel (his brother) a lot with a three-story brick building situated on the east side of King Street for $3200.[1] In a later directory Charles L. Desel is listed as a physician.[2]

Samuel Desel's will, dated September 30, 1814, directs "that my tools, furniture of every Kind; Boards, Benches and so forth be sold by my executors at their discretion." Samuel also mentions his brother Charles Lewis Desel who is to get his share of his estate when he reaches the age of twenty-one.[3] The will was probated November 30, 1814.

On January 3, 1815, the following notice appeared in the *City Gazette and Commercial Advertiser*: "Will be sold Mahogany Boards and Slabs, Cedar Boards, with Benches, Cabinet Makers Tools . . . Finished and unfinished Furniture being the property of Mr. Samuel Desel, deceased."

Lewis Disher
−1835   WORKING 1809−?

Though Disher's name appears only in the 1809 directory, it is thought that he worked in Charleston for many years. At one time his shop was located on the east side of King Street between Columbus and Line Streets. The fact that the area was then outside the city limits may explain why Disher's name does not appear in subsequent directories.

The Health Department Records reveal that Disher died in July, 1835, at the age of fifty-one. The Records state that he was born in Charleston, died of inflammation of the brain, and was buried in the Trinity Church burying ground. Family tradition, however, says that Disher was born in England and came to this country as a young boy. We are indebted to his great-grandson, Lewis Disher, for this information.

John Dobbins
WORKING 1768−

In 1768 John Dobbins purchased from Thomas Mills, another cabinet-maker, the 1/5 part of the estate of Timothy Bread, ship carpenter, for £63.[1] In the same year Dobbins advertised in the *South Carolina Gazette* of August 12, 1768, that he "intended to depart the province for some time." Just when he left Charleston is not known. However, two years later the following advertisement appeared in the *South Carolina Gazette; And Country Journal* of November 27, 1770: "John Dobbins. The subscriber, departing the Province in the Spring, will sell, by public vendue, . . . a neat assortment of Cabinet Work, consisting of Chairs and Tables of all kinds, Chinese Tables, carved & plain mahogany bedsteads, neat double and half chests of drawers; French chairs; brass nailed ditto; . . . He returns thanks to all his friends for their past favors, and hopes for a continuance of them to John Forthet, who carries the business on in the same shop."

Nothing more is heard of Dobbins for many years, until September, 1789, when he married Ann Pots.[2] Again he "departed the province," for on October 17, 1792, John Dobbins "late of the City of Charleston in the Province of South Carolina in America, but now of London in England, Cabinet Maker, appoints wife Ann now living in Charleston his attorney with power to dispose of his lot in Charleston and his plantation."[3] It is interesting to note that even at so late a time the British still spoke of South Carolina as a Province.

Two years later John Dobbins and Ann his wife sold 350 acres in St. Thomas' Parish to Elias Smerdon.[4] Whether John had returned to Charleston by that time or the sale was made by Ann, using his power of attorney, is not clear. His will does not appear in the records of the Probate Court, so in all probability he spent the remainder of his life in London.

James Douglas
–1816

James Douglas was primarily a turner and undoubtedly did work for cabinet-makers. He is listed as a turner in the directories from 1802 through 1809. However, in the 1816 directory James Douglas is listed as a cabinet-maker. Either this is an error or Douglas in later years branched out into cabinet-making.

His will is dated May 1, 1815, and was probated on August 1, 1816, presumably shortly after his death.

John Douglas
1773–1805   WORKING 1799–c. 1805

Even as a young man, John Douglas must have been a very successful cabinet-maker, for in 1799 he purchased from Richard Dennis a lot on the east side of Meeting Street for 650 Guineas,[1] a considerable sum of money for those days. His name appears in the 1801 directory as a cabinet-maker at No. 138 Meeting Street. When Douglas took out his citizenship papers in 1802, he declared that he was twenty-nine years old, a native of Edinburgh, Scotland, and by profession a cabinet-maker.[2] In the next year Douglas purchased another piece of property, again on Meeting Street but on the west side.[3]

Douglas must have died in 1805; on October 25 of that year Letters of Administration Intestate were granted to James Douglas, turner, to administer the estate of John Douglas.[4] His inventory made on December 31, 1805, listed five sideboards valued at $250; two secretaries

appraised at $90; and a quantity of mahogany, cedar, and pine.[5] The pine was probably used for the structural members and drawer linings of his sideboards.

James Duddell
WORKING c. 1801–c. 1806

James Duddell appears for the first time in the 1801 directory as dwelling at No. 251 Meeting Street. The following year he is shown as being at No. 209 Meeting Street.

In 1803 Duddell was one of the appraisers of the estate of Mary Ann Clark.[1] His name appears for the last time in the 1806 directory as a cabinet-maker but without an address. After that date there are no further records of him.

Lewis Duval
–1724   WORKING?

Though Lewis Duval is spoken of as a planter by one of his executors, the articles listed in his inventory indicate that at some time during his life Duval made furniture. The inventory of his estate includes a number of saws, hammers, axes, and squares, in addition to an entry of sixty-one old and new chisels and eleven hollow and round planes.[1] It is unlikely that a carpenter, at that time, would have had such an array of tools.

Duval's will is dated June 9, 1724; it was probated in the following month. In it he mentions his daughters, Ann, Martha, and Susanna.[2]

Joshua Eden
1731–1802   WORKING 1767–1801

Joshua, son of James and Jane Eden, was born on September 14, 1731.[1] Eden was a turner and chairmaker, but there is nothing to indicate under whom he learned his trade. He advertised for the first time on January 19, 1767, in the *South Carolina Gazette*, stating that he did turning "in its several branches, such as banisters, column bedposts, table frames. . . . In the meantime he continues to make straw bottom chairs; which he will sell very reasonable."

No further information concerning Eden appears until 1775, when a lot of things happened to him. In February of that year Thomas Robinson was charged with assault on Joshua Eden, and it was ordered that the Petit Jury be charged with the issue. The accounts fail to indicate how the altercation ended, but in May of the same year Eden himself became a member of the Petit Jury.[2] In August he is listed as a member of Capt. Charles Drayton's Volunteer Company.[3] On November 7, 1775, he advertised in the *South Carolina Gazette* stating that he has for sale, "some extraordinary good Spinning-Wheels . . . also for sale some very good straw bottom Chairs."

Then Eden disappears from the records for fifteen years, until the directory of 1790 names him as a turner at No. 15 Beresford Alley. In 1791 he was one of the sureties for the estate of Joseph Whilden, Sr.[4] The directory of 1801 shows that he had moved to Church Street and lists him as a chairmaker. Eden died on March 26, 1802, in the seventy-first year of his age.[5] In his will he leaves to William, "a negro man I emancipated," all of his working tools and wearing apparel.[6] His inventory reveals that his estate amounted to only a little over eleven hundred dollars.[7]

John Godfrey Ehrenpford
1786–   WORKING C. 1809–1813

John Godfrey Ehrenpford was living in Charleston by 1809; the directory of that year lists him as a cabinet-maker at No. 28 Meeting Street. Three years later, when he took out his citizenship papers, he announced that he was twenty-six years of age, a cabinet-maker by profession, and a native of Oldenburg in Germany.[1] The 1813 directory shows him as being at No. 27 Broad Street. After that all trace of him is lost. He may have moved to some other locality.

Thomas Elfe
1719–1775   WORKING C. 1747–1775

It is a matter of record that on November 28, 1775, died Thomas Elfe, Charleston cabinet-maker, in the fifty-sixth year of his age.[1] He must have been born, therefore, about 1719, and since family tradition says he came from London, it is a fair assumption that London was the place of his birth. Nothing, in fact, is known of his early years, but if it may be supposed that, like so many other craftsmen of the period, Elfe came to South Carolina after he had reached maturity, it is likely that he served his apprenticeship in England. The excellence of the workmanship in the pieces of furniture now attributed to Elfe argues that he received his early training under an excellent master.

Elfe was twenty-eight years old before his name appears in any Charleston records. On September 28, 1747, the following advertisement appeared in the *South Carolina Gazette*: "To be Raffled for, On Tuesday the 6th of October in the Evening, at the House of Mr. Thomas Blyth in Broad-street a pair of large Gilt Sconces, valued at 150£ Currency. The said Sconces and the Conditions of the Raffle may be seen at Mr. Thomas Elfe's Cabinet-maker, near Doct. Martini's." In the same year Elfe purchased a negro woman named Rinah, together with her three children, for £500 current money from one Jemmitt Cobley.[2] A financial transaction of such proportions argues that Elfe was by that time well established in Charleston. Rinah, it may be noted, was not a very satisfactory investment; she ran away and Elfe was forced to advertise for her in the *Gazette* of August 15, 1748. Shortly after her apprehension and return Elfe sold her and her children to John Dobell for £550 (September 20), thereby making a neat profit.[3]

Still further evidence of Elfe's prosperity appears in the fact that on October 3, 1748, Elfe was advertising in the *South Carolina Gazette* that he had "A very good House in *Tradd-street* near the *Printing-Office*, to be lett . . ." A few months before, he had married Mary Hancock, a widow; but the year ended tragically for Elfe with the death of his wife, whose burial is recorded on November 19.[4] Elfe remained a widower until 1755, when, on December 29, he married Rachel

Prideau.[5] By this second marriage he had several children.

The newspaper notices of the 1748–49 period yield a few other details of less importance concerning Elfe's life. In 1748, for example, John Lewis, a shoemaker from London (possibly an acquaintance of Elfe from the London years) advertised that he was "at Mr. Thomas Elfe's Cabinet-maker, who lives at the Corner opposite Mr. Eycotts . . ." In April of the following year Elfe purchased from John Brodie, Practitioner of Physick, a mulatto boy named Jemmy for £300 current money.[6]

As a maker of furniture Elfe did very little advertising. It is possible that he had become so well established that he did not think such advertising necessary. The longest advertisement which he published during his career as a craftsman appeared in the *South Carolina Gazette* of January 7, 1751. It deserves full quotation for what it reveals concerning the nature and extent of Elfe's business at this time: "Thomas Elfe, Cabinet-Maker, having now a very good upholsterer from London, does all kinds of upholsterer's work, in the best and newest manner, and at the most reasonable rates, viz: tapestry, damask, stuff, chints, or paper hangings for rooms; beds after the newest fashion, and so they may be taken off to be washed without inconvenience or damage; all sorts of festoons and window curtains to draw up, and pully rod curtains; chairs stuff covered, tight or loose cases for ditto; All kinds of Machine Chairs are likewise made, stuffed and covered for sickly or weak people, and all sorts of cabinet work done in the best manner, by the said Thomas Elfe."

The next four years are a complete blank in Elfe's biography. His name does not appear again until 1755, when he was one of the witnesses for Andrew Rutledge, one of Charleston's eminent lawyers.[7] By the next year Elfe seems to have formed a business association with Thomas Hutchinson, who was also a cabinet-maker. Working together, they made some of the balusters for the steeple of St. Michael's Church, then in the course of construction. As late as 1761 they submitted a bill to the same church for some interior woodwork they had produced.[8] At a vestry meeting held on March 7, 1763, the Church Wardens of St. Michael's were directed to employ Elfe and Hutchinson for the making of a "Mahogany Communion Table in such Demensions (*sic*) as will fit the Velvet Covering to be ready against Easter Sunday." The two cabinet-makers appear also as associated in the making of the chairs and tables for the Council Chamber. On May 19, 1758, the Council passed an act under "Extraordinary Charges" for the sum of £728.02.06 to pay for that work.[9] That the association of Elfe and Hutchinson may have been in the nature of a partnership is suggested by the fact that on August 9, 1756, they together purchased from Robert Liston, another cabinet-maker, a negro boy named Mingo for £157 current money.[10] There is nothing to indicate when Elfe and Hutchinson terminated their professional association, but they appear to have remained good friends. Hutchinson was the godfather of Thomas Elfe, Jr., and Elfe chose Hutchinson as one of the executors of his will.

All the records dealing with Thomas Elfe as a craftsman indicate that he had risen high in the estimation of his contemporaries. At the same time, he was accumulating wealth. In 1760 he found himself in a position to purchase a pew in St. Michael's Church;[11] and on April 27, 1765, he was elected a warden of the St. George's Society.[12] From this period to the end of his life there are frequent notices of his dealings in property and slaves. One notable transaction was his purchase from Mary Bryan, widow, on April 17, 1758, of two lots (Nos. 181 and 198) on the east side of Friend [Legare] Street and on the south side of Broad Street, for £575 "lawful current money of the province."[13] Apparently he built two tenements on these lots, for in his will he bequeathed one tenement to his daughter Hannah, the other to his son George. Again, on June 9, 1763, Elfe sold to Richard Hart, a chairmaker, part of Lot No. 250, situated on the north side of Queen Street.[14] The amount involved in this transaction is not given. From Benjamin Guerard, Elfe purchased, in 1765, half of Lot No. 243 for £1000 currency and 172 acres of land on what is now Daniel's Island for £500.[15] These and similar transactions later on reveal Elfe to have been a steady dealer in real estate, with an eye for good investments. At the time of his death he was, by the standards of the province, a wealthy man.

From time to time also Elfe made purchases of slaves. It is impossible to conjecture what degree of success he had in such ventures. The newspaper notices give emphasis to his difficulties rather than to his successes. On April 26, 1760, for example, Elfe was forced to advertise in the *South Carolina Gazette* for a runaway named Bob, formerly the property of Luke Stoutenburgh. Then there was the unfortunate affair of Cato, one of Elfe's slaves who was charged with having "feloniously & Burglariously, broke open the dwelling House of Lachlin Mackintosh Esquire & stealing therefrom, sundry sums of money . . ." Cato was tried before two Justices and four free holders, found guilty, and sentenced "to be hanged by the Neck until his Body should be dead." Elfe interceded on his behalf, arguing "that the Said Cato is a very young man & that it was chiefly from his own Confession, that he was convicted of the said Crime & therefore hath humbly besought & hath also undertaken & promised that the said Negro Cato, shall be transported & Shipped from off the Limits of our Province, never to return therein again that Mercy may be extended to him." Elfe's eloquence so moved the court that it was decided to "Pardon Remit & Release the said Cato, as well the felony aforesaid, Whereas he was tried & Convicted as also the Punishments, he became liable to by Reason of the same. Provided always & upon this expressed Condition that the said Cato do & shall within three Calendar Months from the Date hereof transport himself from this Province." If Cato ever returned the pardon was to become void. The degree was signed on June 18, 1771, by William Bull, Lieutenant-Governor.[16]

Elfe took apprentices as a matter of course. The kind of problems which the conscientious master was sometimes called upon to solve may be inferred from an item on January 19, 1770, reporting that Elfe entered a complaint to the Grand Jury against "Daniel Caine, living behind the Beef Market, for keeping a disorderly tipling and Gaming House; where apprentices and other youth are entertained and debauched."[17] Unfortunately, the story is incomplete: there is nothing to indicate whether Elfe succeeded in having the house closed.

It is difficult to derive any very clear information about Elfe's contacts with his fellow-craftsmen in Charleston. The records are sparse. Mention has already been made of his association with Thomas Hutchinson, the cabinet-maker. It appears also that toward the end of his life Elfe entered, for a short time, into partnership with John Fisher, but the fact must be deduced from the notice of the dissolution of the partnership, published in the *South Carolina and American General Gazette* of May 27, 1771: "The co-partnership of Elfe and Fisher being dissolved some time, and all debts due to them assigned over unto Thomas Elfe, he hopes all indebted to them will pay off the same or settle as soon as possible. I am much obliged to all Friends for their Favours, and hope for a continuance of them, as I shall carry on the Business of Cabinet-and-Chair-Making as usual, at my old Shop in Broad-street, and am their humble servant, Thomas Elfe." Fisher seems to have been a newcomer to Charleston. It is probable that he inserted the following announcement in the *South Carolina Gazette; And Country Journal* (May 5, 1767) shortly after his arrival: "John Fisher, Cabinet-Maker from London, Takes this method to acquaint the Publick, That he has taken part of the House in Tradd-street, where Mr. Wise formerly lived, and intends carrying on the Cabinet Business in all its branches. Those Gentlemen and Ladies who please to favour him with their commands, may depend upon having their orders well executed, and on the shortest notice. N. B. Venetian Window Blinds made as in London." Elfe's contact with W. Russell, "Upholsterer, Lately arrived from London," appears to have been only transient. Russell announced himself in the *South Carolina Gazette*, November 9, 1773, as humbly taking "the Liberty of informing the Ladies and Gentlemen, and the Public in General, That he has taken apartments at Mr. Elfe's, Cabinet-

Fig. 67 CABINET Height 8'5½"

Fig. 68 CABINET Height 61½"

Fig. 70 DESK CLOCK
Height 16¼″
Dial inscribed:
Himley, Charletown (sic)

Fig. 69 TALL CLOCK
Height 8′6½″
Dial inscribed:
Joshua Lockwood, Charles town

Fig. 71 TALL CLOCK
Height 8′3¾″
Dial inscribed:
Joshua Lockwood, Charles town

Fig. 72 CELLARETTE
Height 29½"; diameter 25⅝" x 18⅝"

Fig. 74 CELLARETTE
Height 26½"; diameter 19⅛"

Fig. 73 CELLARETTE
Height 24½"; diameter 24½" x 18"

Fig. 75 WALNUT SIDE TABLE
Height 28½″; width 32″; depth 21½″

Fig. 76 SIDE TABLE
Cedar, Cypress, and Long-leaf Pine
Height 26⅞″; width 36″; depth 23⅛″

Fig. 78 WALNUT AND CYPRESS
GATE-LEGGED TABLE
Height 29¼″; width (open) 58⅛″;
depth 47⅞″

Fig. 77 CEDAR AND CYPRESS
GATE-LEGGED TABLE
*Thought to be the earliest piece of
Charleston furniture*
Height 29⅞″; width (open) 67⅛″;
depth 52¼″

Fig. 79 WALNUT DINING TABLE
Height 27⅞″; width (open) 53⅛″; depth 42⅜″

Fig. 80 DINING TABLE
Height 28″; width (open) 50⅛″; depth 42″

Fig. 81 DETAIL OF
FOOT *(see Fig. 80)*

Fig. 82 WALNUT (?) DINING TABLE
Height 27¾″; width (open) 57½″; depth 46½″

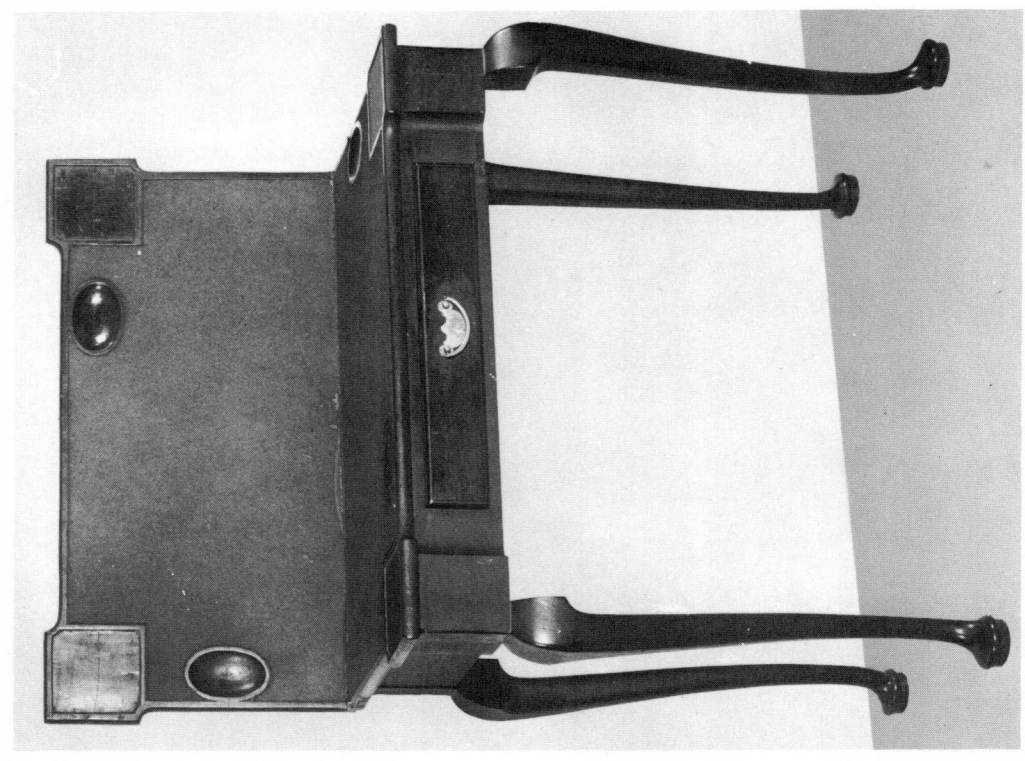

Fig. 84 GAMING TABLE
Height 28⅛"; width 32"; depth (open) 31½"

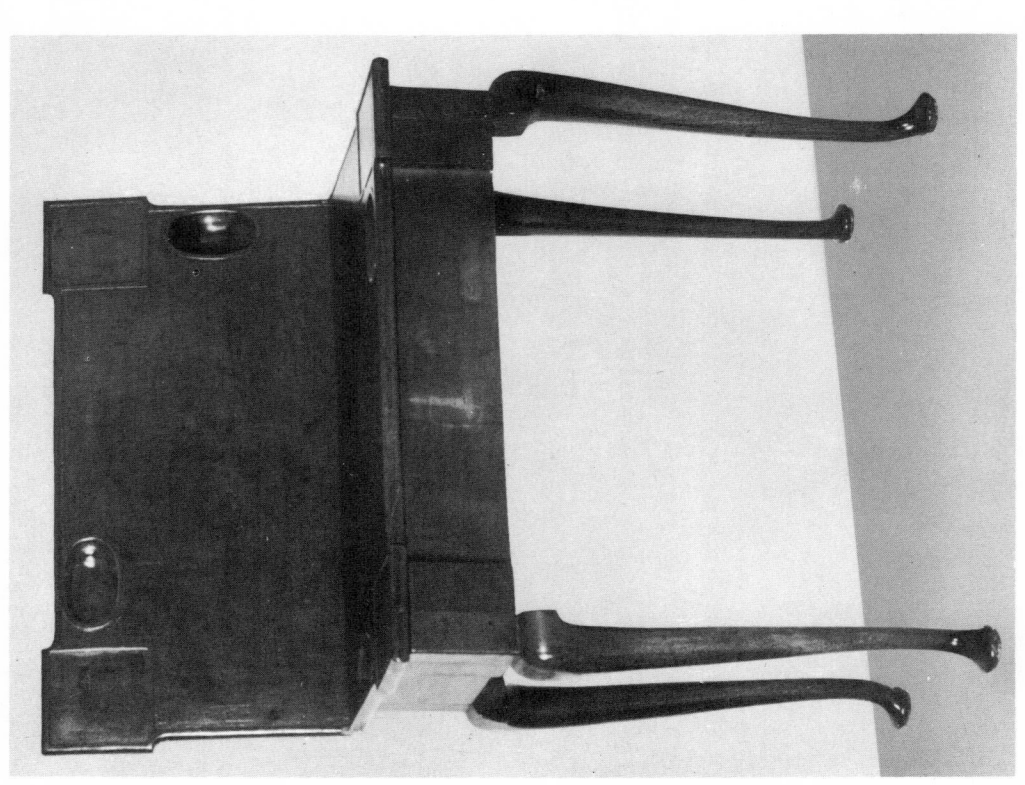

Fig. 83 GAMING TABLE
Height 28"; width 31½"; depth (open) 30¾"

Maker, in Broad-Street until he can conveniently suit himself with a house proper for his purposes. Influenced by his Acquaintances and Friends, he solicits the Favours of the Public, and hopes for their kind Indulgence and countenance . . ."

Elfe's will is dated July 7, 1775, a few months before his death.[18] To his wife, Rachel, he left interest in the plantation on Daniel's Island, together with its slaves, cattle, plantation tools, and household furniture. Rachel also received a town lot on Broad Street with two tenements on it. At her death the property was to go to four of his children, Hannah, Thomas, George, and Benjamin. To his son Willam, Elfe left the plantation in Amelia Township "upon which he resides," eight Negroes, and £1000 currency. To each of the other children Elfe left a Town House and £1000 currency. To Thomas, the only one of his sons who was a cabinet-maker, he left in addition "three negro fellows brought up to my Business named Joe, Jack and Paul together with all the working tools and benches." Elfe named his wife, Rachel, executrix, and his friends, Thomas Hutchinson and Benjamin Baker, executors of his will.

The inventory is a long one and reveals that Thomas Elfe was a man of substantial wealth.[19] It shows that Elfe possessed two "Double Chests of Drawers," one of which had a "Desk Drawer," the latter appraised at £100; four bedsteads with "Eagle Claws"; two "Desk & Bookcase[s]," one valued at £130; a Harpsichord valued at £500; several dozen chairs; a "Parcel Brass furniture, locks, screws, hinges," etc., appraised at £1000; one "Horse Flesh * Table"; and quantities of furniture, some of which was in the process of construction. There were thirty-six slaves listed in the inventory, and the silver was appraised at £622.

The inventory also shows the amount and kinds of woods used by Elfe in making his furniture:

17 Mahogany Logs	£ 680
200 feet of Mahogany Boards	£ 300
a parcel of mahogany about 10 M feet	£1000

* Mahogany from the Bahamas.

about 2 M feet Cypress & plank	£ 60
17 Poplar Plank	£ 9
a parcel Ash Plank	£ 15
a parcel Mahogany in boards	£ 300
a parcel Cedar in ditto	£ 9

Fortunately for students of Charleston furniture one of Thomas Elfe's account books has survived. It is an interesting document, now in the archives of the Charleston Library Society. It covers an eight-year period from 1768 to 1775, the economic peak of pre-Revolutionary Charleston. It is much more than an ordinary account book. It gives not only a detailed description of the various kinds of furniture which Elfe made and the price he charged for it: It lists also the names of his customers, and furnishes incontrovertible evidence that Elfe, during this period at least, supplied furniture of some kind to nearly every outstanding family in Charleston.

The account book also shows the monies due him from various people, many of whom were cabinet-makers. It gives the amount and cost of the various kinds of woods Elfe purchased for use in his shop. It sometimes gives little intimate pictures of Elfe, as when he repaired a bird cage and made a squirrel house, probably for a child of one of his patrons. Elfe, it may also be noted, was too good a business man not to charge for even this small service. Entries in the book show the amount Elfe charged for sending one of his workmen to take down or put up a four-posted bed or to make a minor repair to a piece of furniture. However, Elfe's scrupulous attention to charges, large and small, was matched by his generosity; one entry at least, shows that he gave away £50 at Christmas.

The account book, written in such a careful hand and kept in such detail, must have been only one of several; Elfe constantly makes reference to "Ledger A." It is an invaluable document and one of the few such records on cabinet-making extant in America.

Elfe made the following pieces of furniture during the eight-year period covered by his account book:

Mahogany Bedsteads	68
Poplar Bedsteads	55
Double Chests of Drawers	28

Half-Drawers and Dressing Drawers	51
Mahogany Desks	22
Clothespresses	7
Side Chairs	643
Easy Chairs	9
French Chairs	9
Miscellaneous Chairs	14
Card Tables	39
Tea Tables	52
Slab and Side Board Tables	41
Breakfast Tables	36
Dining Tables	132
Miscellaneous style Tables	70
Large articles consisting of Library Bookcases; Desk and Bookcases with glass doors; Sofas; Couches; and Clock Cases	26
Small articles consisting of Fire Screens; "Bason Stands;" Bottle Boards; Tea Trays; Mahogany Brick Moulds; Mahogany Picture Frames; Candle Stands; etc. Approximately	200
	——
	1502

In addition to his apprentices, Elfe had the assistance of several handicraft slaves; of these the account book lists four sawyers, valued at £1400, and five joiners and cabinet-makers, valued at £2250. Occasionally Elfe employed other independent cabinet-makers to assist him. Nevertheless, Elfe must himself have been a prodigious worker to have turned out so much furniture during an eight-year period. Though it is probably true that at this particular time Elfe was at the height of his productivity, it must not be forgotten that he worked in Charleston for over twenty years prior to the period covered by the account book. The total amount of furniture that came from Elfe's workshop must have been fantastic. Undoubtedly many pieces of furniture made by Elfe have survived and are now scattered throughout the country. It is hoped that in time they will be recognized and attributed to their rightful maker.

Thus far not a single piece of furniture with an Elfe label has been found. Elfe, who was trained in London, was probably following the English custom of omitting labels.

Even if he had pasted labels on his work, it is doubtful that they would have survived Charleston's humid summers and glue-eating insects.

It is logical to ask, then, how one may recognize a piece of furniture made by Elfe. First, it is positively known that Elfe made large quantities of furniture, a fact which increases the possibilities of finding authentic Elfe pieces. Again, a few pieces have been traced through families. Finally, certain characteristics to be found in several large pieces of furniture now in Charleston or definitely known to have come from Charleston clearly indicate that the pieces were made by the same craftsman.

The furniture attributed to Elfe has these outstanding characteristics: The fret, as shown in the line drawing, is found on many of these pieces and is usually applied. Though it cannot be said that Elfe was the designer of the fret which he commonly used, his consistent use of it made it virtually his, and its occurrence on any piece of Charleston furniture suggests Elfe's hand almost to the exclusion of that of any other craftsman. It was used on desk and bookcases, library bookcases, and many double chests of drawers still to be found in Charleston. Elfe made an extra charge for a fret to go on a double chest of drawers.

This same style fret, as shown in the line drawing, is found on the over-mantel of the Heyward-Washington House, a branch of the Charleston Museum. It is made of mahogany. Elfe's account book shows that he made frets for chimney pieces at a cost of £10.

The style foot as shown in the line drawing is found on double chests of drawers, as well as on desk and bookcases. While there is nothing particularly remarkable about it, the foot is well-proportioned and generally pleasing.

The interior construction of the large drawers in these pieces is unusual. The thing first to be noticed is a cross member running from front to rear in the center of the large drawers. This member is usually one and three-quarter inches in width, grooved on both sides for its entire length, and dove-tailed into the front of the drawer. The sides of the drawer are also grooved and the drawer bottoms, which are slightly tapered on both ends, are inserted from the rear and nailed in place.

The wood used in the construction of the drawers, both sides and bottoms, is cypress (*Taxodium distichum*). Upon first examination, many of the bottom boards appear to run the length of the drawer, but close scrutiny reveals that the board is grooved into the cross members. In many cases, the two boards were cut from the same piece of wood, thereby giving the illusion of a single board continued across the entire width. Elfe's account book reveals that he made frequent purchases of cypress in large quantities.

Another feature of the drawer construction is the manner in which the beading is handled. Other cabinet-makers often attached a thin strip of mahogany slightly wider than the drawer-facing to the outside of the four sides of the facing so that the beading projects. Usually in Elfe's method the four sides of the drawer-facing have been rabbeted out by five-sixteenths of an inch and a mahogany strip inserted. This piece makes the beading, which is kept in place by both glue and nails.

The bottom of many of the pieces attributed to Elfe are constructed with a small cove, a small fillet, a taurus, and a square base.

In the foregoing account, the point has been emphasized that Thomas Elfe's account book covers only the eight-year period from 1768 to 1775. Those were the closing years of his life and probably represent the point of his greatest productivity. Yet before 1768 Elfe had lived and worked in Charleston for not less than twenty-one years. Even if it be assumed that Elfe spent many of his early years in getting himself established as a cabinet-maker, it may also be assumed, by the most conservative estimate, that during the twenty-one year period for which there are no extant account books, he turned out as much work as he did in the shorter period for which the record is complete. In short, Elfe's total output must have been not less than three thousand pieces of furniture. It was probably much greater than that.

Thomas Elfe, Jr.

1759–1825   WORKING C. 1778–

Thomas Elfe, Jr. was the only son of Thomas Elfe, Sr. to adopt the trade of his father, under whom he undoubtedly learned it. At the death of his father, Thomas inherited three Negroes who had been brought up in the business, together with his father's working tools, benches, and other property.[1]

In 1778 Thomas married Mary Padgett.[2] During the occupation of Charleston by the British, he was one of the petitioners to Sir Henry Clinton, requesting that he be returned to the status of a British subject. When peace was declared, Thomas, along with many others, was ordered banished and his property confiscated. As it turned out, he was not banished but his property was amerced 12%.[3]

Probably feeling that he would be in a more friendly atmosphere Thomas had moved to Savannah by 1784; on May 11 of that year he sold a lot on the east side of King Street for £870 Sterling,[4] at that time stating that he was formerly of South Carolina but was now of Savannah. During the following year he sold another piece of property, and in 1786 he sold the property situated on Friend [Legare] Street which he inherited from his godfather, Thomas Hutchinson.[5]

Ultimately he returned to Charleston. In the 1801 directory a Thomas Elfe is listed as a cabinet-maker at No. 2 West Street. The following year he is listed as a carpenter at No. 17 Wentworth Street and in all subsequent directories he is spoken of as a carpenter. In 1807 Thomas Elfe was secretary of the Carpenters Society.[6] Nothing more is known of his activities. He died on November 12, 1825, at the age of 66 and is buried in St. Paul's [Episcopal] Church yard.

Elfe and Fisher

–1771

It is not known when the copartnership of Thomas Elfe [Sr.] and John Fisher (*q.v.*) was formed. Since Fisher was advertising independently in 1767 the partnership must have been entered into after that date. It was dissolved by 1771. On May 27 of that year

Elfe inserted an advertisement in the *South Carolina and American General Gazette* explaining that "the co-partnership of Elfe and Fisher being dissolved some time, and all debts due to them assigned over unto Thomas Elfe, he hopes all indebted to them will pay off the same or settle as soon as possible."

Elfe and Hutchinson

For many years Thomas Elfe [Sr.] and Thomas Hutchinson (*q.v.*) worked together in some kind of business association. Whether it was a copartnership is not clear. In 1758 they were paid £728 by the Council for making the chairs and tables for the Council Chamber. Two years later they were making the interior woodwork for St. Michael's Church, which was then being built. As late as 1763 Elfe and Hutchinson were directed by the Church Wardens of St. Michael's to build the communion table. Elfe and Hutchinson terminated their business association at a date unknown, but they remained good friends. Hutchinson was the godfather of Thomas Elfe, Jr., and was one of the executors of the Elfe estate.

Matthew Ellis
WORKING c. 1803–c. 1806

Matthew Ellis, a little known cabinet-maker, probably worked for someone else. His name does not appear in the 1803 directory, but on January 7 of that year he qualified as an administrator of the estate of William Ireland, silver-plate worker, and at that time he is spoken of as a cabinet-maker.[1] His name appears in the directory for 1806, without an address. Thereafter he completely disappears.

Peter Emarrett
WORKING 1809–1811

Only two facts concerning Peter Emarrett have survived. He is named for the first time in the 1809 directory as dwelling at No. 1 Union [State] Street. Two years later George Edwards, an orphan house boy, was bound to Emmerrett[1] (*sic.*). His will is not filed in the

Probate Court nor do the records of the Register of Mesne Conveyance provide any evidence that he owned any property.

Robert Fairchild
1729–1775   WORKING c. 1750–c. 1775

Robert, the son of Thomas Fairchild and Elizabeth his wife, was born on November 10, 1729.[1] It is not known under whom he learned his trade. He was married by 1750 for we find that at that time James Taylor conveyed some property on James Island to his daughter, "wife of Robert Fairchild, cabinet-maker and joiner of James Island."[2] James Island lies across the harbor from Charleston.

After the death of his first wife, Fairchild on February 14, 1754, married Sarah Wigg. By this marriage he had a son and two daughters. His wife Sarah died on September 20, 1770. On March 19, 1772, Fairchild married, for the third time, Christiana McLoud. By this marriage there were two sons.[3]

There is reason to believe that at the time of the second marriage Fairchild moved to Beaufort, South Carolina, where he presumably worked until his death in 1775.[4]

Hance Fairley
1771–1815   WORKING 1799–1815

When Hance Fairley took out his citizenship papers on March 4, 1799,[1] he stated that he was a native of County Antrim, Ireland. However, there is nothing to indicate how long he had been in this country before applying for citizenship. Fairley is listed in the various directories as a cabinet-maker on Meeting Street. He seems to have been a man of small means; there is no record of his having purchased any property. He died in January 1815 at the age of forty-four leaving his wife, Martha, and four young children.[2]

Mungo Finlayson
–1793   WORKING 1768–1793

Presumably Mungo Finlayson and Thomas Elfe, Sr., (*q.v.*) were friends. The first record that we have of Finlayson is dated January,

1768, when he borrowed £60 from Elfe. Two months later Elfe again made a loan to him, this time for £200. It was not until three years later that Finlayson paid back £50 on his debt. In January, 1774, Elfe paid Finlayson £20 for some work that he had done for him.[1]

Mary Ann Hartley and Mungo Finlayson were married on March 20, 1769.[2] Their son Mungo Graeme was baptized on August 25, 1776.[3]

We have no information concerning Finlayson during the Revolution. In fact, nothing more is heard of him until January, 1784, when he was granted letters of administration for the estate of Mary Wall, widow.[4] In the directory for 1790 he is listed as dwelling at No. 32 Queen Street.

Finlayson died on November 29, 1793.[5] According to the inventory his estate was valued at £302.[6]

Mungo Graeme Finlayson
-1799   WORKING 1795–1799

Mungo Graeme Finlayson, the son of Mungo Finlayson, in all likelihood learned his trade under his father. In 1795 he formed a copartnership with Hance Fairley (q.v.) The partnership was of short duration, for Mungo Graeme died a young man and was buried on June 26, 1799.[1]

Finlayson and Fairley
WORKING 1795

In the *South Carolina Gazette* for February 9, 1795, appeared the following advertisement: "The subscribers having entered into Copartnership under the firm of Finlayson & Fairley, Intend to carry on the Cabinet-Making Business in all its branches, and in the most fashionable and approved taste, the knowledge of which H. Fairley is perfectly acquainted with, being lately from London. Any order that they may be favoured with, will be executed on the most reasonable Terms, and at the same time in such a manner as they flatter themselves will give satisfaction to their employers. The above business will be carried

on at the shop formerly occupied by Mr. Mungo Finlayson, deceased, in Queen-street, where the upholsterer's business likewise be conducted by Mr. Henry Campbell, from Boston, who through this means offers his best services to the public in said line, with assurances of his best endeavours to merit their favours."

Both Fairley and Mungo Graeme were about twenty-four years old when they formed their copartnership. It was of short duration, however, for Finlayson died in 1799.

John Fisher
WORKING 1767–c. 1782

The advertisement of John Fisher, cabinet-maker from London, in the *South Carolina Gazette; And Country Journal* of May 5, 1767, states that he "intends carrying on the Cabinet Business in all its branches" and that he will produce "Venetian Window Blinds made as in London."

The will of Ezra Waite, drawn up on October 12, 1769, leaves £50 currency to his friend John Fisher.[1] Waite was the builder of the famous Miles Brewton House and it is quite possible that Fisher helped him with some of the interior woodwork.

It is not known when Fisher formed a copartnership with Thomas Elfe, but by 1771 the copartnership had been dissolved for Fisher advertised in the *South Carolina & American General Gazette* of June 3 of that year that he had "purchased of Mr. Stephen Townsend his Stock in Trade and Negroes brought up in the Business, which he now carries on at the House in Meeting-Street where Mr. Townsend formerly lived."

In spite of the dissolution of their copartnership, Elfe and Fisher remained on business terms; in May, 1773, Elfe paid Fisher 40 shillings for cutting a frett (*sic*) and 30 shillings for cutting a pediment board. That same year he had Fisher turn "2 Setts bed Posts."[2]

In 1774 John Fisher served on a jury that sentenced Isaac Reeves to death by hanging for the crime of horse stealing. The fact that it was Reeves's second offense probably accounts for the severity of the sentence.[3] There is nothing to indicate whether the sentence was carried out.

Fisher apparently prospered. On April 13, 1778, he purchased lot No. 39 on Tradd Street from John Wells, Jr., printer, and in 1781 he purchased 893 acres of land in the Goose Creek section.[4]

After the capitulation of Charleston to the British, Fisher along with others petitioned General Clinton to be restored to the status of a British subject.[5] With the evacuation of the British in December, 1782, Fisher left with the fleet.[6] His property was confiscated, and in 1783 at the sale of Confiscated Estates, James Fallan purchased a lot on the north side of Elliott Street with a three-story unfinished brick house formerly the property of John Fisher.[7]

Nothing is known of Fisher's later life or the time of his death.

John Forthet

WORKING 1770

The only information we have about John Forthet comes from a single advertisement in the *South Carolina Gazette; And Country Journal* for November 27, 1770: John Dobbins (*q.v.*) advertised that he was "departing the Province in the Spring" and that "He returns thanks to all his friends for their past favors, and hopes for a continuance of them to John Forthet, who carries the business on in the same shop." Forthet did no advertising. The records of the Register of Mesne Conveyance provide no evidence that he owned any property nor is his will filed in the Probate Court.

William Foulds [Fowles]

WORKING 1809–1813

A William Fowles is listed in the directory for 1813 as a cabinet-maker at No. 62 Meeting Street. This was very probably the William Foulds who was a partner of John McIntosh. In the 1809 directory Mackintosh (*sic*) and Foulds are shown as being at the same place of business. Although Foulds seems to have worked with McIntosh for a number of years,

no specific information can be found concerning him. The records of the Register of Mesne Conveyance do not reveal that he purchased any property and his will is not to be found in the Probate Court.

James Freeman

WORKING C. 1738

The fact of James Freeman's tragic death provides the only information we have of him and the information comes only indirectly from an advertisement in the *South Carolina Gazette* for April 8, 1745: "Either in the Year 1738 or 39, one James Freeman, a Joyner and Cabinet maker, fell out of the Ashley Ferry Boat and was drowned; he left a Son who I believe is now about 16 Years of Age of the Name of his Father. If the Lad be living, let him apply to me who have very good News for him. John Laurens." It is not known whether young Freeman was ever located and received the "very good News."

Theodore Freling

–1799   WORKING PRIOR TO 1799

Records incidental to the death of Theodore Freling give us our only intimation of his existence. On September 9, 1799, letters of administration were granted to James Fife, cooper, to administer the estate of Theodore Freling, cabinet-maker. The surety was John Watson, another cabinet-maker.[1] Though it is purely a surmise, Freling may have been employed by Watson. The inventory of Freling reveals that he was a man of small means.[2]

John Frew

1776–1799   WORKING 1795–1799

John Frew seems to have been a rather precocious young man, for at the age of nineteen he "Informed his friends in particular, and the Public in general, that he has commenced business for himself at his Shop No. 124 Queen-street and executes in all its various branches every article of the Cabinet Making Business." The advertisement continues, "As no person in this city has ever publicly offered to take charge of, and conduct funerals, he offers himself in that line." Finally, he expressed the need for "Two or Three Journeymen, Also One or two apprentices." [1]

A career which gave promise of so much was cut short. On November 10, 1799, Frew died on Sullivan's Island, South Carolina, at the age of twenty-three.[2]

John Fyfe
WORKING C. 1775–C. 1777

On July 2, 1775, John Fyfe and Sarah Dott, a widow, were married.[1] This constitutes the first record we have of him. Two years later John Fyfe, cabinet-maker, sold a house and lot on Colleton Square to Charles Desel, another cabinet-maker, for £800 current money of South Carolina.[2] That Fyfe died prior to 1779 is indicated by the fact that in that year Captain Andrew Quelch was married to Sarah Fyffe (*sic*), widow.[3]

Henry Gaskins
WORKING 1784

There is only one record of Gaskins. In 1784 he was appointed one of the executors of the estate of Benjamin Wheeler, another cabinet-maker. Whether Gaskins worked with Wheeler or was simply a friend is not known. The records of the Register of Mesne Conveyance Office fail to show that he ever purchased any property, nor can his will and inventory be found in the Probate Court. Though such evidence is completely negative, it suggests that Gaskins remained in Charleston only a short time.

Andrew Gifford
WORKING ? 1790

Whether Gifford actually worked in Charleston as a cabinet-maker is not clear. The only record that we have of him comes from a single advertisement in the *City Gazette and Daily Advertiser* of March 16, 1790: "Andrew Gifford, Cabinet Maker, Just arrived from New York, at the store on the head of Champney's Wharf, . . . has for sale on moderate terms, for cash or produce, An excellent assortment of Mahogany Furniture, Consisting of Desk and book-cases, Secretary ditto, Wardrobes, Side boards plain and inlaid, . . . N. B. The above articles are warranted good."

Inasmuch as Gifford was located at the head of a wharf, it is quite possible that he had just arrived with some New York-made furniture. As nothing more can be found about him and he did no more advertising it is quite possible that, finding the competition too keen from the local cabinet-makers—of whom there were many—he returned to New York.

James Gilmer
–1772   WORKING PRIOR TO 1772

The only extant record of James Gilmer is contained in his inventory, dated April 19, 1772.[1] From the articles listed in it he appears to have been a chairmaker. Besides leaving numerous chisels, gouges, and saws he also left "12 new chairs" and "2 dozn of chairs" and in addition "14 sides of leather." The latter was probably used for chair bottoms.

John Gough
WORKING 1783

There seem to have been several John Goughs living in and around Charleston at about the same time. The only record pertaining to John Gough, the cabinet-maker, comes from a single deed recorded September 25, 1783, when he and his wife Margaret sold a lot in Charles Town to Stephen Shrewsbury.[1]

Richard Gouldsmith
1790–   WORKING C. 1816–C. 1852

Gouldsmith, a native of Sussex, England, took out his citizenship papers in 1825. At that time he stated that he was thirty-five years of age.[1] However, Gouldsmith was in Charleston for many years prior to his taking out his naturalization papers, for in 1816 he is listed as a cabinet-maker at No. 104 King Street.

On July 25, 1822, he purchased from City Council the property on the southwest corner of King and Market Streets for $4,400.00.[2] Gouldsmith is listed in all subsequent directories as a cabinet-maker. The last time that his name appears is in the one for 1852 at which time he is shown as being at No. 91 Wentworth Street. It is not known when he died.

Thomas Graham
−1820   WORKING 1809–1820

Thomas, the son of the Reverend William E. and Sarah Graham was born on February 19, 1786.[1] Whether or not this was the future cabinet-maker is problematical. A Thomas Graham is listed for the first time in the 1809 directory as a cabinet-maker at No. 67 Meeting Street. On January 5, 1813, a marriage settlement was drawn up between Margaret Corre and Graham. Margaret owned five Negroes and a lot on the west side of King Street.[2] Presumably Graham and Margaret were married shortly afterwards. In 1818 Graham leased from John White the northwest corner of State and Amen Street for sixty dollars per annum.[3] On May 4, 1820, the following notice appeared: "The Friends and Acquaintances of Mr. & Mrs. Thomas Graham are requested to attend the Funeral of the former, from his late residence, No. 58 King street, This Afternoon, at 3 o'clock." [4]

Walter Greenland
WORKING 1763

Walter Greenland is known to us only from one advertisement which appeared in the *South Carolina Gazette* of October 29, 1763: "WALTER GREENLAND, Cabinet-Maker and Joiner, Begs leave to acquaint his friends and customers that he has taken a shop on Queen-street . . ." The advertisement seems to indicate that Greenland had just started in business for himself.

Ephraim Griffen
WORKING 1809

The name of Ephraim Griffen appears in

but one directory, that of 1809, where he is shown as dwelling at No. 14 Archdale Street. There are no other extant records.

John Gros
1780–1853   WORKING c. 1804–c. 1831

John Gros was born in Charleston in 1780. It is not known under whom he learned his trade but by 1804 he and Thomas Lee, another cabinet-maker, had formed a copartnership under the name of Gros and Lee. This copartnership probably lasted until Lee's death, which occurred in 1814. After the death of his partner, Gros continued in business by himself.

Gros and Elizabeth Catherine Love were married on May 10, 1807.[1] By this marriage there were several children.[2]

Either Gros was connected with the Schirmer family or he was a very close friend. On May 27, 1829, Aaron Smith either sold or transferred some property on Queen Street and some Negroes to Gros in trust for the Schirmer children.[3]

On July 2, 1828, Gros advertised in the *Courier* of that date that he had for sale "a few Charleston made Ice Houses of a superior kind for family use cheaper than those imported from the North."

Gros died of "old age" at the age of seventy-three and was buried in the French Burying Ground.

Peter Hall
WORKING 1761–c. 1768

Peter Hall, cabinet-maker from London, advertised for the first time in Charleston on December 19, 1761, in the *South Carolina Gazette*, stating that "gentlemen and ladies of taste may have made, and be supplied with, *Chinese* tables of all sorts, shelves, trays, chimney-pieces, baskets, &c. being at present the most elegant and admired fashion in London." The following year he says that he will "continue to make Chinese tables" and that in addition he "also intends to carry on the UPHOLSTERING business in all its branches." He further indicates that he will give good encouragement and constant employ to journeymen cabinet-makers and will also take two apprentices.[1] The inference is clear that he was prospering.

Hall advertised for the last time in the *South Carolina Gazette* for August 10, 1765. On that date he had for sale "Two large elegant pier glasses, and one Chimney ditto, just imported from London." The only other reference to Hall is contained in a single item in the account book of Thomas Elfe (*q.v.*). "January 1768 Peter Hall note for £100 due Thomas Elfe."[2]

The records of the Register of Mesne Conveyance Office do not show that Hall purchased any property and his will is not to be found in the Probate Court, possibly because he remained in Charleston for only a short time.

Thomas Hamett
WORKING 1755

On October 9, 1755, Thomas Hamett, cabinet-maker of Charleston, advertised in the *South Carolina Gazette* that he "intends to remove from *Charles-Town* to *Jackson-Borough* in about a month, and has a house and lot well situated on *King-street*" which he desires to sell. Hamett may have moved to Jacksonboro, according to plan, but he retained his Charleston property; two years after the advertisement the Provost Marshal seized his house and lot on King Street for a judgment brought against Hamett by Thomas Corker and Moses Mitchell for a debt. It is not known how long Hamett worked in Charleston prior to his removal to Jacksonboro.

William Hammet
WORKING PRIOR TO 1738

William Hammet, at the sign of the Coffin and Chair, was a chairmaker, and his inventory clearly reveals that he made chairs as we now know the term rather than riding chairs. His inventory, which was recorded on January 8, 1738, lists "14 Mahogany chairs about a forth part done £30; also about 160 feet of Mahogany and about 150 feet of Red Bay."[1] Mahogany was definitely established in Charleston by this time, and Red Bay, while probably becoming scarcer, was still being used for articles of furniture.

Nothing further concerning William Hammet has come to light. It cannot be said with certainty that he was related to Thomas Hamett, the cabinet-maker. The possibility cannot be summarily dismissed, however, on the ground that their names are differently spelled. In a period of phonetic spelling, identities are easily confused.

William Hampton
WORKING 1786–1806

A William Hampton, who may have been the future cabinet-maker, was baptized on May 19, 1758.[1] Twenty-eight years later, in 1786, William Hampton's name appears as that of one of the witnesses to a deed between James Graves and Eleazer Phillips, a cabinet-maker.[2] It is possible that he was working for Phillips at this time. Hampton as a cabinet-maker appears in the 1790 directory and in the subsequent ones.

Nothing specific is known about him until the following item appeared in the *Courier* of October 21, 1806: "An inquest was held in the Poor-house yesterday morning, on the body of MARY ROBERTSON, a girl of about 19 years of age, who was shot on the top of her head, on the 21st of Sept. last, by WILLIAM HAMPTON, a cabinet-maker living in Coming-street, with a musquet loaded with small shot: She was immediately placed in the Poor-house, under the care of the Physician of that institution—and died yesterday, the 20th inst. The Jury brought in a verdict 'that the deceased, MARY ROBERTSON, came to her death in consequence of a gun-shot wound she received from WILLIAM HAMPTON, on or about the 21st September last, on the top of the head, under which she languished until seven o'clock this morning, at which time she died of a *tetanus*, or locked jaw, occasioned by the said gun-shot wound.'"

Search has failed to reveal whether Hampton was apprehended and convicted for the crime.

George Hancock
1789–   WORKING 1813–

Hancock's name appears for the first time in the 1813 directory where he is listed as a cabinet-maker at No. 3 Hard Alley. The following year he took out his naturalization papers. At that time he stated that he was a native of London, twenty-five years of age and a cabinet-maker by profession.[1] Nothing further can be found about him.

Joel Harden
–1731   WORKING PRIOR TO 1731

Joel Harden, "Joyner," died intestate. On September 11, 1731, letters were granted to William Randall and Mary his wife to administer his estate. Harden's inventory, made a week later,[1] indicates from the tools listed, as well as other articles, that he must have made furniture. Hence the inclusion of his name in this work.

John Hefferman [Heffernan]
1765–   WORKING 1806–1818

When John Hefferman received his citizenship papers in 1814, he gave his age as forty-nine, and his occupation as that of a cabinet-maker; and he stated that he was a native of Tipperary, Ireland.[1] Hefferman, however, was working in Charleston several years before he became a citizen, his name appearing for the first time in the 1806 directory. His name is spelled in various ways. It occurs frequently as Heffernan, not only in the directories, but in certain deeds.

In 1809 Hefferman made a bookcase and table for James Jervey, for which he charged $90.[2]

Being a good Irishman, Hefferman joined the Hibernian Society in 1814. His wife, Margaret, died in 1817.[3] Nothing more can be found about his activities in Charleston. However, on May 5, 1821, a John Hefferman of

Columbia, South Carolina, was married to Miss Eliza McCormick of Charleston.[4] This may have been the Charleston cabinet-maker, who had moved to Columbia after the death of his first wife.

Julian Henry
WORKING 1802–1822

For a man who worked as a cabinet-maker in Charleston for at least twenty years, surprisingly little is to be found about Julian Henry. His name appears for the first time in the directory of 1802, the last time in the 1822 directory. There is a reasonable probability that Henry was of French extraction and that he anglicized his name to Julian Henry.

Diligent search of the Register of Mesne Conveyance and the Probate Court has failed to reveal any record of Henry.

David Hodge
WORKING 1809

The name of Hodge appears only in the directory of 1809, where he is listed as a cabinet-maker at No. 62 Meeting Street.

Thomas Holton
–1732   WORKING 1720–1731

On June 27, 1720, Thomas Holton, chair-maker, appointed "his loving friend, John Stone, clockmaker, of Charleston" his attorney.[1] The following year Holton married Anne Mindemen.[2] Shortly after their marriage Holton and his wife sold lot No. 222 in Charleston to Joseph Danford for £70 current money. This lot was located on the west side of King, just below Tradd Street.[3]

In 1729 Holton executed a mortgage to John Herring of Middlesex, England, for £57 Sterling of England, giving as collateral three Negro men by name "Seasar, Will and Jack by Trade Chairmakers."[4] This is one of the early records which show that slaves were being taught their master's trade.

It would appear that Holton and his wife did not get on well together, for in 1731 articles of separation were drawn up. The articles mention their three children, William, Thomas, and Mary.[5] Holton did not long survive; a few months later, letters of administration were granted to Ann (sic) Holton to administer his estate.[6]

On August 5, 1732, the following advertisement appeared in the *South Carolina Gazette:* "At the House of the late T. Holton, Chairmaker, on the Green, the same Business is carried on, where Chairs and Couches are made and mended, after the same Manner, and at reasonable Rates." No mention is made of the person who took over his business.

Thomas Hope
WORKING 1790

The name of Thomas Hope appears in but one directory, that of 1790, where he is listed as a cabinet-maker living at No. 15 Friend [Legare] Street. Presumably Hope was a journeyman cabinet-maker who kept moving from place to place. No further records can be found.

How and Roulain
WORKING 1762

On November 13, 1762, the following advertisement appeared in the *South Carolina Gazette:* "HOW & ROULAIN, JOINERS & CABINET-MAKERS, *next door to Miss Hester Simons, in King-street,* Gives notice, that they carry on the said business in all its branches . . ." Such an association of names suggests a copartnership, but the advertisement is the only record upon which to base such a conjecture. Roulain may have been Abraham Roulain (*q.v.*), who later advertised as a cabinet-maker. On September 30, 1761, Thomas How sold three Negroes to John How.[1] Unfortunately, no mention is made of the occupation of either seller or purchaser.

Jay Humiston
WORKING 1802

Jay Humiston is listed in the 1802 directory as a Windsor chairmaker at No. 136 Meeting Street. He was probably the partner of Stafford although the spelling of his name underwent a slight change. As Humiston's name does not appear in the directory of 1803, he presumably left the city before the directory was compiled.

Humiston and Stafford
WORKING 1798

All that is known about Humiston and Stafford comes from a single advertisement which appeared in the *Charleston City Gazette and Advertiser* for November 29, 1798: "Humiston & Stafford, Chair Makers. Warranted Windsor Chairs and Green Settees, Of the newest fashion, and of an excellent quality, superior to any ever imported into this city, . . . Also, for sale as above—A Quantity of Cheese, and a large Parcel of Onions." The emphasis upon "superior" Windsor chairs is quite evidently an effort to meet the competition of those who were bringing in such chairs from other American cities.

In the 1802 directory a Jay Humeston (sic), Windsor chairmaker, is shown as being at No. 136 Meeting Street, and a Theodore Stafford is listed as a chairmaker at No. 42 Queen Street. Presumably these were the two partners; however there is nothing to indicate the length of their business association.

Thomas Hutchinson
–1782   WORKING c. 1757–1782

Hutchinson, a close friend of Thomas Elfe, Sr., was associated with him in business for a number of years. It is not known whether Hutchinson was native born or, like Elfe, came from London. The earliest mention we have of him occurs in 1757, when he was made sole executor of the estate of his kinsman, Ribton Hutchinson.[1] In 1774 Hutchinson was one of the wardens of the St. George Society.

During the Revolution Hutchinson was a member of Capt. James Bentham's Company of Militia.[2] During the siege of Charleston, he petitioned General Lincoln, together with many others, to surrender to the British.[3] After the fall of the city Hutchinson petitioned Sir Henry Clinton to be returned to the status of a British Citizen.[4] Hutchinson died during the period of the British occupation and was buried on July 21, 1782.[5]

In his will Hutchinson leaves most of his property to his godson, Thomas Elfe, Jr.[6] For signing the petitions to General Lincoln and Sir Henry Clinton, Hutchinson was ordered banished and his estates to be confiscated.[7] He died before the order of banishment could be put into execution. Thomas Elfe, Jr., eventually received the property bequeathed to him, but it was probably amerced 12% of its value before Elfe got a clear title to it.

William Jasper
WORKING 1819

William Jasper's name appears but once; in the 1819 directory he is listed as a cabinet-maker at No. 351 King Street. Nothing further is known about him.

Henry Jocelin
WORKING 1807

Henry Jocelin may have been a peripatetic cabinet-maker, for his name appears only in the 1807 directory. His will is not filed in the Probate Court nor do the records of the Register of Mesne Conveyance provide any evidence that he owned any property. It is not known what ultimately happened to him.

Edward Johnston [Johnson]
–1796   WORKING 1796

Edward Johnston may have served his apprenticeship under a local cabinet-maker, but his career as an independent craftsman was of short duration. He advertised for the first time in the *South Carolina Gazette* on April 23, 1796: "Johnson, Edward, Cabinet Maker, late from Philadelphia, Begs leave to inform the public in general, that he has opened a Ware-Room in Meeting-street, nearly opposite the Scotch-Church, where he has for sale, A general Assortment of Modern and Elegant

Cabinet work, Finished in a style of Elegance and Neatness that surpasses anything of the kind, hitherto offered for Sale in this City. Amongst which are: Capital cylinder fall desks and book cases, side boards, ladies commodes, drawers of different patterns, card tables of various patterns, and figures, breakfast ditto, ditto; and a variety of Chairs of newest patterns, with sundry other articles in the above branch. Likewise, Two suits of Tables, superbly finished for a Drawing-Room, Beautiful Japanned Chairs, or painted for do. or bed chambers. And various kinds of Fire Skreens. N. B. E. Johnson having engaged workmen of the first abilities, intends carrying on the Cabinet-Making Business, in all its various branches at his Wareroom, where orders are received and executed with dispatch."

Four months later letters of administration were granted to Mrs. Catherine Coates to administer the estate of Edward Johnston, cabinet-maker.[1] It is not known from what cause he died or how old he was at the time of his death.

Abraham Jones
–1857   WORKING 1813–c. 1857

Abraham Jones worked as a cabinet-maker in Charleston for many years. His name first appears in the 1813 directory and in most of the subsequent ones up until the time of his death, which occurred in 1857. He appears to have been something of a "joiner," for we find that on April 1, 1811, he was admitted a member of Orange Lodge (Masonic); he became a member of the German Friendly Society on March 3, 1819;[1] and he joined the Charleston Ancient Artillery Society on October 12, 1820.[2] He subsequently became Vice-president of both the German Friendly and the Artillery Societies.

During the long period that he worked at his trade he appears to have had his shop always on Beaufain Street. In 1818 he purchased a lot on the south side of Beaufain Street from the heirs of Patrick Hinds, and four years later he bought the adjoining lot.[3]

The German Friendly Society awarded Jones a contract to build a bookcase for

$110.50. Unfortunately, its present whereabouts is unknown.

Jones died on January 13, 1857.[4] In his will he mentions four children.

Robert W. Jones
WORKING 1807

A Robert Williams, son of Jesse and Margaret Jones, was baptized on January 1, 1788.[1] Whether this is the future cabinet-maker is not known. However, a Robert W. Jones is listed as a cabinet-maker for the first time in the 1807 directory. This is the only time that his name appears in any of the directories, and nothing further can be found about him. Presumably he left Charleston and plied his trade elsewhere.

William Jones
−1792   WORKING 1790–1792

The name of William Jones appears for the first time in the 1790 directory. He is listed as being a cabinet-maker at No. 51 Broad Street. The following year he advertised that in addition to carrying on the cabinet-making business "he also intends carrying on the Upholstering Business"; that he "Wanted, one or two journey-men cabinet-makers"[1] shows that he must have been fairly successful.

Jones died in 1792. His will, which is very short, was made on October 29, 1792, and was probated the following month. He left £20 to Miss Rebecca Minskey; the remainder of his estate was bequeathed to his daughter, Harriot.[2] His inventory reveals that he had an inlaid cellaret—probably made by him—a pair of caned Mahogany Bedsteads, and some ash and pine boards.[3] These were, of course, used as secondary woods in the construction of furniture made by Jones.

Jones and Harper
WORKING 1809

In the 1809 directory appear the names of Jones and Harper as copartners in cabinet-making working at No. 14 Archdale Street.

It is not known when the copartnership was formed or how long it lasted. Jones may have been Abraham Jones, who later worked independently from 1813 to 1857. Nothing is known concerning Harper.

John Keckley
WORKING 1809–1822

Notwithstanding the fact that Keckley worked for many years in Charleston little is known about him. His name appears for the first time in the 1809 directory; the last time in the one for 1822. The records of the office of Register of Mesne Conveyance do not reveal that he purchased any property and his will is not listed in the files of the Probate Court. It is not known what happened to him.

Alexander Kinkaid
WORKING 1809

To the unfortunately long list of cabinet-makers about whom virtually nothing is known must be added the name of Alexander Kinkaid. It appears but once. In the 1809 directory Kinkaid is shown as being at No. 84 Tradd Street.

James Kirkwood
1716–1781   WORKING C. 1747–1781

The earliest mention of James Kirkwood occurs in the notice of the birth of his daughter Catherine on October 6, 1747.[1] Nothing more appears concerning Kirkwood until January 27, 1761, when he purchased part of lot No. 18 from Isabella Finch. On the following day James Kirkwood and Mary his wife sold the same piece of property to Thomas Smith, Jr.[2] The price is not stated but the quick re-sale suggests that Kirkwood made a profit on the transaction.

At this time Kirkwood was living on Broad Street.[3] Three years later William Murdaugh, an apprentice who lived with him, died and was interred without a minister.[4] The record provides no reason for so curious a procedure. Kirkwood himself was buried on July 20, 1781.[5]

Francis Joseph Lacroix
1775–1806   WORKING 1806

There is little reason to suppose that Lacroix worked in Charleston for any great length of time. His name appears only in one directory, that of 1806, as a cabinet-maker at No. 53 Meeting Street. He died intestate on August 17, 1806, after an illness of only three days. The obituary notice states that he was thirty-one years of age and that he was a native of the Province of Champagne, France.[1]

Esparee Lamare
WORKING ? 1753

The only thing known about Lamare is from an advertisement in the *South Carolina Gazette* for September 10, 1753: "RUN AWAY from the Subscriber, on Tuesday the 4th of *September, John Daniel,* a *French* man, by trade a shoe-maker, and can work very well at the ship carpenter's business: . . . He is supposed to be gone with another *French* man, one *Esparee Lamare,* by trade a cabinet-maker, a thin man, *Roman* nosed, and can speak little or no *English* . . . Benjamin Godfrey." Whether Daniel was apprehended is not recorded.

Gilbert Bernard James Lapiere
1774–1814   WORKING 1806–1814

When Lapiere took out his citizenship papers on November 13, 1807, he stated that he was a cabinet-maker by trade, a native of Metz, France, and thirty-three years of age.[1] He had been in Charleston at least a year before that time, however, for he is listed in the 1806 directory as being at No. 30 Union Street.

Lapiere died at the age of forty and in his will, probated on October 28, 1814, he leaves all his tools to his copartner, Thomas Lejeune, and the remaining half of his estate to Docile "as a Proof of my gratitude for the care she has had of me and the attention she Paid to our common interest." [2]

James Lardant
WORKING PRIOR TO 1697/8

The name of James Lardant, joiner, is contained in the list of French Huguenots to be found in "An Act for the making Aliens free of this part of this Province, and for granting liberty of conscience to all Protestants." This act was ratified on March 10, 1696/7.[1]

Just when Lardant arrived in Charleston is not known but on May 9, 1694, he was granted lot No. 224.[2] On March 16, 1697/8 Martha Lardant and Noah Roy gave a performance bond of £2000 Sterling to the Governor who ordered them to take an inventory within ninety days of the estate of James Lardant. Strangely enough the inventory is not listed.[3] It must have been made, for otherwise there would have been some record of the Governor's having collected the bond.

Francis Larue
–1804   WORKING 1802

Larue, another French cabinet-maker, was in Charleston by 1802; the directory of that year lists him as being at No. 81 Meeting Street. In the same directory a Madame Larue is shown as a shopkeeper at the same locality. In the following year Larue is also listed as a shopkeeper, suggesting that by that time he had given up cabinet-making.

Larue probably died in the early part of 1804. On May 11 of that year letters were granted to Francis Soult, Commissary of Commercial Relations of the French Republic, to administer Larue's estate.[1] Obviously Larue was a French citizen at the time of his death.

Thomas Lee
1780–1814   WORKING 1806–1814

A native of Scotland, Thomas Lee probably served his apprenticeship there. It is not known when he came to Charleston but in 1804 he and John Gros (*q.v.*)[1] appear to have formed a copartnership which apparently lasted until Lee's early death on February 10, 1814, at the age of thirty-four.[2]

Letters of Administration were granted to Sarah Lee, his widow, on February 25, 1814.[3] The surety was Thomas Wallace, another Scotch cabinet-maker.

Solomon Legare, Jr.
1703–1774   WORKING c. 1754–c. 1765

Solomon Legare appears to have only made chairs. On September 26, 1754, he inserted the following advertisement in the *South Carolina Gazette:* "ANY Person may be supplied with black chairs at 12 1 per dozen, white ditto a 9 1. low chairs at 15 s a piece, and children's chairs at 12 s. 6 d. and 15 s. by applying to me at my plantation on *John's-island,* or Mr. *Thomas Legare* next door to the EXCHANGE COFFEE-HOUSE in Charles-Town. *Solomon Legare,* junior." Legare did no more advertising but he continued to make chairs, for we find the following item in the Statutes at Large: "January 1—December 31, 1765 . . . For the Public Buildings. Solomon Legare Jr. for chairs for the jury room £18 05 00." [1]

Solomon, the chairmaker, was the son of Solomon Legare, a local silversmith. Solomon, Jr., in addition to chairmaking cultivated his plantation on John's Island, a few miles from Charleston, and later in life operated a tannery. In his will he leaves his tannery, which was in Charleston, to his son Thomas. To his other sons, Solomon and Daniel, he left his lands on John's Island.[2] His wife's name was Amy. Solomon, Jr., died in November, 1774, at the age of seventy-one.[3]

Thomas Lejeune
WORKING 1814–

Although Lejeune's name appears for the first time in the 1816 directory, he must have been working in Charleston some time before that date. There is a record of his copartnership with Bernard Lapiere (*q.v.*) who died in 1814.

The Societe Francaise of Charleston was founded December 17, 1816. A Lejeune, probably the cabinet-maker, is given as one of the founders.[1] Nothing further is known of his activities or what eventually happened to him.

William Lewis
WORKING 1809

The name of William Lewis appears only in the directory of 1809; there he is listed as a cabinet-maker at No. 99 Queen Street. Nothing is known of his activities. A William Lewis, who may have been the cabinet-maker, died in the Poor House on August 29, 1828,[1] at the age of fifty-three.[1]

Thomas Lining
–1763   WORKING 1748–1763

It is not known when Thomas Lining arrived in Charleston but on May 2, 1748, his advertisement in the *South Carolina Gazette* stated that he had "lately arrived from London" and that he made "Cabinet and Chair Work, and Coffins plain and otherwise . . . in the neatest and cheapest Manner" at his shop on Broad Street.

Thomas Lining and Mrs. Ann Ware were married on March 1, 1753.[1] Before his marriage Lining had joined the St. Andrews Society and the Charles Town Library Society.[2]

In 1754 Lining moved to another location on Broad Street. The notice of the removal appeared in the *Gazette* of July 4: "Thomas Lining, Cabinet and Chair Maker from London, has removed into the House lately possessed by Mr. *Macarton* . . . opposite to *Isaac Mazyck* Esq; in *Broad*-street." He added that he would "sell all sorts of CABINET and CHAIR work, well finished in the most fashionable manner" and that "*All Letters and Orders for the Country shall be punctually answered; and the Goods put up in a safe Manner for Carriage, and sent by whatever Conveyance directed.*"

Two years later fire broke out in his shop, "but by the timely Assistance of the Engines, it was extinguished before the roof was entirely burnt." [3]

In 1750 a Dutch lad named Jacob Echard

was bound out to Lining.[4] Apparently they could not get on together; the Records of the Vestry of St. Philip reveal that on June 13, 1757, "Mr. Thomas Lining will pay the Church-wardens £25 for the use of schooling Jacob Echard, that then all disputes . . . between them shall cease." Whether Echard finished his apprenticeship with Lining is not known. He later became organist of St. Michael's Church.

Lining was paid £49 out of the General Tax for lodging Lt. Colonel Grant,[5] who arrived in Charleston on January 6, 1761. Grant was in command of 1200 British Regulars making up a part of the expedition which was being sent against the Cherokees.

Lining died intestate in September, 1763.[6] His inventory shows that he was a man of some wealth.[7] In it are listed "9 logs of Mahogany plank and boards" valued at £869 and "Three lots of Cypress" valued at £92. Lining, like many of his contemporaries, used cypress as the secondary wood in the construction of his furniture.

Henry Lipper
WORKING?

Nothing is known of Henry Lipper apart from the fact that on March 4, 1808, letters were granted to Alexander Calder to administer on Lipper's estate.[1] The inventory made the following month shows that the total estate amounted to $63.25.[2] It is probable that Lipper arrived in Charleston only a short time before his death and that he worked for Alexander Calder (q.v.).

Robert Liston
–1760   WORKING 1756–1760

Robert Liston may have been the son of another Robert Liston, a local shipwright. There is no record of his apprenticeship but by 1756 he was working as a cabinet-maker. On August 9 of that year he sold a negro boy named Mingo to Thomas Elfe and Thomas Hutchinson for £157 current money.[1] That he prospered seems indicated by the fact that three years later he purchased two Negro

girls from John Poinsett.[2] Liston married Mary Toomer on May 1, 1756.[3]

The date of his death is not known but the following notice of the closing of his estate appeared in the *South Carolina Gazette* for April 26, 1760: "To be Sold, *On Friday the 30th Instant, at* 10 *of the Clock in the Forenoon, at the House of the late* Robert Liston, *deceased, in* Tradd-street. The Estate of said deceased, consisting of 3 SLAVES that have had the Small-Pox, household Furniture, Cabinet-makers Tools, &c. . . . *Mary Liston.* Admx." His inventory includes a parcel of mahogany plank and a parcel of poplar plank.[4] The latter item leads to the supposition that Liston probably differed from his contemporaries in using poplar instead of cypress as a secondary wood in the furniture which he made.

John Litle
1769?–1818   WORKING 1816

John, son of Aaron and Elizabeth Little (*sic*) was born on September 11, 1769. This may have been the future cabinet-maker. The first certain reference to John Litle the cabinet-maker occurs in the 1816 directory. He appears to have died some time in 1818, letters having been granted on August 22 of that year to James Litle to administer the estate of John Litle, saw-gin maker.[1] It would appear that between 1816 and the time of his death he gave up cabinet-making for the manufacture of saw gins. The inventory, made on August 29, 1818, lists a "Turning Lathe & Tools" valued at $40.00.[2]

William Little
WORKING 1800

Little came to Charleston in 1799 from Marlsgate, England. In 1800 he received a letter from his brother George addressed to "Mr. William Little, Charleston, S. C. Cabinet Maker to the cair (*sic*) of John Watson, Kingstrail [King Street], No. 12." John Watson, a cabinet-maker who had worked in Charleston for many years, was then living at No. 21 King Street. No doubt while he re-

Fig. 85 BREAKFAST TABLE
Height 27¾″; width (open)38⅞″; depth 35⅞″

Fig. 86 CARD TABLE
Height 29⅜″; width 34½″; depth 17½″

Fig. 87 BREAKFAST TABLE
Height 28″; width (open) 53¼″; depth 26⅝″

Fig. 88 BREAKFAST TABLE
Height 28¾″; width (open) 42″; depth 26″

Fig. 89 DETAIL OF BREAKFAST TABLE *(see Fig. 88)*

Fig. 90 DRESSING TABLE
(Cross member under drawer missing)
Height 27¾″; width 33″; depth 20¼″

Fig. 91 DRESSING TABLE
Height 31½″; width 33⅞″; depth 20⅜″

Fig. 92 DRESSING TABLE
(Lower moulding of leg not applied)
Height 27⅝″; width 30¼″; depth 19⅜″

Fig. 93 DRESSING TABLE
Height 29¼″; width 30½″; depth 19½″

Fig. 94 MARBLE TOP SIDE TABLE
Height 37⅛″; width 48″; depth 25″

Fig. 95 MARBLE TOP SIDE TABLE Height 35″; width 6′9″; depth 36½″

Fig. 96 CARD TABLE
Height 27¾″; width 36⅞″; depth (open) 35¼″

Fig. 97 CARD TABLE
Height 28½″; width 35″; depth (open) 34½″

Fig. 98 CARD TABLE
Height 29⅛″; width 34⅝″; depth (open) 34″

Fig. 99 CARD TABLE
Height 29¼″; width 35″; depth (open) 35″

Fig. 100 PEMBROKE TABLE *(Bilston Handles)*
Height 28¾″; width (open) 37½″; depth 30″

Fig. 101 PEMBROKE TABLE
dimensions not available

Fig. 102 PEMBROKE TABLE
Height 29½″; width (open) 43½″; depth 30½″

Fig. 103 PEMBROKE TABLE
Height 28½″; width (open) 39⅜″; depth 29⅞″

Fig. 104 SEWING TABLE
Height 28″; width 19¼″; depth 16½″

Fig. 105 SEWING TABLE
dimensions not available

Fig. 106 PEMBROKE TABLE
Height 28⅜″; width (open) 40½″; depth 32″

Fig. 107 SEWING TABLE
Height 28¾″; width 26¹³⁄₁₆″; depth 18¾″

mained in Charleston Little worked for Watson.

There is a family tradition to the effect that a member of St. Michael's church engaged Little to make a complete set of furniture, for which Little was never paid. It is thought that Little stayed only a short time in Charleston before moving to Sneedsboro, North Carolina. Either while he was in Charleston or at a later date "he bought a real native African to whom he taught his trade and afterwards made his assistant."

The foregoing information on William Little has been supplied through the courtesy of Colonel and Mrs. Jeffrey F. Stanback, of Mt. Gilead, North Carolina.

William Lupton
WORKING 1743–1751

William Lupton, cabinet-maker from London, advertised for the first time in the *South Carolina Gazette* on September 19, 1743. He informed the public that he lived on Broad Street and that he would make "all sort of Cabinets and Chairs in the best and neatest Manner, and at the lowest Prices."

William Lupton and Alice North were married on March 3, 1744.[1] Six years later, on December 10, 1750, he inserted an advertisement in the *Gazette* stating that he did "All Kinds of Upholsterer's Work, as Beds, window-hangings, easy chairs, &c. . . . by a person lately arrived from *London*, and all kinds of cabinet-work as usual." The last statement clearly indicates that Lupton had been carrying on his trade in the intervening years. It also implies that easy chairs had become common in and around Charleston during that period.

During the following year Lupton got into financial difficulties. A statement in the *Gazette* of July 8, 1751, tells something of the story: "To be held on the first Tuesday in August for the benefit of my creditors, a lot with a good dwelling-house upon it, . . . with good conveniences for a cabinet-maker. Any person inclinable to purchase the same before the day of sale, may treat with *William Lupton*."

It is thought that Lupton left Charleston and moved to the vicinity of Georgetown, South Carolina.

William Luyten
–1800   WORKING c. 1764–c. 1784

Mary Ann Collins and William Luyten were married on May 29, 1764. If Luyten was old enough to acquire a wife he certainly must have been a full-fledged cabinet-maker at that time. Mary Ann died on September 9, 1770, in the 27th year of her age, and was buried in St. Michael's churchyard. Her tombstone was a cypress bedstead. It can be seen to this day and is a tribute to the lasting qualities of cypress.

In 1774 Luyten had numerous business transactions with Thomas Elfe and in fact appears to have worked for him for a short period of time. Again there is a lapse of several years during which nothing is known of Luyten. His name next appears in 1780 when he, together with many others, signed a petition to General Lincoln requesting him to surrender the City to the British. The records do not indicate whether his property was subsequently amerced the usual 12% for signing the petition, as was usually the case.

In 1784 Luyten and John Ralph were sureties for the estate of Mary Monck. At that time both he and Ralph are spoken of as cabinet-makers. Then Luyten appears to have given up cabinet-making, for he is frequently spoken of as a merchant. He remarried and his second wife Mary died in Camden, South Carolina, on November 29, 1792. Luyten died there also on October 24, 1800.

His will is very forthright and clearly expresses his views. In fact, it is so interesting that it deserves to be quoted in part:

"Item; I first say that I wish the Carcass Box maker to be paid, but the Box must be procured in a most frugal manner—a priest or a Ridiculous prayer Reader I can dispense with, and I hope my friends will not admit such stuff at my interment, as I am sure their prayers were never of any Service or Use to me in my Lifetime, So of Course, they can be of no profit to me after my Death, a pound saved for the Survivor is better than Lost,—my Confidence is in my God, he is my Saviour, my Hope, my all,—neither do I want Organs or Bag-pipes as I am sure that my Sense of hearing will depart from me—and I hope my friends will be so obliging as to Lay me in a Hole as far from any Church as possible, particularly from these Canting Hypocrites— . . ."

Richard Magrath (McGrath)
WORKING C. 1771–

If one may judge from his advertisements, Magrath wanted to be considered the most fashionable cabinet-maker in Charleston. His first and rather pretentious advertisement appeared in the *South Carolina Gazette* on August 8, 1771. He there announces that he is lately from London, the inference being that he learned cabinet-making in that fashionable metropolis. The advertisement adds that "he intends to remove up the Path, a little way without the Town Gate; where the Cabinet-maker's and Upholsterers Business will be carried on in a more extensive Manner." Evidently he had been in Charleston for some time. Finally he announces that he will sell at Public Auction at his house on King Street the following Goods: "Half a dozen Caned Chairs, a Couch to match them, with commode fronts, and Pincushion seats, of the newest fashion, and the first of that construction ever made in this province"; also sofas "made in the genteelest manner, Easy Chairs, Double Chest of Drawers, and Half Chest of Drawers."

In the following year we find Magrath back in King Street. He then advertises "That he now carries on the above branches in a more extensive manner than it was in his power formerly to do." Evidently his business was increasing. He could supply "Double chest of Drawers, with neat and light Pediment Heads, which take off and put on occasionally; Ditto with a desk Drawer; Dining-Tables; commode Card Tables; Breakfast ditto, with stretchers; China Tables; Sophas, with Commode fronts divided with three sweeps, which give them a noble look;

caned Chairs of the newest fashion, splat Backs, with hollow slats and commode fronts, of the same Pattern as those imported by Peter Manigault, Esq.—He is now making some Hollow-seated Chairs, the seats to take in and out." [1] From such an advertisement it certainly appears that Magrath was making furniture in the latest prevailing style, which at that time would have been in the London manner. Peter Manigault, one of the richest merchants in the colony, had imported a set of chairs and allowed Magrath to copy them. Also Magrath's statement that he is making "Hollow-seated Chairs, the seat to take in and out" would lead one to believe that heretofore all Charleston-made chairs during this period were constructed with solid seats, the covers being put on with brass nails. Unfortunately the "neat and light" pediment heads for his double chests of drawers, "which take off and put on occasionally" were taken off so "occasionally" that only a few have survived.

In the *Gazette* for May 10, 1773, Magrath again advertised a public sale of "Sophas, French chairs, conversation stools, and Easy chairs, of the newest fashion and neatest construction, such as were never offered for sale in this Province before."

As the unsettled time of the Revolution drew on, Magrath inserted his final advertisement in the *Gazette:* "He at the same Time acquaints them [his Friends], that he is obliged to continue following his Business; as the Times do not admit to his settling his affairs; nor do his Circumstances enable him to stand still to wait for better" and that "he has moved from King-street to Broad-street, almost opposite to JOHN RUTLEDGE, Esq. . . ." [2] This certainly indicates that Magrath would have discontinued his business if he could. Nothing further can be discovered concerning Magrath. It is quite possible that his sympathies were with his mother country and that he returned to England before the outbreak of hostilities in the South.

James Main
WORKING 1813–1822

James Main and Mary Ann Smith were

married on March 18, 1813. In the same year Main's name appears for the first time in the directory. In the directory for 1822 he is listed as a cabinet-maker at No. 63 Broad Street, this being the last record we have about him. Nothing is known of his activities during the intervening years.

William Marlen
WORKING C. 1799–1809

It is not known when Marlen started working in Charleston as a cabinet-maker. His daughter, Mary Stephens, was buried on September 19, 1799.[1] His name appears as a cabinet-maker in the 1803, 1807, and 1809 directories. After that there is no trace of him. The records of the Register of Mesne Conveyance Office do not show that he owned any property nor is his will to be found in the Probate Court.

John Marshall
–1820 WORKING 1790–c. 1820

At the time John Marshall, the cabinet-maker, was working in Charleston there were two other John Marshalls in the city: one a planter, the other a cutler. All three were probably Scottish. John Marshall, the cabinet-maker, is first made known to us in the 1790 directory, where he is listed as being at No. 219 Meeting Street.

On August 22, 1793, Marshall advertised in the *State Gazette of South Carolina* that a horse had strayed from his plantation on Ashley River, and two days later he advertised for a negro man who ran away from his plantation on Daniel's Island. The ownership of two plantations can certainly be taken as an indication that he must have been a very prosperous cabinet-maker.

The following year Marshall was one of the sureties of the estate of Thomas Philips.[1] Two years later, Marshall leased from Christopher Gadsen a lot on Wall Street for a term of fourteen years at a rental of $40.00 per annum.[2] By 1800 Marshall appears to have left Charleston or given up cabinet-making, for in a lease between him and Ann Purcell

Gillon he is spoken of as "late of the City of Charleston" and in other indentures made at the same time he is spoken of as "formerly of Charleston."[3] However, in the 1803 directory he is again listed as a cabinet-maker at the upper end of Meeting Street.

In 1814 a John Marshall joined the St. Andrews Society. This is thought to have been the cabinet-maker. John Marshall, the cabinet-maker, died in June, 1820.[4]

John May
1792–1859 WORKING 1822–1855

When he was still a young man, John May formed a copartnership (?) with Munro. This appears to have lasted only a few years; the 1822 directory lists May as an independent cabinet-maker at No. 61 Queen Street. May maintained his cabinet shop on Queen Street for over thirty years. During the last years of his life he appears to have discontinued furniture making and to have become an undertaker. Like so many other cabinet-makers he probably made coffins during his entire career.

In 1833 May received $50.00 as payment in full from James Jervey for making a mahogany bedstead and a mahogany set of drawers.[1] In the same year Joel R. Poinsett wrote to J. B. Campbell relative to having May do over some of his furniture: "I just recollect to have forgotten to call and tell Mr. May the Cabinet maker Qn. St. what is to be done with my card tables—tell him they are to be levelled nothing more and especially let him abstain from cleaning them up and making them look new—a thing I abhor—I like old looking furniture and as they will probably go to the Cottage newness must be avoided."[2]

May died on July 31, 1859, in his sixty-eighth year and was buried in the churchyard of the Circular Church.[3] In his will he mentions his son James and his wife Mary.[4]

May & Munro
WORKING 1819

This copartnership (?) appears to have been of but short duration. The names appear in only one directory—that of 1819, when they are shown as being at No. 29 Queen Street. John May was probably one of the partners. Nothing is known of Munro.

James Mazett
WORKING 1816

James Mazett, as cabinet-maker, is only a name on a list. Evidently he worked in Charleston for but a short time. He is listed only in the 1816 directory.

James McClellan
WORKING 1732?–1738?

McClellan was one of the first advertisers in the *South Carolina Gazette*, which was founded in 1732. On January 27 of that year he inserted the following advertisement: "James McClellan, Cabinet-Maker, from London, living next door to Mr. *Joseph Massey*, in *Church-Street*, Makes and sells all sorts of Cabinet Ware, viz. Cabinets, Desks & Book-Cases, Buroes, Tables of all sorts, Chairs, Tea-boxes, and new-fashioned Chests &c. . . ." It is not known how long McClellan had been working in Charleston before 1732. It is interesting to conjecture at this late date just what McClellan meant by "new-fashioned Chests." Unfortunately none of his furniture appears to have survived.

Some years later, for reasons unknown, McClellan decided to leave Charleston; he inserted the following announcement in the *South Carolina Gazette* of March 30, 1738: "As *James McClellan* of *Charles-Town*, designs to leave this Province soon, he desires all those indebted to him, to pay their respective Debts in *May* next, or they will be sued without further Notice. . . ." Presumably he left the province; no further record of him can be found.

In 1733 he became a member of the St. Andrews Society. The records of that Society reveal he died a member but give neither the time nor the place.

M'Donald & Bonner
WORKING 1819–1822

M'Donald and Bonner are listed as cabinet-makers at No. 48 Broad Street in the 1819 directory. Three years later they are shown as being at No. 85 Broad Street. No further information has been found about M'Donald. Presumably the other partner(?) was John Bonner, who worked as an independent cabinet-maker for many years.

Farquhar [McGilvrey] McGillivray
–1770   WORKING 1760–1770

Farquhar McGilvrey was in the province by 1760. On August 6 of that year he purchased some tacks from James Poyas.[1] On March 1, 1765, McGilvrey executed a mortgage for £2500 current money, putting up as collateral his two Negroes.[2] Like almost every cabinet-maker of the period, McGilvrey had some sort of business contacts with Thomas Elfe.[3] People with whom he dealt experienced difficulty with the spelling of his first name; they usually spelled it phonetically and the form varies greatly.

McGilvrey died on August 20, 1770,[4] apparently unmarried, for a citation was issued to George Gray "to administer on the Estate and Effects of Farquhar McGilvrey late of Charles Town Cabinet maker as nearest of kin." [5]

John McIntosh [M'Intosh]
1771–1822   WORKING C. 1806–1822

A native of Edinburgh, John McIntosh took out his citizenship papers on August 25, 1813.[1] However, it is thought that he was in Charleston several years before that time. The 1806 directory lists M'Intosh (*sic*) and Foulds as cabinet-makers at No. 133 Meeting Street. This was probably John McIntosh. He seems to have worked with Foulds until 1813. After that he appears as an independent cabinet-maker.

No doubt McIntosh served his apprenticeship in Scotland. The date of his marriage is unknown, but his son David Neal was baptized on August 7, 1812.[2]

McIntosh appears to have died intestate, probably in the latter part of 1822 at the age of fifty-one. His inventory is dated January

2, 1823.[3] In it are listed 32 Mahogany "Bedstead posts," some unfinished furniture, and a lot of mahogany and pine boards.

M'Intosh & Foulds
WORKING C. 1806–1813

The copartners (?) M'Intosh and Foulds, listed together for the first time in the 1806 directory, were probably John McIntosh (*q.v.*) and William Foulds (*q.v.*). They were still working together in 1809, it being recorded that in that year they were paid $65.00 by James Jervey for making a pair of sofas.[1] The present whereabouts of the sofas is unknown. In the 1813 directory the two men are listed as independent cabinet-makers.

Thomas Mills
WORKING 1766–1771

On March 29, 1766, a marriage license was granted to Thomas Mills and Sarah Breed.[1] Two years later Mills purchased from John Dobbins 1/5 part of the personal estate of Timothy Breed, who was his father-in-law.[2]

Thomas Elfe, having more business than he could handle, got Mills to make a sofa for him.[3] This was in August, 1771. There is no further information to be had about Mills. Some years later the name of a Reverend Thomas Mills appears in the records [4] but it is doubtful that this was the cabinet-maker.

Philip Mintzing
WORKING 1788

Philip Mintzing, the cabinet-maker, was probably the son of Philip Mintzing, a blacksmith, who died in 1781. Nothing is known about the activities of the cabinet-maker except for a single instrument. On December 22, 1788, Mintzing was a surety for the estate of William Sutcliffe, at which time he is spoken of as a cabinet-maker.[1] The records of the Register of Mesne Conveyance contain no records of his ownership of property. His will is not filed in the Probate Court.

Richard Moncrief [Muncreef]
–1789   WORKING C. 1749–c. 1754

Richard Moncrief was not simply a cabinet-maker: he devoted much of his time to house building. On March 27, 1749, he inserted the following advertisement in the *South Carolina Gazette:* "THIS is to give Notice . . . that the subscriber is now at leisure, and will be obliged to any person that will employ him to do all the carpenter's and joiner's work in any one building. At whose shop in Queen-street all sorts of cabinet work is neatly made, and all kinds of lumber sold." In a deed dated January 13, 1754, between Samuel Ball and Moncrief he is spoken of as a cabinet-maker.[1] After that time he is generally spoken of as a house carpenter.

Moncrief was elected to the South Carolina Society on January 25, 1743. Two years later he was elected constable. He was probably well established as a cabinet-maker by that time. In 1748 Governor Glenn ordered that the Free School house be repaired. Moncrief submitted an estimate of £800, but it is not known whether he was awarded the contract.[2] He furnished some timber that was used in the construction of St. Michael's Church. His bill, amounting to over £12, is dated June 12, 1754.[3]

For many years Moncrief was paid out of the General Tax for taking care of the Fire Engines.[4] In 1771 he was a member of the Grand Jury and the following year a member of the Petit Jury.[5] Moncrief must have been pleasantly surprised when he received a small legacy from his kinswoman, Elizabeth Gordon, of London.[6]

In 1782 the estate of Richard Moncrief was amerced 12%.[7] No reason is recorded, but probably Moncrief signed, with many others, a petition to General Lincoln asking him to surrender the city to the British.

Moncrief probably died in September 1789, his will having been probated on the eighteenth of that month,[8] and the inventory of his estate was made three weeks later.[9] In his will Moncrief mentions his wife Susannah and makes his son Richard his executor. Moncrief had four children—Robert, Elizabeth, Richard, and Susannah.[10] His inventory reveals that among his household furniture he had a "double chest of draws."

Philip Moore
WORKING c. 1797–c. 1809

In 1779 a Philip Moore was a private in Captain Felix Warley's Company.[1] This was probably not the cabinet-maker, but his father. Our first certain information concerning Philip Moore the cabinet-maker is his marriage to Besheba Hariet Hanlins, April 16, 1797.[2] Two years later his daughter Mary was baptized.[3]

In 1800 Moore leased from John McIver for five years the east side of Meeting Street "bounded on the South on an alley called Rope Lane."[4] For the next nine years he is listed in the directories as having his shop at No. 28 Meeting Street, undoubtedly the location of the property that he had leased.

In the *Times* for May 21, 1806, Moore advertised that he had for sale a Mahogany Double Desk.

By 1816 Moore seems to have given up cabinet-making and become a lumber sawyer. In later directories he is spoken of as a lumber merchant. The last time that his name appears is in the 1831 directory. After that nothing is known about him. There is in existence a will of a Philip Moore, planter, that was probated July 7, 1857.[5] This may have been the cabinet-maker turned planter.

Simon Morison
1796–1839   WORKING 1817–1836

Simon Morison came to Charleston in 1817 at the age of twenty-one.[1] In taking out his citizenship papers he stated that he was a native of Fifeshire, "North Britain," that is, Scotland. Morison died of "Country Fever" on September 23, 1839, at the age of forty-three.[2] His obituary states that "In his vocation as a Cabinet Maker he was indefatigable; by his industry he had secured a competency for life, and about three years since, retired from the business."[3] In his will he mentions his wife Maria and several sisters. His brother Thomas was one of the executors.[4]

Michael Muckenfuss
1774–1808   WORKING c. 1795–c. 1806

Michael Muckenfuss was born in 1774, probably in Charleston. His name is indicative of his German ancestry, and he was actively associated with the German element in Charleston; he was admitted to the German Friendly Society on March 16, 1796, made a Steward in 1799, and elected President of the Society in 1803, at the age of twenty-nine.

It is not known under whom Muckenfuss served his apprenticeship. It may have been Charles Desel, who, it is believed, married Muckenfuss's sister, Mary Barbara.

By the time he was twenty-four years old he was well on the way toward becoming a wealthy man. In 1798 he was able to purchase three lots in the town of Jacksonboro, South Carolina. In the following year he bought 200 acres in Craven County and 1000 acres in Granville County.

Muckenfuss died on August 2, 1808, at the age of thirty-four, after a long and painful illness. "He left a disconsolate widow, a son and a number of relations and friends, to bemoan their irreparable loss."[4] His wife was Elizabeth Custer. He left to his son, James Custer Muckenfuss, all of his cabinet stores which included some mahogany, cedar, and pine. The two latter woods were probably used by Muckenfuss as secondary woods in the construction of his furniture.[5] His inventory included "1 Shower Barth [Bath] $2."[6]

Josiah Murphy
WORKING PRIOR TO 1771

On November 23, 1771, a citation was granted to Charles Harris, a silversmith, to administer the estate of Josiah Murphy, late of St. Michael's Parish, cabinet-maker.[1] In all probability Murphy had died not more than a few weeks before. Among the items listed in Murphy's inventory, which was taken the following month, is a mahogany camp bedstead, and a mahogany chest of drawers, the latter appraised at £80. Judging from its value, it was probably a double chest of drawers. Thomas Elfe, who made so many double chests of drawers, usually received either £75 or £80 for new ones. Also listed in his inventory is a parcel of mahogany boards and a lot of cypress boards.[2]

Frederick Naser
1786–1860   WORKING 1807–c. 1827

Frederick Naser, of German descent, was the son of Frederick Naser and the grandson of Philip Naser. On October 29, 1807, Naser married Ann Custer, the daughter of James Custer. Michael Muckenfuss, another cabinet-maker, married Elizabeth Custer, a sister of Ann. Two years later Naser is listed in the 1809 directory as a cabinet-maker at No. 58 Meeting Street.

Naser became a member of the Charleston Artillery Society on February 8, 1821, and was admitted to the German Friendly Society on February 7, 1827.

Henry W. and Joshua Neville
1768–1840
1796–1857   WORKING c. 1801–1840

For over forty years Joshua Neville worked as a cabinet-maker in Charleston. Joshua was from Queen's County, Ireland. In taking out his citizenship papers in 1814, he stated that he was forty-six years of age.[1] It is not known when he came to Charleston but he was working here in 1801, for the directory of that year lists him as dwelling at No. 11 Clifford Alley. The following year Joshua moved to No. 43 Tradd Street.

Henry, Joshua's son, was born in 1796. By 1819 he was working as an independent craftsman at No. 134 East Bay. However, the next year Henry was working with his father.[2] This association lasted for over twenty years. The 1840 directory lists Joshua Neville as a cabinet-maker at No. 98 Church Street. It is thought that he died the same year. If this is correct he would have been eighty-three years old. No doubt he did very little cabinet work during the latter years of his life.

In the fall of 1820 the Nevilles moved from Meeting Street to No. 282 King Street, opposite Beaufain Street. They advertised that they had on hand a variey of Charleston-made furniture,[3] an indication that they were feeling the results of importations from the North. By 1828 they had again moved, this time to a location on Wentworth between King and Meeting Streets. In the *Courier* for September 22, 1828, they advertised "Funerals, furnished . . . on the shortest Notice and most reasonable terms"; they also "WANTED, three or four BOYS, to learn the Cabinet Making business, either white or colored." Apparently it was a custom of the time to take either white or colored apprentices. Many of the colored apprentices must have ultimately become independent cabinet-makers.

Henry Neville was buried in Magnolia Cemetery on December 28, 1857. He died at the age of sixty-one.[4] It is thought that he gave up cabinet-making at the time of his father's death.

James Neville
WORKING 1801

It is not known whether James Neville was in any way related to Joshua Neville. James is listed in the 1801 directory as a cabinet-maker on Broad Street, but his name as a cabinet-maker does not appear in any of the subsequent ones. On March 20, 1817, a James Neville, carver, purchased a lot on the south side of Queen Street.[1] This may have been the former cabinet-maker, who by this time was devoting his entire energies to carving.

Thomas Newton
WORKING 1744–1747

Thomas Newton, carpenter, joiner, cabinet-maker, and frame maker from London, advised the public in the *South Carolina Gazette* of June 4, 1744, that he was "at Mr. *Graham's* Wig maker in Broad-street," and that he was "ready to serve Gentlemen, Ladies, or others, in these Branches of Trade, which shall be perform'd in the neatest Manner, and at reasonable Rates."

Newton and Sarah Hawk were married in 1744. On January 17, 1747, their daughter was baptized.[1] Nothing further is known of

Newton's activities. It is very likely that he left the Province.

James C. Norris
–c. 1853   WORKING C. 1819–c. 1822

James C. Norris worked as a cabinet-maker on King Street from about 1819 to 1822.[1] After that period it is thought that he gave up cabinet-making. Norris joined the Charleston Ancient Artillery Society on November 11, 1813, and served as secretary of that organization from 1820 to 1853. He was elected a member of the South Carolina Society on August 9, 1831. Norris was married on January 24, 1830, to a Miss Hayden.[2]

The date of his death is not known but it was probably about 1853, that being the last date given for his secretaryship in the Artilley Society.

John Nutt
WORKING 1770

The only information we have about John Nutt comes from a single advertisement in the South Carolina Gazette of August 2, 1770: "To Be Sold, for Ready Money, At the very Lowest Prices, by John Nutt, Cabinet-Maker, Facing the Cross-Keys in King-Street, A parcel of Well Manufactured Mahogany Furniture, consisting of Chairs of different patterns, Dining Tables of different sizes, Tea-Tables, Half Chest of Drawers & & . . ."

The advertisement conveys the impression that Nutt was selling out his stock of furniture. This is substantiated by the fact that no later information can be found concerning him. Presumably he left the Province.

John Packrow
WORKING C. 1761–c. 1767

John Packrow was born in Charleston of Huguenot ancestry. The name was originally Pasquereau but was later anglicized to Packrow. On August 21, 1762, Packrow advertised in the South Carolina Gazette "that he still continues to carry on his business of CABI-NET and CHAIR-MAKING, &c. at his shop in Charles-Town, and will be obliged to those who will favour him with their custom, and he engages to have their work done well, and with the greatest dispatch, having very good workmen."

There are two things of special interest in this advertisement; one is that Packrow must have been working in Charleston for some time if he "still continues to carry on his business"; the other that he must have been successful if he was able to employ some "very good workmen."

On May 20, 1761, Elizabeth Packrow, widow, gave to her son, John Packrow, lot No. 115 on Tradd Street. The following month John mortgaged the property for £3000 "lawful money." John Rutledge may have assumed the mortgage; in any event on February 25, 1765, the property was conveyed to Rutledge. At that time Elizabeth Packrow is spoken of as the widow of Lewis.[1]

Packrow moved to Jacksonboro, South Carolina, about 1763, perhaps thinking that he could build up a lucrative business among the plantation owners of the Edisto River area. Apparently this did not occur, for in the South Carolina Gazette of November 12, 1764, he states "That, having given over his business in Jacksonborough, a few months ago, he has now resumed his said business again in all its branches; and having provided a set of good workmen for that purpose, . . . And, after returning thanks to his country and town customers for their favours, hopes for a continuance of them."

A marriage license was granted on March 4, 1762, to John Packrow and Jane Singleton, a widow. Jane did not live long after her marriage. We find that a marriage license was granted to John Packrow and Sophia Harvey, another widow, on February 12, 1766.[2] Packrow appears to have had a liking for widows. His son Benjamin, a child of his second marriage, was buried on July 12, 1767.[3]

It is not known what happened to Packrow after the death of his son. He no longer advertised nor is his will listed in the records of the Probate Court. His widow Sophia Packrow appears to have died in 1798.[4]

Abraham Pearce
WORKING 1766–1782

It is not known when Abraham Pearce came to the Province, but by 1766 he had been granted 100 acres near Long Canes by the Provincial Council.[1] Two years later he advertised in the *Gazette*, as a cabinet-maker and carver from London, that he was opening his shop on Broad Street "two doors from the Beef Market," and that "Orders from the country, or any of the southern provinces, will be punctually complied with."[2] The latter statement is very significant as an indication that it was the custom of the local cabinet-makers to export some of their furniture.

Pearce did no more adverising. According to the Elfe account book, Pearce devoted some of his time to carving chair splats for Elfe.[3] Presumably during this period he made furniture on his own account. After Elfe's death, which occurred in 1775, Pearce remained in Charleston. After the city was captured by the British in 1780 he was one of those who petitioned Sir Henry Clinton to be admitted to the status of a British citizen. In 1782, while the city was still under British occupation, Pearce is listed in the directory as an undertaker at No. 32 Broad Street. Presumably he left with the British when they evacuated Charleston in December, 1782. It is recorded that for having signed the petition to Clinton he was ordered banished and his estate confiscated.[4] After that date there is no further record of him.

James L. Peigne
1784–1839　　WORKING 1809–

James L. Peigne was a native of France, but the date of his arrival in Charleston is not known.[1] His name appears for the first time as a cabinet-maker in the 1809 directory. The next we hear of him is in 1816, when he is listed as a grocer. Three years later he is shown as being the assistant engineer for the city. He probably held that position until his death, which occurred in August, 1839. He died of "Cholera Morbis" at the age of fifty-five and was buried in the French Protestant [Huguenot] Churchyard.[2]

Martin Pfeninger, Sr.
–1782　　WORKING C. 1772–1782

The first mention of Martin Pfeninger occurs in an item of the account book of Thomas Elfe: in May, 1772, Elfe "paid Martin Pfeninger for work £40." Pfeninger advertised in the *South Carolina Gazette* on April 12, 1773, that his Shop was in New Church Street opposite the Scotch Meeting and Parsonage House.

Evidently Pfeninger was a successful cabinet-maker. On October 2, 1777, he purchased from Michael Kalteisen a lot "on the N. E. side of the High Road leading from Charles Town or King Street." The following year he purchased 200 acres in St. George's Parish.

On October 28, 1777, he inserted the following advertisement in the *South Carolina Gazette:* "Martin Pfeninger—is sorry for want of material to oblige him to leave off his business of Cabinet-making &c. . . . As soon as material [Mahogany] can be had, he will be obliged to the public and his customers for a continuance of their favor." Obviously Charleston was feeling the effect of the British blockade. It was probably an easy task for the British cruisers to intercept all shipments of mahogany from the Indies and Honduras. The advertisement may also be an indication that the inhabitants of Charleston were so used to mahogany that they would have no other wood as a substitute.

During the siege of Charleston by the British in 1780 Pfeninger, with many others, signed a petition addressed to General Lincoln urging him to surrender to the British.

Pfeninger was admitted to the German Friendly Society on June 5, 1776. The records of the Society show that he died on September 20, 1782. His will was not probated until April 2, 1783, delayed no doubt by the British occupation which terminated in December, 1782.

In his will Pfeninger mentions his wife Hannah and his son Daniel.

[111]

Martin Pfeninger [II]
-1796   WORKING C. 1796

It is not known what relation this Martin Pfeninger was to the one who died in 1782. He may have been the nephew of the elder Martin. Nothing is known of his activities as a cabinet-maker. On January 21, 1796, letters were granted to William Goodson to administer on the estate of Martin Pfeninger, late of Charleston, cabinet-maker.[1] The inventory of his estate, which amounted to £157, was taken two weeks later.[2] Pfeninger probably died in January, 1796.

Eleazer Philips [Phillips]
                                       WORKING 1784–1793

The first knowledge that we have of Eleazer Philips is on November 9, 1786, when he was a surety for the estate of Henry Leiber. The same year Philips and his wife Martha sold a lot on Smith Lane to James Gravers for £175 Sterling, "of the State." The only other record we have of Philips is dated February 3, 1793, when he and his wife Martha sold another piece of property on Smith Lane. It is not known when or how they acquired this property. It is quite possible that it was an inheritance of Martha's.

The records of the Probate Court fail to reveal his will or inventory.

John M. Philips [Phillips]
-1825   WORKING 1796–1813

John M. Philips joined the German Friendly Society on April 20, 1796; this leads us to believe that he was of German extraction. In the same year he was working as an independent craftsman on Beaufain Street.[1] In 1801 he inserted the following advertisement in the Times of August 22: "CAUTION. Being apprehensive that my apprentice boy, JOHN HODGE, intends leaving the country, without my approbation or consent; this is to forewarn (sic) all captains of vessels and others concerned, from taking him away as they will be prosecuted to the utmost rigour

of the law." It is not known whether Hodge was ever apprehended.

For the next few years John M. Philips is listed in the directories as a painter and glazier, and it is not until 1809 that his occupation is again given as that of a cabinet-maker. He is also shown in the 1813 directory as a cabinet-maker. As his name does not appear in any of the later directories it may be supposed that he gave up cabinet-making about this time.

Benjamin R. Porter
-1825   WORKING 1798–1822

As a young man Porter formed a copartnership (?) with Labach.[1] The association seems to have been of short duration. In 1798, when he was twenty-three years old, Porter started working as an independent craftsman.[2] For the next twenty-four years his name appears as a cabinet-maker in the various directories, although he appears to have moved the location of his shop at frequent intervals.

Porter died of consumption at the age of fifty on September 13, 1825. The Health Department Records make note of the fact that he was born in Charleston.

Porter & Labach [or Fabach]
                                       WORKING 1797

This copartnership (?) is known from a single advertisement that appeared in the South Carolina Gazette on June 20, 1797: "Cabinet Makers. The Subscribers beg leave to inform their friends and the public, that they have commenced the Cabinet-making Business, No. 187, Meeting-street," and "that all orders will be thankfully received and executed with neatness at a low price, for Cash, Benj. Porter, Jacob Labach." This partnership was of short duration, for in January of the following year Porter was advertising as an independent craftsman.

John Powell
-1789   WORKING C. 1789

Nothing is known concerning Powell except what is recorded in his will and inventory. In the former, made October 28, 1789, and recorded a week later, Powell stipulated that his goods are to be sold and the proceeds given to his "friend Wm. Walters for his full demand against me for boarding, Lodging and nursing." [1] Powell does not mention any family. His inventory amounted to £22. [2]

Thomas Price
−1797   WORKING C. 1797

On November 3, 1797, letters were granted to Mrs. Elizabeth Price, widow, and Samuel Salter, carver, both of Philadelphia, to administer the estate of Thomas Price, cabinet-maker. [1] The circumstance leads to the supposition that Price was from Philadelphia.

A few months before his death Price leased, for seven years, from John McCrady, the corner of Queen and Union Street continued. [2] Price's inventory reveals that he owed small sums of money to four of the local cabinet-makers. [3] It is not known whether he worked for them or was an independent craftsman.

John Prue
WORKING C. 1746–1772

For one who did no advertising and apparently made no money out of real estate, Prue became a fairly well-to-do man. During the time that Prue worked in Charleston he must have made a substantial amount of furniture if his wealth was derived solely from that source.

The first and only record we have of Prue in Charleston occurs in a deed dated March 10, 1746, when he purchased two lots on the west side of King Street from Jordan Roche. His workshop was situated in his yard.

His will was dated August 28, 1772, and probated the following February. Prue, after leaving certain bequests, left his money (other than that left to his wife Sarah) to the Commissioners to be appointed by an act passed by General Assembly for erecting, founding, or endowing a College in this Province.

The difficulty of securing the bequest is best told by Dr. J. H. Easterby in his *History of the College of Charleston:*

"A third benefactor was John Prue who describes himself in his will as a cabinet-maker of Charles Town. By this instrument the college was made the ultimate heir of property valued at £2000 sterling. . . . According to the will . . . the college which the general assembly was endeavoring to establish in 1770 was to receive the residue of the estate on the death of the testator's widow. This lady subsequently married a Mr. Creighton, who, being a loyalist, retired to Scotland at the beginning of the Revolution. When Charleston was taken by the British in 1780, however, he returned and seems to have sold certain bonds which should have been reserved for the residuary heir. Whether the former Mrs. Prue participated in this procedure is not known, but it is certain that she died before Feb. 10, 1785. On that day the general assembly ordered John Baker, who had been named as executor in the will but had never qualified, to take possession of a house at 96 King Street formerly occupied by Mr. Prue. This apparently was all that was left of the residue. Under the authority of an act passed the next year . . . the property was sold . . . by a board of commissioners appointed from the trustees of the three colleges. The deed has not been found, and it is not known how much was realized."
Prue's wife Sarah was the daughter of Daniel Townsend.

W. W. Purse
1797–1858   WORKING 1822–1831

W. W. Purse has the distinction of being one of the few Charleston cabinet-makers to whom a definite piece of furniture can be attributed. On November 8, 1822, Purse billed James Jervey for $38.00 for making a bookcase. Both the bookcase and receipt are in existence and are owned by one of Jervey's descendants. The bookcase is made of mahogany, and as the price would indicate, is quite plain and was probably made for Mr.

Jervey's office. White pine is used as a secondary wood in its construction. This in itself is of great interest, for it shows that the local cabinet-makers were still using this imported pine instead of the more abundant, and doubtless cheaper, long-leaf pine.

It is not known when Purse started working as an independent cabinet-maker, but his name appears for the first time in the directory for 1822. Four years later his shop was destroyed by fire.[1] His wife was the former Miss Mary T. Fendin.[2]

Purse's name appears for the last time in the 1831 directory. The Health Department records reveal that a "Mr. Purse," who may have been the cabinet-maker, died on January 26, 1858, at the age of sixty-one.

Laurence Quackinbush
WORKING C. 1801–C. 1808

Laurence Quackinbush (or Quackenbush) must have been working in Charleston before 1801; on September 3 of that year he and Mary Pringle were married. Their son Alexander was baptized the following August.[1] Quackinbush is listed in the 1806 directory as being at No. 3 Cock Lane. On January 1, 1808, his daughter Ann Caroline was baptized.[2] As no further record can be found about him, it is possible that he moved to some other locality.

John Ralph
–1801   WORKING C. 1773–1801

As a young man, John Ralph worked for Thomas Elfe. In the account book, kept in so meticulous a manner by Elfe, it is recorded that during the latter part of 1773 and the early part of 1774, Elfe paid Ralph £35 every month.[1] This, of course, was in local currency, but it probably is a good indication of the wage scale of a cabinet-maker during that particular period. It is not known when Ralph started working for himself independently (Elfe died in December, 1775), but he was sufficiently prosperous to purchase a lot on the Bay on February 27, 1778. In the follow-

ing year he bought a piece of property in Unity Alley.[2]

During the Revolution, Ralph became a member of the County Militia and during the siege of Charleston he was one of those who petitioned General Lincoln to surrender to the British.[3] After the surrender of the city to the British, Ralph petitioned Sir Henry Clinton to be allowed to resume the status of a British citizen.[4] While the British forces occupied the city Ralph remained in Charleston and probably continued working as a cabinet-maker. On September 24, 1781, still during the occupation, Ralph purchased a piece of property from John Robertson on the west side of Church Street.[5]

For signing the petition to General Lincoln, Ralph was ordered banished and his estate confiscated. Ralph probably talked himself out of being banished and may have gotten off with a 12% fine on his estate. In 1784 he was one of the sureties for the estate of Mary Monck.[6]

The 1790 census shows Ralph as being the owner of one slave. His wife Ann died in January, 1792.[7] In the following year Ralph formed a copartnership with Nicholas Silberg which lasted for about three years. After the dissolution of the copartnership Ralph again became an independent cabinet-maker, but was probably not as successful as heretofore for we find that in 1797 he gave a mortgage for £410, putting up as collateral his property on Church Street.[8] The mortgage was not satisfied until after his death.

It is not known when Ralph remarried but after Ralph's death, which occurred in September, 1801,[9] letters were granted to Mrs. Jane Ralph, widow, to administer his estate.[10] Among the items listed in his inventory are 9 Windsor chairs (which probably had been made by Ralph), 12 mahogany chairs, 5 beds, and some mahogany.[11]

Ralph & Silberg
WORKING 1793–1796

The copartnership of John Ralph and Nicholas Silberg was formed in October, 1793. Their advertisement states that they were "Cabinet Makers, Chair Makers, and Undertakers" at No. 52 Church Street.[1] On

April 1, 1796, a notice of the dissolution of the partnership appeared in the *City Gazette and Daily Advertiser*. After that time both men worked in Charleston as independent cabinet-makers.

William R. Rawson

Though Rawson's name appears in the 1819 directory as a cabinet-maker, it is probable that he was primarily an importer of furniture. On March 15, 1819, he inserted the following advertisement in the *City Gazette and Commercial Advertiser:* "Mahogany Furniture. Selling off cheap. W. R. Rawson, 86 Meeting Street. Has just received from his Manufactury at the North 22 Boxes Cabinet Furniture . . . Side Boards, Grecian Couches and Sofas . . . Mahogany and Burch Bedsteads." For some reason Rawson's importations were not successful, for another advertisement three months later in the same paper reads: "Positive Sale of New and Handsome Furniture . . . at W. Rawson's Furniture Warehouse, No. 87 Meeting Street, will be sold without reserve, as the proprietor intends to decline business . . ." It is not known what happened to Rawson after he "declined" business.

There is in existence a chest-of-drawers with mirror attached bearing Rawson's label. It is believed, however, to be one of Rawson's New York importations. A photograph of this piece appears on Plate XI, facing page 159 in *Southern Antiques,* by Paul H. Burroughs (1931).

Andrew Redmond
–1791   WORKING C. 1774–1790

Although he was by trade a turner, Andrew Redmond also made Windsor chairs. His only advertisement, which appeared on January 13, 1784, in the *South Carolina Gazette and General Advertiser* says that Redmond "still carries on, at No. 27 Meeting-street, near the New Church [St. Michael's], or corner of St. Michaels Alley, Turnery in all its Branches, All kinds of House, Cabinet and Ship-Joiner's Work; Jobbing ditto, etc. Likewise Philadelphia Windsor Chairs, either armed or unarmed, as neat as any imported, and much better stuff; Common Chairs, etc."

Redmond was obviously meeting the competition of imported Windsor chairs. These chairs were sporadically brought into the port of Charleston from the North, the majority of them coming from Philadelphia. The fact creates a problem: if Redmond made his Windsor chair similar to those of Philadelphia manufacture, how can they be distinguished today? The kind of wood used in their construction may be the answer.

It is not known whether Redmond was a native of Charleston. He was here, however, by 1774, for in that year he did some work for Elfe.[1] The following year an Andrew Redmond is listed as a sergeant in the troop of Capt. Thomas Pinckney,[2] but there is nothing to indicate the nature of his service in the Revolution. In his will, probated on February 1, 1791, he mentions his brother and sister.[3]

William Reside
WORKING 1797–1809

William Reside was active in Masonry. On January 1, 1799, he was admitted to Orange Lodge No. 14 (Masonic) and by 1806 was elected Treasurer of the Ancient York Masons.[1] He was working as a cabinet-maker by 1797 [2] and advertised in the *City Gazette and Daily Advertiser* on April 9, 1799, that his shop was at No. 131 Meeting Street. A few months before this he purchased from Helen Perry a lot on the east side of Meeting Street.[3]

On July 13, 1800, a marriage settlement was made between Reside and Mary Magdeline Clarkson, widow of Alexander Clarkson. Mary had inherited seven slaves and a lot on the north side of Tradd Street. The slaves she transferred to Joseph Gaultier as trustee for her daughter Elizabeth Clarkson.[4] The marriage between Reside and Mary Magdeline took place on August 3, 1800, the ceremony being performed by the Rev. John C. Faber.[5] Within a few months Mary was dead. On April 2, 1801, letters were granted to Reside to administer the estate of Mary Magdeline Reside.[6]

Reside appears to have prospered. On July 14, 1804, he purchased from John Drayton, Grand Master of the Grand Lodge of South Carolina, Ancient York Masons, two lots on the east side of New Street, south of the Charleston Theatre.[7] At that time the theatre was situated on the corner of Broad and New Streets.

On June 1, 1808, Reside became involved in a lawsuit with William Wightman. Wightman claimed that he had sold a piece of property to Reside for £600, payable in three equal installments, and that Reside had only paid him £116, taken possession of the property, and built a house upon it. The Court decreed that Reside must comply with the original contract.[8]

Reside's name appears for the last time in the 1809 directory, where he is listed as being on Church Street. It is not known what happened to him after this time.

John Riley
1751–1804   WORKING c. 1784–1804

In July, 1775, a John Riley was a private in the Company commanded by Captain Charles C. Pinckney.[1] This may have been the cabinet-maker who enlisted as a young man. Nothing is known of his activities during the Revolution. Presumably he served his apprenticeship in Charleston and may have worked there in his early days. After the Revolution it appears that he moved to Jacksonboro, South Carolina, a small community on the Edisto River about twenty-five miles south of Charleston. On March 31, 1804, Riley was granted letters to administer the estate of Samuel Davidson, a schoolmaster.[2] At that time Riley is spoken of as a cabinet-maker of St. Bartholomew's Parish, in which Jacksonboro is located.

Riley married Frances Morgandollar on November 23, 1797. The marriage took place at Coosewhatchie, Beaufort District, the home of the bride.[3] Presumably Riley remained in Jacksonboro. He died there on February 23, 1804, at the age of 53.[4]

[116]

Paul Rosse
–1807

When Paul Rosse took out his citizenship papers on January 14, 1806, he stated that he was a cabinet-maker by profession, thirty years of age, and a native of Italy.[1] It is not known that Rosse practiced his profession while he was in Charleston. In the directory for 1806 he is listed as a print seller and frame maker at No. 31 Broad Street. In September of that year he applied for a license to retail spiritous liquors.[2]

The following obituary notice appeared in the *City Gazette* of October 28, 1807:

"Died, on Tuesday last, Captain Paul Rosse, in the 37th year of his age. He was interred in the Roman Catholic Church with military honors, by a detachment of fifty men from the 28th regiment. The officers of which regiment, with many from the Legionary Corps, attended their deceased Brother Soldier to the grave. Captain Rosse was a native of Italy; and had, in a residence of six years in this city, established the character of an honest man and good citizen."

Presumably this was the same man in spite of the discrepancy in the ages given by the two records.

George D. Rou
WORKING c. 1815–c. 1819

A George D. Rou was admitted to the German Friendly Society on November 11, 1815. In the 1819 directory he is listed as a cabinet-maker on Warren Street. The only other available information concerning him is contained in the Records of the German Friendly Society, which show that he was "excluded" on August 9, 1825. Whether he was still working in the city at that time is not known.

M. Rou, Jr.
WORKING 1802–1806

M. Rou is listed as a cabinet-maker at No. 22 George Street in the 1802 directory. At that time he is spoken of as "Junior." In the directory for 1806 he is shown as still being on George Street but by this time the term "Junior" has been dropped. His name appears for the last time in the directory of 1806. The name Rou being an unusual one, it seems likely that George D. Rou and M. Rou, Jr., were in some way related.

Abraham Roulain
1738–1787   WORKING C. 1768–1787

Of French Huguenot extraction, Abraham Roulain was born on August 6, 1738,[1] the son of Abraham Roulain and his wife, Mary Ann Guerin. It is not known under whom he was apprenticed. The first information we have of him as an independent cabinet-maker comes from an advertisement in the *South Carolina Gazette; And Country Journal* for December 6, 1768: "ABRAHAM ROULAIN, Acquaints the Public, in General, and his friends and former customers, that he hath removed into Tradd Street, next Door to George Saxby, Esq, where he carries on the Joiners and Cabinet Business; he will be much obliged to those Ladies and Gentlemen who please to favour him with their custom.—Mrs. Roulain carries on the Mantua-Makers Business at the same place."

Roulain appears to have had some business transaction with Thomas Elfe. In 1772 Roulain owed Elfe £23; three years later he owed Elfe another £6.[2] Roulain got into an altercation with Francis Bayle in the same year. The Grand Jury brought in a bill of assault and battery against Roulain, but after due deliberation the Jury returned the verdict of "we can't say."[3] Presumably the charges were dropped.

There seems to be no record of Roulain during the Revolution and the British occupation of the city. On December 23, 1783, he mortgaged his plantation in St. Thomas's Parish for the sum of £226 Sterling of Great Britain.[4] He had probably inherited the property, which consisted of 197 acres; there is, at least, no record of his having purchased it.

In his later years Roulain probably devoted some of his time to cultivating the plantation. In his will, which was made on May 7, 1787, he is spoken of as a planter.[5] However, in a deed dated August 7, 1787, Lewis Fogartie, executor of the estate of Abraham Roulain, sold some property to Andrew Guillebar, at which time Roulain is spoken of as a cabinet-maker.[6] Roulain must have died between the date of his will and the execution of the deed.

There is nothing unusual in his inventory except 9 Hickory chairs valued at 20 shillings each. His total estate was appraised at £531.[7]

James Roushan [Rousham]
–1754   WORKING 1731–1754

The first record of James Roushan is to be found in a bill of sale dated August 28, 1731, when he purchased from William Brace "his household goods, Indian Wench named Sarah, one lot in new London," all for £5 current money.[1] It was a remarkable purchase for such a sum. By 1733 Roushan was living in Dorchester, a small village at the headwaters of the Ashley River, near Summerville, South Carolina.[2] On June 30, 1744, a marriage license was granted to Roushan and Catherine Van Velsin, spinster.[3] Presumably this was his second marriage, for in that same year Roushan gave a Negro to his daughter Sarah.[4]

Roushan was primarily a carpenter and in all deeds and other records is so referred to. His name would not be included in this work were it not for the fact that his inventory reveals that he had "1 desk unfinished."[5] Also listed in the advertisement of the sale of his effects, which appeared in the *South Carolina Gazette* for February 27, 1755, is some cedar and mahogany plank. It is more than likely that the mahogany was being used to make furniture.

Roushan's will is dated December 8, 1754, and was probated on January 10, 1755.[6]

George Daniel Row
WORKING 1800–1819

On January 1, 1800, Rev. John C. Faber, Executor of John Eberley, sold to George Daniel Row, cabinet-maker, lot No. 222 on the east side of Meeting Street for 410 Guineas.[1] In the following year a Daniel Row is listed in the 1801 directory as a cabinet-maker, at No. 11 Federal Street. And in the 1819 directory a George D. Rou is listed as a cabinet-maker. It is just possible that George D. Rou and George Daniel Row could be one and the same person. Certainly the similarity in given names, as well as in the surname, would lead to such a conclusion.

Edward George Sass
1788–1849   WORKING 1809–1849

Edward George Sass followed in the footsteps of his father, Jacob Sass, and undoubtedly served his apprenticeship under him. Born on March 5, 1788,[1] he was working with his father in 1811, for on February 12 of that year they advertised in the *Courier* as Jacob Sass and Son. In the 1813 directory Edward is shown as being located at No. 38 Queen Street, which is the same address as that given for his father.

Edward became a member of the German Friendly Society in 1809 at the age of twenty-one. He was made a Steward in 1811 and elected Junior Warden the following year. He married Mary, the daughter of Rudolph Switzer, on April 2, 1809.[2] By this marriage they had nine children.[3]

In the 1822 directory Edward Sass is listed as being at the Northern Warehouse at No. 77 Queen Street. About this time Charleston was feeling the impact of furniture imported from the North. Perhaps Edward, realizing that mass produced furniture from New York could probably be imported more cheaply than furniture which was being made by local craftsmen, opened up a warehouse to take care of these importations.

In December, 1823, Jacob Sass conveyed some property inherited by his wife to John C. Schirmer in trust for his two surviving sons, Edward G. and William H. Sass.[4]

A month after the death of Jacob Sass, which occurred in February, 1836, Jacob F. Schirmer, Wm. H. Schirmer, and others conveyed No. 77 Queen Street to Edward Sass for $5,500; this included the three-story brick dwelling house, workshop, and other buildings.[5]

Immediately after his father's death Edward advertised in the *Courier* of February 24, 1836, that he intended to continue the business formerly carried on by his father and that "he was grateful for the patronage so long bestowed on his deceased father."

Mary, the wife of Edward, died in 1834 at the age of forty-three. Edward died on January 20, 1849, at the age of sixty-one. Both are buried in the churchyard of the First Baptist Church. His tombstone states that "For many years he was a Warden of this Church." [6] It is not known when Sass left the Lutheran Church and joined the Baptist Church.

In his will Edward gives specific instructions to his son, Jacob Keith Sass, to put his body "in a thin Spanish Cedar Coffin to be covered with lead and enclosed in a Mahogany coffin made of thick Mahogany boards." He left all his tools and workbenches to his son, George Washington Sass.[7]

Jacob Sass
1750–1836   WORKING 1774–c. 1828

For nearly fifty years, Jacob Sass worked as a cabinet-maker in Charleston. During that period he must have produced a prodigious amount of furniture. It is regrettable that none of his account books has survived. Sass ultimately became a man of wealth, owning much property. The funds to purchase these properties must have been derived solely from the sale of furniture. Undoubtedly an appreciable amount of Sass's furniture must still be in existence, even though it may be scattered throughout the country.

There is in existence a desk and bookcase of large proportions now (1955) in the Miles Brewton House. Written in ink, in an old-fashioned hand, on the side of one of the smaller drawers is "Made by Jacob Sass, October 1794." It is reasonable to assume that the piece was actually made by Sass. Unfortunately, because of the large size of the bookcase it is difficult to make comparison with some of the smaller pieces attributed to Sass.

A native of Schenstad, Hessen, Germany, Sass arrived in Charleston in the year 1773.[1]

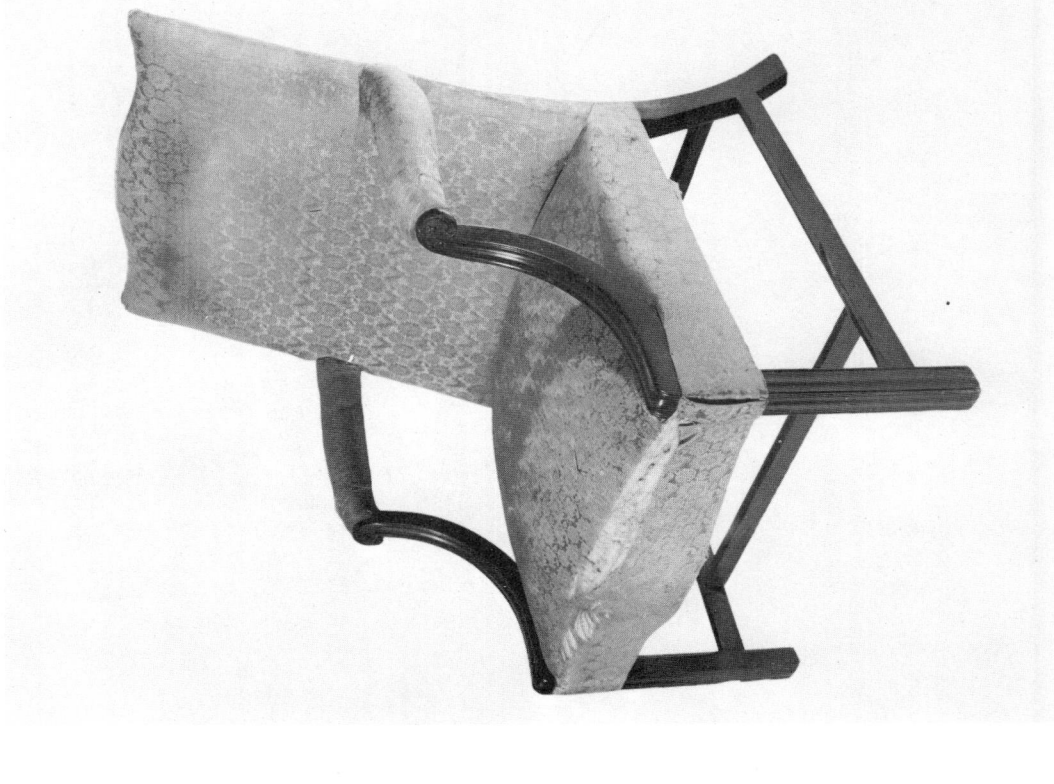

Fig. 109 FRENCH CHAIR dimensions not available

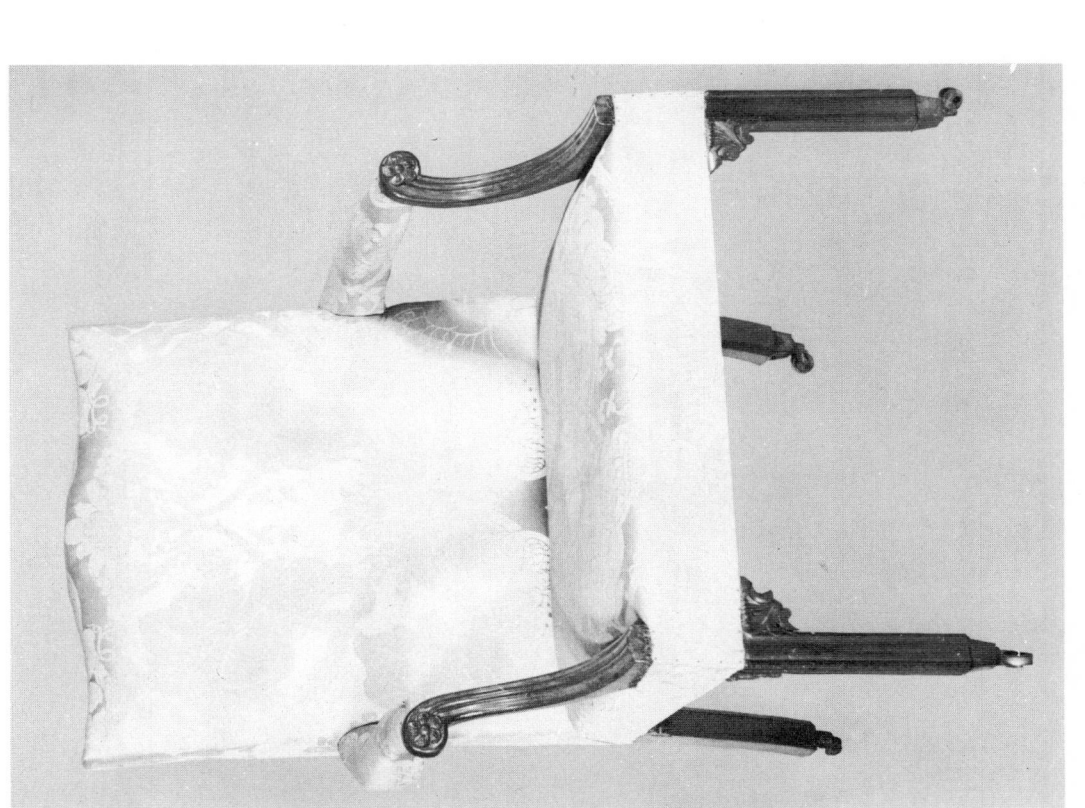

Fig. 108 FRENCH CHAIR Height 40"; width 27"

Fig. 110 CHIPPENDALE STYLE CHAIR
Height 37¾"; width 21⅝"

Fig. 111 CHINESE CHIPPENDALE
STYLE CHAIR   Height 37"; width 22⁷⁄₁₆"

Fig. 112 CHIPPENDALE STYLE CHAIR
(Corner brackets missing)
Height 38⅛"; width 21⅞"

Fig. 113 CHIPPENDALE STYLE CHAIR
Height 37⅜"; width 21¼"

Little is known of the early period of his residence in Charleston. In 1776 he married Dorothea Vielham, the daughter of a German planter residing at Goose Creek. By this marriage they had five girls and three boys. That Sass prospered is indicated by his purchase on September 3, 1777, of lot No. 97 on Archdale Square from John Ward.

During the Revolution Sass gave his wholehearted support to the Colonies. In 1777 he was elected a 2nd Lieutenant of the German Fusiliers, a local militia company. The Fusiliers participated in the disastrous siege of Savannah in 1779. During the siege the company was conspicuous for its bravery and suffered heavy losses. Sass returned to Charleston and later on joined the brigade led by the gallant General Francis Marion. After the war when the German Fusiliers was reorganized, Sass was elected 1st Lieutenant and afterwards Captain. He was in command for several years until he was promoted to Wagon Master General, with the rank of Colonel, on the Governor's Staff.[2]

Sass was admitted to the German Friendly Society on July 9, 1777. He was elected Steward in 1783 and became President of the organization in 1789. His portrait, in uniform, hangs in the Hall of the Society along with those of many of its other Presidents. Sass was also active in other organizations. In 1807 he became President of the corporation of the local Lutheran Church and was one of the founders of the German Fusiliers [military] Company and Society.

After the Revolution, Sass began acquiring property in and around Charleston. On June 30, 1790, he purchased from Sir John Nesbit a lot on the south side of Queen Street, adjacent to a piece of property already owned by him. Sass apparently stayed in the locality during the greater part of his lifetime. In 1802 Sass purchased a piece of property on the north side of Queen Street and conveyed it to John Elias Schirmer, who had married Sass's daughter, Margaret Helen. The value of the property was estimated at £900 sterling. Not only was it a munificent gift but it gives an indication of Sass's wealth.

The following item appeared in the *Times* for January 29, 1802: "FOR PRIVATE SALE. An elegant BROAD CLOTH CARPET. Wrought with different kinds of Fruits and Flowers, to be seen at the subscriber's House, No. 35 Queen Street. Price, One hundred Guineas. If not sold before the commencement of the Races, it will then be raffled for. Jacob Sass." During Race Week practically every wealthy planter within the area touched by Charleston came to town, not only to see the races, but to participate in the social whirl which occurred during the week. One hundred Guineas was no small sum, particularly in those days. But it must not be forgotten that the preceding cotton crop had sold for 44 cents per pound. Doubtless, Sass disposed of the carpet with no difficulty to some rich planter or merchant.

Mrs. Sass died on March 31, 1812, after a long illness of nearly eight years. Jacob Sass died in February, 1836, at the age of eighty-seven and was buried next to his wife in the churchyard of St. John's Lutheran Church. Some idea of the esteem in which he was held by friends and the public in general is found in an article which appeared in the *Courier* of February 18, 1836: "At an extra Meeting of the German Fusiliers convened on the 15th. inst. for the purpose of testifying their respect to the memory of their deceased Member, Col. Jacob Sass . . . the last of the founders of the German Fusilier Company and Society.

"*Resolved:* That our Hall of Meeting shall be hung with the emblem of mourning, during three successive Meetings. *Resolved,* That we will wear Crape on the left arm for three months, in token of our loss and affection . . ."

Harry Saunders
−1787   WORKING C. 1786

Nothing is known about Harry Saunders except from his obituary notice, which appeared in the *Charleston Morning Post and Daily Advertiser* for June 16, 1787: "DIED . . . Also, Mr. Harry Saunders, cabinet maker, of this city."

On December 1, 1786, a Harrie Sanderson, cabinet-maker, was surety for the estate of

Malcolm Smith.[1] This is probably the same man.

Edward Scull
-1744   WORKING C. 1727–1744

Edward Scull presents a problem, since he is nowhere listed as a cabinet-maker. However, he is spoken of both as a joiner and as a chairmaker and it is probable that he actually made chairs as we now know them. In 1727 he executed a bond to Joseph Hunt for £433 current lawful money.[1] In the *South Carolina Gazette* for February 20, 1744, occurs the following advertisement: ". . . to be sold a small Pettiaugua . . . Whoever has a mind to purchase her, may treat with the said John Hogg, next door to Mr. Scull, Chairmaker." It is not known how long Scull worked in Charleston. On October 20 of that same year the will of Edward Scull, Joiner, was probated. In it he mentions his mother, Mary Forster, living in Pennsylvania, and his wife Ann.[2]

Among the items listed in Scull's inventory are "one mahogany table, one mahogany tea table, and one cypress Press."[3]

John J. Sheridan
WORKING C. 1825

A strong advocate of local industry, John J. Sheridan started working in Charleston about 1825. On April 26 of that year he advertised for the first time in the *Courier* that he had "GRECIAN SOFAS, Easy Chairs," and other articles of furniture for sale. For the next few years nothing is known of his activities except from an item that appeared in the Weekly Report of the Stewards of the Orphan House: "Sept. 10–16, 1829 Marinus Vannifer [apprenticed] to Mr. John J. Sheridan, Cabinet maker."

By 1830 the importation into Charleston of mass-produced furniture from New York had reached such proportions that it was working an economic hardship on the local cabinet-makers. Many Charleston cabinet-makers handled these importations, finding, no doubt, that even with the freight added, the imported piece could be made and sold more cheaply than one made by a local artisan. Sheridan appeared determined to combat these importations by arousing the civic pride of the Charlestonians. During the next three years his advertisements in the *Courier* laid particular stress on "CHARLESTON MADE FURNITURE," which consisted of "Dressing and plain Bureaus; Sideboards of the latest fashion; Mahogany and plain bedsteads; Pillar and Claw Tea Tables . . . Wardrobes; Sofas of various patterns—Also, Windsor and Easy-chairs . . ." Just how successful Sheridan was in influencing the purchases of the Charlestonians does not appear.

Information on Sheridan's later life is scant. On April 20, 1855, he executed a mortgage to Thomas W. Gadsden, giving as collateral a lot and building on the south side of Ann Street.[1]

Thomas Sigwald
WORKING C. 1797–1816

Thomas Sigwald, who was of German extraction, became a member of the German Friendly Society on July 26, 1797. Two years later letters were granted to him to administer the estate of Christian Sigwald, Inn Keeper.[1] This may have been his father. In 1801 Sigwald sold a lot on the north side of Montagu Street to Jacob Sass for 250 Guineas.[2] It is quite possible that Sigwald was apprenticed to, and worked for, Sass during his early life.

His name appears for the first time as an independent cabinet-maker in the 1806 directory where he is listed as being on the southwest corner of King and Queen Streets. He is listed as a cabinet-maker for the last time in the directory for 1816. After that nothing is known about him. His will is not recorded in the files of the Probate Court.

Nicholas Silberg
-1801   WORKING 1796–1801

Nicholas Silberg, a native of Sweden, formed a copartnership with John Ralph (*q.v.*) in 1793. This association lasted about three years. Both Silberg and Ralph were probably very young men when they formed this copartnership. By 1796 Silberg was established as an independent cabinet-maker and undertaker at No. 132 Queen Street.[1]

Silberg and Mrs. Margaret Clark were married on March 28, 1797.[2] The marriage was of short duration. Silberg was buried on December 27, 1801, having died of "strangers" fever.[3] In his will he leaves the residue of his estate to his wife Margaret for her lifetime, then to relatives in the Town of Carlscrona, Sweden.[4] Among the things listed in his inventory are some chests of drawers, 1 lot of mahogany, 1 lot of cedar boards, 1 lot of pine boards.[5] The latter wood by this time had supplanted cypress as a secondary wood.

James Simmons
WORKING 1790

James Simmons, like some of the other Low Country cabinet-makers, apparently thought that Jacksonboro, South Carolina, would be a lucrative place to establish his shop. This small community is about twenty-five miles south of Charleston on the Edisto River and in the center of several rice plantations. It is not known when Simmons moved to Jacksonboro or how long he worked there. On April 7, 1790, letters were granted to Mrs. Sarah Horn to administer the estate of James Simmons, cabinet-maker of Jacksonboro.[1]

George Elias Smith
WORKING 1806–1816

Although George Elias Smith worked in Charleston for many years, little is known of his activities. His name appears for the first time in the directory of 1806, where he is listed as being at No. 115 Meeting Street. A decade later he is still spoken of as a cabinet-maker, but in the 1819 directory his occupation is given as that of carpenter.

On August 18, 1810, George Elias Smith and Margaret Morgan were married.[1] The records contain no further data concerning him.

John Smith
WORKING ? 1774

John Smith, cabinet-maker, aged twenty-two, left the port of London during the first week of August, 1774, on the *Carolina Packet*. He stated that his destination was Carolina [Charleston], where he intended to settle.[1] There is, however, no record of his working in Charleston.

Richard Smith
–1857   WORKING 1809–1857

Richard Smith worked for nearly fifty years as a cabinet-maker in Charleston. He began working in 1809, (the year in which his name first appears in the directory) and until the time of his death, which occurred in 1857, Smith produced furniture. Even if he had no one to help him, he must have produced, during that length of time, a prodigious amount. There is a record where Smith was paid $4.00 by James Jervey for a wash-hand stand. The payment was made on December 6, 1824.[1]

Ann Wood and Richard Smith were married on December 24, 1812.[2] Two years later their son Richard was baptized.[3] In his will, which was probated on August 25, 1857, Smith provides for his wife Ann and leaves his estate to his children, "share and share alike."

Theodore Stafford
WORKING 1801–

Theodore Stafford appears to have been the former partner of Jay Humiston. Under the name of Humiston and Stafford they advertised in 1798 as Windsor chairmakers. It is not known how long this partnership lasted, but in the 1801 directory Stafford's name appears as that of a chairmaker at No. 98 Tradd Street. He is again listed in the 1802 directory but after that there is no record of him. It seems fairly certain that he left the city to work elsewhere.

Charles Stewart
WORKING C. 1794–C. 1800

Charles Stewart states that he is from London. He is primarily interested in furthering a new type sunshade for windows "a specimen of which, may in the course of a few days be seen on the house of the hon. John Rutledge; . . . The utility of this invention has been fully proved by the approbation of all persons of taste, and the encouragement given by people of property in England." Stewart adds that he is engaged in "Cabinet Making in all its branches, from a tea caddy to a library bookcase." [1]

Esther Brindley and Charles Stewart were married on June 16, 1794.[2] In 1800 Stewart took out his citizenship papers.[3] His age and birthplace were not recorded at the time. Stewart must have prospered, for on November 23, 1795 he bought some land situated near the headwaters of the Ashley River. Three years later he purchased a lot on the south side of Broad Street.[4]

A Charles Stewart died on November 14, 1817, at White Bluff, Savannah, at the age of fifty-seven.[5] This may have been the cabinet-maker.

George Stewart
WORKING PRIOR TO 1785

The only records of George Stewart are those which were made after his death. On March 11, 1785, letters were granted to Isabelle Stewart, widow, to administer the estate of George Stewart, cabinet-maker.[1] His inventory, taken three months later, lists only two chests of carpenter and cabinet-makers tools.[2] Stewart must have worked in Charleston immediately after the Revolution when economic conditions were still chaotic. It is not known whether he worked independently or for some one else.

Thomas Stocks
–C. 1760   WORKING C. 1758

There appear to have been three Thomas Stocks living in the vicinity of Charleston during the same period. One, a planter, died in 1742; one, who speaks of himself as "Gentleman," died in 1766; the third was the cabinet-maker, who died in 1760. Practically nothing is known about the cabinet-maker. On October 1, 1758, Thomas Stocks, cabinet-maker, and his wife Sarah conveyed the southeastern part of lot No. 254 to Philip Mensing for £660 local currency.[1] In the same year Stocks' daughter Eleanor was baptized.[2]

Stocks formed a copartnership with Stephen Townsend though the date is not known. The one fact about it is contained in a single advertisement published in the *South Carolina Gazette* for April 7, 1760: "The co-partnership of the late *Thomas Stocks* deceased, and *Stephen Townsend*, being expired, all persons indebted to them are desired to settle their accompts with all convenient speed . . ."

William Swaney
WORKING 1803–1807

William Swaney's name appears in only two directories, those of 1806 and 1807. An earlier notice of him provides the information that he was admitted to Orange Lodge (Masonic) on February 9, 1803. Since at that time he could not have been less than twenty-one years old, and since he is not mentioned as a cabinet-maker until three years later, it is possible that in 1806 he was still comparatively young and that he had spent his early years either as an apprentice or as the employee of an established cabinet-maker. After 1807 all trace of him is lost.

Christian Tamerus
WORKING 1805–1810

On November 24, 1805, Christian Tamerus sold a lot on the east side of King Street and another piece of property "up the path in St. Phillip Parish fronting on the Broad Road leading to and from Charleston." [1] There are no earlier records to indicate how he acquired the property; it may have come to him by inheritance. The next year Tamerus appears in the directory as being at No. 9 East King Street Road. During the succeeding years

Tamerus purchased some additional property on King Street.

On January 24, 1809, Miss Fanny Moran and Christian Tamerus were married by the Rev. Charles Faber.[2] As his will cannot be found in the records of the Probate Court and no other records can be found concerning him it is thought that he moved to some other locality.

John Teachester
WORKING 1822

The name of John Teachester appears only in the directory of 1822; there he is listed as being at No. 11 East Bay. No other records of Teachester have been found.

Thomas Tennant
1776–1838   WORKING 1816–1819

It is not known how long Thomas Tennant worked as a cabinet-maker in Charleston. His name appears only in the directories of 1816 and 1819. In 1832 Tennant and his wife Elizabeth conveyed some property on the south side of Queen Street.[1] Tennant died in 1838 at the age of sixty-two and is buried in the churchyard of the French [Huguenot] Church. The records of the Health Department state that he was born in Germany.

Jacob Thom
WORKING 1800–1803

Jacob Thom and Susan Quackinbush were married on May 25, 1800.[1] Susan may have been the sister of Laurence Quackinbush, another cabinet-maker, with whom Thom entered into partnership for a time. The directory of 1802 shows them as being at the same address, No. 68 Meeting Street. The directory of the next year lists Thom as an independent craftsman.

There are no records of Thom after 1803.

Thom and Quackinbush
WORKING 1802

This copartnership (?) between Jacob Thom and his brother-in-law, Laurence Quackinbush, apparently lasted but a year. They are shown in the 1802 directory as being at No. 68 Meeting Street. After that time their names appear separately and at different locations.

James H. Thompson
WORKING 1819

There appear to have been more than one James Thompson living in Charleston during the early 1800's; hence it is difficult to know which of the various records refer to the James H. Thompson who is identified in the directory as a cabinet-maker, on St. Philip's Street. Whether he moved to some other city or gave up cabinet-making and took up some other trade, nowhere appears.

William Thompson
WORKING 1803–1806

William Thompson devoted himself to the making of Windsor chairs. In the directories of both 1803 and 1806 he is listed as a Windsor chairmaker. During that period numbers of such chairs were being imported into Charleston from Philadelphia. No doubt Thompson, along with some other Charleston chairmakers, was trying to meet this competition. Whether he was successful is not known.

Stephen Townsend
–1799   WORKING c. 1760–1771

The first reference we have of Stephen Townsend is contained in an advertisement in the *South Carolina Gazette* for April 7, 1760, which states that the copartnership between Townsend and Stocks has been terminated by Stock's death. Apparently Townsend worked as an independent cabinet-maker for three years. Then on February 12, 1763, Townsend and William Axson advertised in the *Gazette* that they were open for business at their shop on Tradd Street. Two years later they suffered from a disastrous fire. At that time they were spoken of as "industrious young men."[1] Their copartnership appears to have lasted until 1768. On April of that year Townsend advertised that he was moving his shop to Meeting Street. Again Townsend appears to have worked as an independent craftsman for about three years. On June 1, 1771, John Fisher (q.v.) announced in the *South Carolina Gazette; And Country Journal* that he was buying out "Mr. Stephen Townsend his STOCK in TRADE and NEGROES brought up in the Business."

Townsend's financial success as a cabinetmaker is indicated by the fact that in 1768 he was able to purchase a lot which is thought to have been on Meeting Street.[2] This is probably the location to which he moved after the dissolution of his copartnership with Axson. In 1770 he purchased 150 acres in St. Thomas and St. Denis Parish.[3] In the same year he purchased six Negroes for £1900 current money.[4] Like almost every other cabinet-maker in Charleston, Townsend appears to have had several business transactions with Thomas Elfe. In April, 1770, the following notation is found in Elfe's account book: "Lent Stephen Townsend on his bond 15 instant £173."[5]

It is thought that Townsend gave up cabinet-making after he sold out to Fisher in 1771, and became a planter in Christ Church Parish. In 1772 he was still buying property, for it is recorded that on May 25 of that year he purchased 663 acres on the Wando River from Charles Pinckney.[6]

Whether Townsend took an active part in the Revolution is not known. During the occupation of Charleston by the British, Townsend was one of those who petitioned Sir Henry Clinton for restoration to the status of a British citizen. After peace was restored Townsend was ordered banished and his estates were confiscated.[7] It is fairly certain that the former order was not put into execution. Probably Townsend got off with a 12% amercement of his estate for having signed the petition. Even as late as 1791 he was still buying property in Christ Church Parish.[8] Townsend died on June 20, 1799. His age is not given in the obituary notice, which states simply that he was one of the oldest inhabitants of Christ Church Parish.[9]

There is no reason to suppose that Townsend was related to the celebrated family of cabinet-makers by that same name from Rhode Island.[10]

Townsend and Axson
WORKING 1763–1768

The copartnership (?) of Stephen Townsend and William Axson (q.v.) was formed in 1763.[1] Their shop was on the northeast corner of Tradd and Church Streets. In 1765 most of their shop was destroyed by a fire which occurred in the early morning hours. Their association terminated in 1768. After that time each worked in Charleston as an independent craftsman.

John Tremain
WORKING 1755

John Tremain is known from only one advertisement which appeared in the *South Carolina Gazette* for July 17, 1755: "JOHN TREMAIN takes this opportunity to inform the public, that he has set up his business of cabinet and coffin making, in *Elliott-street*; where those that please to employ him may be assured of having their work done in the neatest and cheapest manner. . . . Said *Tremain* is inclinable to take an apprentice for 5, 6, or 7 years, if the boy be of a sober family, and well recommended."

The records of the Register of Mesne Conveyance do not reveal that he purchased any property during his stay in Charleston nor is his will filed in the Probate Court.

Matthew Vanoll [Vanall]
WORKING c. 1738–1742

It is only by inference that the name of Matthew Vanoll can be included in this work. The following announcement appeared in the *South Carolina Gazette* on April 3, 1742: "Having been inform'd that for the future no License for retailing strong Liquors will be granted to Trades men in this Province, I find

[124]

myself obliged to leave this Town, wherefore I desire all Persons indebted to me forthwith to discharge their respective Debts. N. B. I have a Press and a red Bay Corner Cupboard, also some Plank and Timber to be sold which I would work up if employed. Matthew Vanoll." His statement that he has some plank and timber that he will work up, as well as having some articles of furniture for sale, leads naturally to the supposition that Vanoll actually made furniture. A Matthew Vanall was one of the appraisers of the estate of Samuel Glaser on November 21, 1739.[1] As no other record of Vanoll can be found it is presumed that he left Charleston.

John Vinyard
WORKING 1801

Vinyard was probably the son of John Vinyard, a leather dresser. His name appears but once as a cabinet-maker. In the 1801 directory he is shown as being at No. 181 Meeting Street. It is thought that Vinyard moved to Orangeburg, South Carolina. On May 4, 1806, at Orangeburg, a John Vinyard was married to Eliza Elliott Lestarjette.[1] In 1821 Sanders Glover gave a power-of-attorney to John Vinyard. The instrument was made in the Orangeburg District.[2]

Robert Walker
1772–1833   WORKING C. 1799–1833

A native of Scotland, Robert Walker probably came to Charleston as a young man. Walker was established in Charleston by 1799; on September 13 of that year he was granted letters to administer the estate of John Gibson, a house carpenter.[1] By 1801 Walker was working as an independent cabinet-maker at No. 57 Broad Street.[2] He must have been successful because on May 21, 1806, he advertised in the *Times* for "Two Journeymen Cabinet-Makers."

Walker appears to have been an active and successful cabinet-maker for the next thirty years. Being a good Scotsman he was admitted in 1801 to the St. Andrew's Society. On March 6, 1809, Walker purchased a lot on

the east side of Meeting Street for "three thousand two hundred dollars Sterling money." Two years later he purchased a lot on the west side of Church Street for $6,400.[3] This property was adjacent to some which he already owned.

On January 31, 1810, Walker advertised in the *City Gazette and Daily Advertiser* that he was removing "his Cabinet ware-room and work shop from No. 39 Church-street to No. 19 Elliott street. . . . also [he had] Mahogany Boards, Plank Veneers, Sattin [*sic*] Wood, Holly . . ." The mention of satinwood indicates that it was in demand and was being used by other cabinet-makers in Charleston.

Walker has the distinction of being the only Charleston cabinet-maker whose label has survived (1955). A satinwood secretary and bookcase has a much faded though legible label still attached to it. It reads:
"Robert Walker
Cabinet maker
No. 53 Church Street, Charleston";
The directory shows him as being at No. 53 Church Street between the years 1813 and 1819.

Walker and Thomas Wallace, another Scottish cabinet-maker, appear to have been friends. Wallace in his will appointed Walker guardian of his infant children.[4]

Walker died on July 30, 1833, at the age of sixty-one. His tombstone states that he was born on January 24, 1772, at Cupar in Fifeshire, Scotland.[5] In his will he mentions his wife Margaret, his daughter Margaret, and his son James Walker. Apparently there were several other children.[6] His inventory, which included a great number of bank stocks, totaled over $37,000.[7]

William Walker
WORKING 1801–1811

Though William Walker and Robert Walker were contemporaries they do not seem to have been related. For several years William's shop is shown in the directories as being located on Hasell Street. On November 5, 1802, he purchased the lot on the southeast corner of Archdale and Beaufain Streets for £550.[1] By 1806 his address is given as No. 12

Archdale Street, doubtless the same property he had purchased a few years earlier. In 1807 Walker and Peter Mood, a local silversmith, were sureties of the estate of George Dennis.[2]

Walker appears to have died intestate. His inventory, which was made by Jane Walker, administratrix, is dated July 5, 1811.[3]

Thomas Wallace
1758–1816   WORKING 1792–1816

Another cabinet-maker of Scotch origin was Thomas Wallace, who was working in Charleston by 1790. In that year he formed a copartnership (?) with Charles Watts. Two years later the association was dissolved and Wallace started working by himself. In an advertisement in the *City Gazette and Daily Advertiser* of March 31, 1792, Wallace speaks of himself as a cabinet-maker and undertaker. There was nothing unusual in the combination, for practically every cabinet-maker made coffins and many conducted funerals. Four years later Wallace advertised that he was moving his shop from Meeting Street to Church Street between Broad and Queen, and that "He has also on hand a quantity of ready made Furniture, among which are, a few dozen of fashionable Mahogany Chairs, which he will dispose of on lower terms than any in this city of the same quality." [1] If one cabinet-maker had a "few dozen" chairs, the number that must have been made in Charleston during this period, when approximately sixty cabinet-makers were working in the city, must have been prodigious. It is regrettable that so few have survived in and around Charleston.

Wallace prospered. In any event, he purchased several pieces of property in the city.[2] He died on November 22, 1816, at the age of fifty-eight. Being a Scotsman he is buried in the graveyard of the Scots Church. His tombstone states that he was born in Ayreshire, Scotland. His wife was Agnes Rogers of Paisley.[3] In his will Wallace appoints Dr. Aaron W. Leland and Robert Walker, another cabinet-maker, as guardians to his three younger children until they reach the age of twenty-one.[4] The inventory of Wallace's personal belongings lists one secretary and bookcase, one set of mahogany chairs, and two mahogany bedsteads. One of the appraisers was Thomas Elfe, Jr.[5]

Wallace & Watts
WORKING 1790–1791

The announcement of the copartnership (?) between Thomas Wallace and Charles Watts appears in the *City Gazette and Daily Advertiser* on March 5, 1790. They speak of themselves as "Cabinet and Piano Forte Makers, From London," and advertise that "They have now on hand, an elegant assortment of cabinet furniture of the most modern taste, . . . Likewise harpsichords and piano fortes repaired." This partnership was of short duration, for we find that the following year Watts announces that "he has moved to the corner of Broad-street and Market-Square, opposite the state house."

Charles Warham
1701–1779   WORKING 1733–c. 1767

Originally from London by way of Boston, Charles Warham was in Charleston by 1733; on July 29 of that year his daughter Ann was baptized.[1] It is reasonable to assume that Warham served his apprenticeship under one of the London cabinet-makers, emigrated to Boston and, not finding it to his liking, moved to Charleston. The city must have appealed to him for he worked here as a cabinet-maker for over forty years.

Warham advertised in the *South Carolina Gazette* on November 2, 1734, that he was late from "*Boston* N. England" and that he made "all sorts of Tables, Chests, Chest-of-drawers, Desks, Bookcases &c. As also Coffins of the newest fashion, never as yet made in *Charlestown*. . . ." It is interesting to conjecture just what Warham meant when he spoke of coffins of the newest fashion.

Warham prospered to such an extent that, on January 1, 1740, he purchased from Ebenezer Simmons lots Nos. 87 and 88 on the north side of Tradd Street. Some years later he purchased lot No. 73 on the south

Fig. 114 CHIPPENDALE STYLE CHAIR
Height 37⅜″; width 20″

Fig. 115 CHIPPENDALE STYLE CHAIR
Height 37⅜″; width 19¾″

Fig. 116 CHIPPENDALE STYLE CHAIR
Height 37½″; width 21¼″

Fig. 117 TRANSITIONAL STYLE CHAIR
Height 36½″; width 21½″

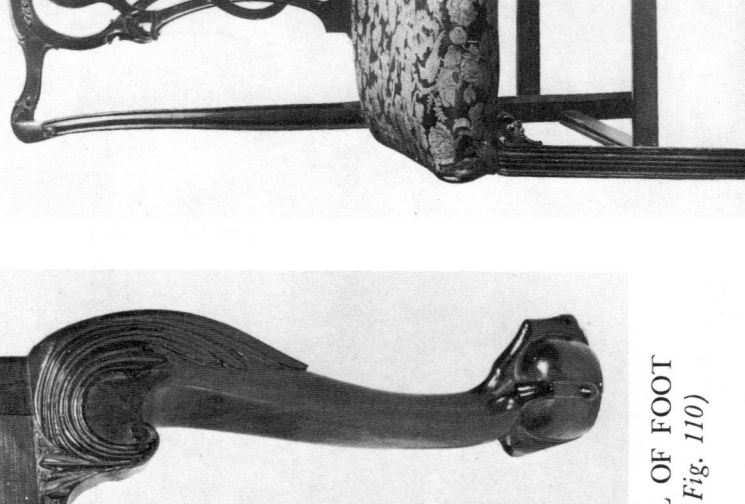

Fig. 121 CHIPPENDALE STYLE CHAIR
Height 37″; width 22″

Fig. 120 MAHOGANY CORNER
BLOCKS OF ARMCHAIR
(*Grain Horizontal*) (*see Fig. 111*)

Fig. 119 DETAIL OF FOOT
OF CHAIR (*see Fig. 110*)

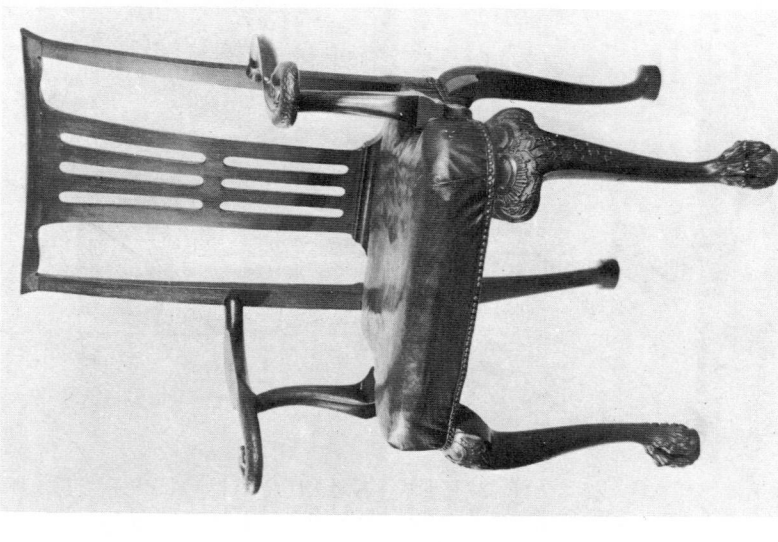

Fig. 118 "STATE CHAIR"
Height 53″; width (seat) 29″; height of
seat 25¾″; mahogany front rail 3⅝″
thick

Fig. 122 CORNER CHAIR
Height 31¾"

Fig. 123 DETAIL OF CHAIR *(see Fig. 127)*

Fig. 124 CORNER CHAIR
Height 31"

Fig. 125 DETAIL OF CHAIR *(see Fig. 126)*

Fig. 126 HEPPLEWHITE STYLE
ARMCHAIR   Height 38¾″; width 21¼″

Fig. 127 HEPPLEWHITE STYLE CHAIR
Height 39″; width 21″

Fig. 128 HEPPLEWHITE STYLE CHAIR
Height 36¾″, width 22″

Fig. 129 HEPPLEWHITE STYLE CHAIR
Height 37¼″; width 20½″

Fig. 130 TEA TABLE
Height 28$\frac{5}{16}$"; diameter 34$\frac{3}{16}$"

Fig. 132 TEA TABLE
Height 27$\frac{3}{4}$"; diameter 28$\frac{15}{16}$" x 28$\frac{3}{4}$"

Fig. 131 CANDLE STAND
Height 25$\frac{3}{4}$"; diameter 18$\frac{3}{4}$"

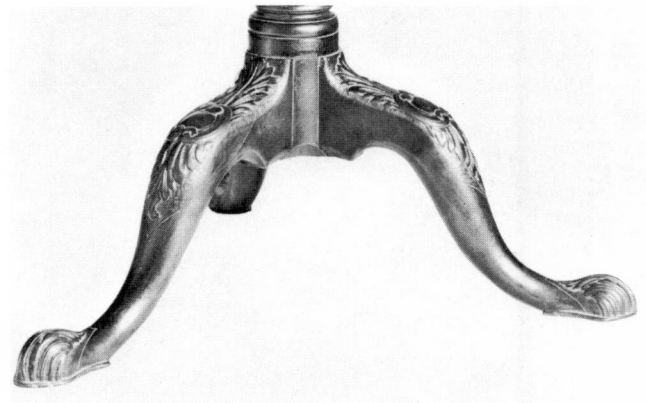

Fig. 133 DETAIL OF FOOT OF TEA TABLE
(see Fig. 132)

Fig. 135 TEA TABLE Height 27⅝″; diameter 28″ x 28⅝″

Fig. 134 TEA TABLE Height 29⅜″; diameter 33³⁄₁₆″ x 33⁷⁄₁₆″

Fig. 136 COMMODE
Height 30¼″; width 25½″; depth 19½″

Fig. 138 TRAVELING HAT BOX
Height 18⅛″; width 25½″; depth 16¾″

Fig. 137 COMMODE, Open *(see Fig. 136)*

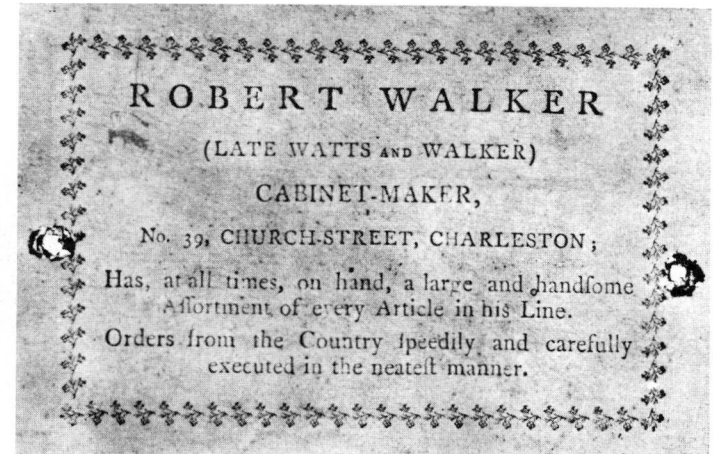

Fig. 139 LABEL OF ROBERT WALKER
(see Page 133)

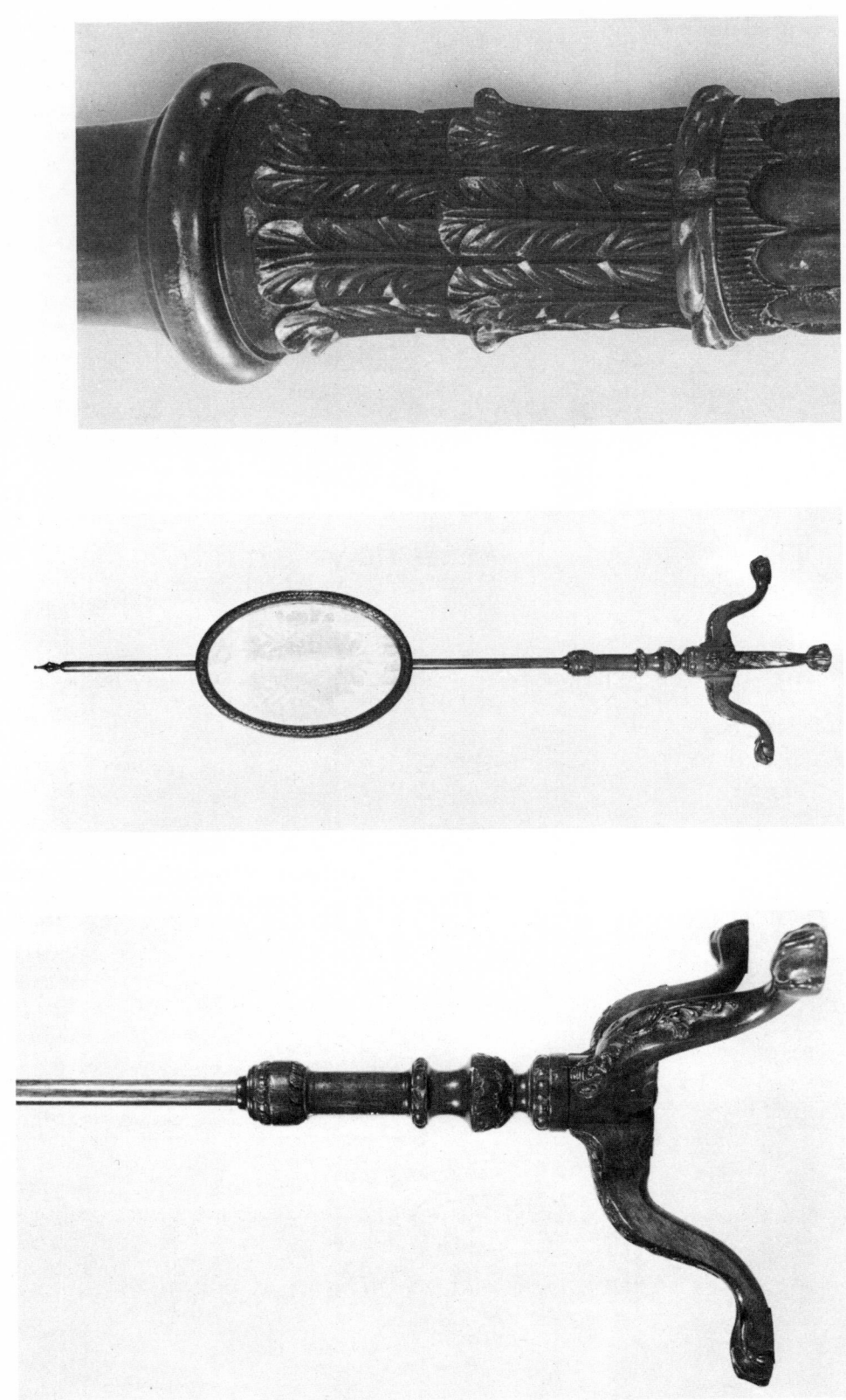

Fig. 140 DETAIL OF FOOT OF FIRE SCREEN (*see Fig. 141*)

Fig. 141 FIRE SCREEN Height 59¼″; end of foot to end of foot 17¼″

Fig. 142 DETAIL OF BED SHOWING DOUBLE-LEAF CARVING (*see Fig. 21*)

side of Tradd Street.[2] Warham was probably so well established by this time that he did not think it necessary to advertise. Little is known of his activities during the following years except that, according to the records, he occasionally purchased some additional property or a Negro slave.

Early in his career Warham, being in need of some money, borrowed £150 current money from Solomon Legare, a local silversmith, putting up as collateral his Negro boy named Boston,[3] a rather unusual name for a slave but undoubtedly given to him in recognition of Warham's former place of residence.

Warham was elected a member of the South Carolina Society on June 29, 1756. He was a member of the Grand Jury in 1768 [4] and a member of the Petit Jury in 1774.[5] The given name of Warham's wife was Martha, whose surname is not known. They had several children, most of whom died young.

Thomas Elfe purchased from Warham his riding chair and harness for £81. This transaction took place in August 1769.[6] During his lifetime Warham acquired an appreciable amount of property. On October 16, 1776, he advertised in the *South Carolina and American General Gazette* that he had for sale 5000 acres of land.

Warham died on July 20, 1779, at the age of seventy-nine. His tombstone records that he was born in London on May 23, 1701.[7]

John Watson

1751–1812   WORKING 1782–1812

John Watson, another Scotsman, was working in Charleston by 1790, being listed in the directory of that year as a cabinet-maker at No. 21 Tradd Street.

The next notice concerning Watson occurs in 1796, when on July 9 he advertised in the *City Gazette and Daily Advertiser* that he was removing his shop to No. 21 King Street and that he also had on hand Dining, Card, and Breakfast Tables, "Secretary and Wardrobes, Wardrobes and Secretaries . . . Chest of Drawers; a few dozen of handsome Drawing and Chamber Room Chairs and Sofas. He

makes up at the shortest notice . . . Venetian Blinds . . . done in a neat manner."

Business was so good that in the following February Watson inserted another advertisement to the effect that he had procured the best workmen from Auld Reekie [Edinburgh], London, and Paris, and that "an Assortment of the most elegant Modern Furniture, of every description, . . . may be seen at his Depository, No. 21 King Street." [1] The use of the word "depository" would lead us to believe that Watson had a warehouse and shop of large proportions.

On January 1, 1798, Watson formed a copartnership with his "step-son" [son-in-law] John A. Woodill under the firm name of Watson & Woodill at No. 21 King Street.[2] It is thought that this partnership lasted until Woodill's untimely death, which occurred in 1805.

Watson was admitted as a member of the St. Andrew's Society in 1792. In 1799 he took out his citizenship papers.[3] He must have owned his shop at No. 21 King Street. In 1795 he executed a mortgage of £300 Sterling to Daniel Martin, giving as collateral a lot on the west side of King Street.[4]

The directories reveal that Watson continued in business on King Street until his death on December 10, 1812.[5]

Watson is buried in St. Michael's churchyard. According to his tombstone, he was sixty-one years of age, "a native of Mussillborough, Scotland, but for 30 years past a respectable inhabitant of this place." If Watson had been a resident of Charleston for thirty years, he must have come over immediately after the British occupation of Charleston; perhaps he came with one of the Scotch Regiments and decided to remain and try his fortune in the new country.

William Watson

–1736   WORKING c. 1723–1736

One of Charleston's earliest furniture makers, William Watson is always spoken of as a joiner. He and Mary Kemp were married on September 26, 1723.[1] It is reasonable to assume that Watson was working in Charleston before his marriage. That he was successful in his trade is manifested by his being able to purchase lots Nos. 236 and 237 and also part of lot No. 115 from John Arnold on March 20, 1729.[2] He purchased these lots before some of the streets had names. For instance, the first two lots were described as being "on a street that leadeth from the White Point to the high Road"; the other as "fronting the street that leadeth to ashley river running the whole breadth there."

Watson was buried on August 10, 1736.[3] In his will he mentions his wife Mary and his daughters, Ann and Mary, and a daughter Elizabeth residing in Boston.[4] It is probable that Elizabeth was a daughter by an earlier marriage.

On August 14, 1736, Mrs. Watson inserted the following advertisement in the *South Carolina Gazette:* "Notice is hereby given, That the Business lately carried on by *Wm: Watson* deceased will be continued by his Widow, who has a considerable stock of fresh goods of all sorts necessary for Funerals, and Workmen fully capable of making Coffins and Cabinet ware, she has also ready made and to be sold cheap, Tables Chests of-drawers, Buroes &c." It would be interesting to ascertain whether Mrs. Watson succeeded in her business venture. Unfortunately the answer does not appear in the records.

Watson & Woodill
WORKING 1798–1805

The only thing known about this partnership is contained in an advertisement in the *City Gazette and Daily Advertiser* for January 1, 1798: "John Watson, Cabinet-maker and Upholsterer . . . on the first day of January next, . . . intends to take into partnership his step-son [son-in-law] Mr. John A. Woodill . . . the above mentioned business will be carried on by them, in all its various branches, under the firm of *Watson and Woodill* at its present shop No. 21 King Street . . . Wanted a complete workman in the Cabinet Branch."

No. 21 King Street was the location of the shop of John Watson. The partnership seems to have lasted until about 1805, the year of Woodill's death.

The date of Charles Watts' arrival at Charleston is not known. In 1790 he formed a partnership with Thomas Wallace. The association was of short duration, for on July 19, 1791, Watts advertised in the *City Gazette and Daily Advertiser* as an independent craftsman, and informed his friends that he had moved to the corner of Broad Street and Market Square opposite the State House. In addition to saying that he was a cabinet-maker he stated that he repaired harpsichords, forte pianos, and spinets.

Watts' shop was destroyed by one of Charleston's innumerable fires. In 1795 he moved to Church Street, explaining that "he has again got his Business in a regular train (since his disaster by the late fire) and has for sale a variety of Cabinet Furniture."[1] In the following year his shop was again destroyed by fire (the great conflagration of 1796) but undaunted, Watts re-established his shop, this time on lower Church Street. In his advertisement which appeared in the *City Gazette and Daily Advertiser* on July 19, 1796, Watts states that he is residing at John Milligan's, No. 6 Bedon's Alley "where he has for sale, A Variety of Cabinet Furniture, The following of which are a part, viz. Sideboards of different kinds, Sets of Dining Tables, Card and Tea Tables, Ladies Commodes, Dressing Chest Drawers, Ward-robes; Secretaries and Desks, and Book Cases."

In spite of his misfortunes, Watts prospered. In 1796 he purchased a lot on the west side of Church Street from Mrs. Mary Magdalen Grimball for £650. The following year he bought, from John Cordes Prioleau, a brick house and lot for £400 Sterling. This was also on the west side of Church Street and next to his property. In later years Watts must have been successful, for he not only added to his holdings on Church Street but also purchased a lot on Broad Street.[2]

His name appears for the last time in the directory of 1803. His will, dated April 2, 1808, states that he is "now residing in Liverpool City of Lancaster." To his wife Catherine he left all of his plate and household furniture. It was specified that his property in South Carolina was to be rented out and kept at interest until his son Charles became twenty-one. Watts also had a daughter named Helen. His will was probated on November 30, 1811, presumably shortly after his death.[3] The inventory of his estate shows that it consisted mostly of stocks and bonds, with some notes from several local cabinet-makers.[4]

Watts & Walker
WORKING 1802

The name of the firm of Watts and Walker appears only in the directory of 1802, at which time they are listed as cabinet-makers at No. 39 Church Street. The two partners (?) were Charles Watts and Robert Walker. Why the association was not continued is not known.

William Wayne
WORKING 1769

Either there were several William Waynes in Charleston during the same period or Wayne had a proclivity for changing his occupation. The first record that we have of any William Wayne is on November 15, 1764. At that time William Wayne, painter, and Catherine his wife, executed a mortgage to William Hall, carpenter, for £1600 lawful money.[1] The next five years are a blank. Then comes an advertisement which appeared in the *Pennsylvania Chronicle* [Philadelphia] on February 20, 1769: "Dissolution of partnership between Robert Moore, cabinet and chairmaker and William Wayne he [Moore] now carries on the business on his own account."[2] The records of the Register of Mesne Conveyance Office in Charleston reveal that on April 5, 1769, William Wayne, cabinet-maker, executed a mortgage to Susannah Hall, Executrix of William Hall, carpenter, for £2100 at 8% per annum.[3] This is apparently the same William Hall who loaned the money in 1764 to William Wayne, painter. Three months later there is a bill of sale from William Wayne, painter, to Daniel

Bourdeaux, for a three-quarters share of a schooner called *Catherine*.[4]

To further complicate matters, on April 16, 1770 the Grand Jury presented "William Wayne Tavern keeper up the path for keeping a disorderly House and secreting and entertaining youth to the corruption of their Morals and loss of Service to their Masters upon information of John Bremar Esquire." Wayne appeared in Court and declared that he was ready to have the matter tried by a jury. He was released under bond of £50 "proclamation money of America."[5] The ultimate outcome of the trial is unknown. In June of the same year Thomas Elfe lent "William Wayne of his Bond this day £300."[6] Wayne and Elfe had numerous business transactions during the next five years. Occasionally Elfe would purchase linseed oil from Wayne; at another time he paid Wayne £13 for a frame of an Easy Chair.[7]

On February 14, 1778, Paul Townsend sold to William Wayne, planter, a lot on the west side of Bedon's Alley.[8] The following year Mary Ellis sold to William Wayne, merchant, a lot on the south side of Broad Street.[9]

Thus we have the name of a William Wayne listed as being a painter, cabinet-maker, tavern keeper, merchant, and planter. How much cabinet-making was actually done by a William Wayne is not indicated.

George Welch
WORKING C. 1804–1819

The marriage of George Welch to Mrs. Christiana Smith, widow, took place on October 10, 1804.[1] In the 1806 directory he is listed as an independent cabinet-maker at No. 21 Pinckney Street.

With the exception of the baptismal records[2] of two of his children nothing further is recorded about Welch before 1819. In that year his address is given as Charlotte Street, which was then outside the city limits. Thereafter he disappears completely.

John Welch
WORKING 1806–1819

Although they were contemporaries, it cannot be said with certainty that John and George Welch were related. Like George, John's name is listed for the first time in the 1806 directory. By 1819 he is listed both as superintendent of the city burying ground and as a cabinet-maker. After that time he appears to have devoted his entire time to supervising the "Burial Ground."

The Health Department Records reveal that a John Welch was buried in December 1832. This may have been the former cabinet-maker.

John M. Werner
WORKING 1819

John M. Werner's name appears in but one directory, that of 1819, when he is shown as being a cabinet-maker on Pinckney Street. Nothing is known of his work or of his later life.

Weyman & Carne
WORKING 1764–1766

The copartnership of Edward Weyman and John Carne (q.v.) was formed in 1764. On March 31 of that year they advertised at length in the *South Carolina Gazette* that they were opening their shop on Queen Street where "any of the several branches of CABINET-MAKING" would be done at their "LOOKING-GLASS shop." Weyman was a maker and importer of looking glass and it is unlikely that he made any furniture. Carne was a cabinet-maker and undoubtedly was the one who made the furniture. Their association lasted about two years. On December 2, 1766, Weyman advertised by himself, explaining "That he still continued the Cabinet and Chair Work business, for which purpose he has furnished himself with good workmen . . ."[1] Unfortunately, the names of the men who worked for him are not known.

Benjamin Wheeler
WORKING 1784

After the capitulation of Charleston during the Revolution, a Benjamin Wheeler was one of the persons sent aboard one of the horrible British prison ships anchored in Charleston harbor. The prisoner is thought to have been the cabinet-maker. A few months later Wheeler's family, along with many others, was banished to Philadelphia.[1] On May 8, 1784, an obituary notice appeared in the *South Carolina Weekly Gazette* reporting the death of Benjamin Wheeler, cabinet-maker. In his will, which was made on April 13, 1784, and probated the following month, Wheeler appointed two cabinet-makers, Thomas Cooke and Henry Gaskins, as his executors.[2]

Charles White
WORKING 1807

White may have been an itinerant cabinet-maker. His name appears in the 1807 directory as a cabinet-maker at No. 36 Broad Street. After that there is no further trace of him.

George White
WORKING 1813

In the 1813 directory George White is listed as a cabinet-maker at No. 120 Church Street. Three years later, though he is listed at the same address, his occupation is given as that of a joiner. Since no other record of him can be found in Charleston, it is thought that he moved to some other locality.

Gottleib White
1762–1822   WORKING 1809–1822

The spelling of White's given name seems to have caused him endless trouble. Frequently it was spelled Gottlys and once it appears as Gudlip. In the directory for 1809 his address is given as No. 36 Broad Street. In 1811 White and his wife Matilda transferred some property on Johns Island to William Champlin and Joseph Maxey.[1] From the deed it appears that the property had been inherited by Matilda from her former husband. White was still working as a cabinet-maker in 1819.[2] His death occurred in December, 1822. The

Health Department Records state that he was sixty years of age, that he was born in Germany, and that he died of consumption.

Jedidiah Whitney
WORKING 1813

Jedidiah Whitney is listed in the 1813 directory as a cabinet-maker at No. 1 St. Philip Street. In the directory for 1819 he is still shown as being on St. Philip Street, but his occupation is given as that of a carpenter. While it is purely a supposition, it is just possible that Whitney may have been forced to change his occupation because so much mass-produced furniture was being brought into Charleston at that time.

George Wilkie
WORKING C. 1786

The only thing known about George Wilkie is that on January 12, 1787, letters were granted to Thomas Mell, planter, to administer the estate of George Wilkie, cabinet-maker.[1] The inventory of Wilkie's estate, which was taken the following month, amounted to £21.[2]

Mathew Will
WORKING 1801–1806

Nothing is known of Mathew Will's activities as a cabinet-maker. In the 1801 directory he is listed as being at No. 205 Meeting Street. The following years he appears to have formed a copartnership (?) with William Marlin. This copartnership could not have been of long duration, for by 1806 Will is again listed as an independent cabinet-maker at No. 41 Trott [Wentworth] Street. There is no further record of him.

Will & Marlin
WORKING 1802

The copartnership (?) of Will and Marlin seems to have been of short duration. The name of Will and Marlin appears only in the 1802 directory. It is probable that the two partners were Mathew Will and William Marlin.

John Williams
WORKING ?

John Williams, aged thirty, "Cabinet" [maker], sailed from London during the third week of January, 1774, on the ship *Carolina*, bound for Carolina (i.e., Charleston) "for employment." [1] As there is no record of the *Carolina* having been lost at sea, Williams must have landed in Charleston some time during the spring of 1774. However, there is no record of his having worked as a cabinet-maker here.

John Wilson
–c. 1808   WORKING 1790–1807

Although John Wilson worked in Charleston as a cabinet-maker for many years very little is known about his activities. What seems to be his only advertisement appeared in the *City Gazette and Daily Advertiser* of March 18, 1790, wherein it is stated that he has "Some very elegant mahogany furniture for sale, consisting of breakfast and dining Tables, bedsteads, a very elegant commode chest of drawers" and that he was at the sign of the Cradle and Coffin at No. 217 Meeting Street.

In 1794 Wilson purchased a lot on the east side of Meeting Street from William Clarkson.[1] He appears to have resided there for the rest of his life, for the various directories list him as a cabinet-maker on Meeting Street.

It is not known when Wilson died. His name appears for the last time in the directory of 1807. On December 24, 1808, Samuel Stine married Barbara Wilson, "daughter of the late John Wilson, Cabinet Maker, of this city." [2] Strangely enough his inventory, will, and letters of administration cannot be found.

John Anthony Woodill
–1805   WORKING 1801–1805

John Anthony Woodill started working in

1798 with his father-in-law, John Watson, under the firm name of Watson & Woodill. The partnership did not last very long. By 1801, Woodill is listed in the directory of that year as being on Lynch's Lane. On April 7, 1801, Woodill purchased a lot on the east side of King Street for 440 Guineas. In the same year he was admitted to the St. Andrew's Society.

It is thought that Woodill died as a young man. His will was made on February 7, 1805, and probated the following month. His wife, Susannah, was named executrix.

Thomas Woodin
−1774   WORKING 1766–c. 1770

Thomas Woodin, besides being a cabinet-maker, was also a carver and a teacher of drawing. The first record we have of him is dated 1766, when he was paid £36 out of the General Tax for plans for the Exchange, at the east end of Broad Street.[1]

On September 7, 1767, Woodin inserted the following advertisement in the *South Carolina Gazette; And Country Journal:* "THOMAS WOODIN Carver and Cabinet-Maker, teaches Drawing in all its Branches at the same place. . . . AND has to sell on the most reasonable terms some curious mahogany work, viz. Desks, and Book-Cases with glass doors, Ladies Dressing-Tables, with all the useful apparatus; Chinese Bamboo Tea-Tables, and Kitchen Stands, &c. . . ." The sale of the Chinese Tea Tables indicates that at this time the Chinese influence was still strong in Charleston.

Woodin prospered sufficiently to purchase in 1770 a Negro, Betty, and her son Jack, for £400 current money.[2] It is thought that about this time Woodin gave up cabinet-making and procured an appointment as "weigher and gauger of his Majesty's Customs." This must have been a fairly lucrative position, for it enabled Woodin, during the next four years, to purchase considerable property along the Edisto River.[3]

Woodin's death occurred on July 26, 1774.[4] In his will he requests that he be buried next to his wife in St. Michael's churchyard.

He also says that he forgives his son John Ash for his misconduct and leaves him some property, household furniture, and working tools.[5] It is not known what John did to incur his father's wrath.

Joseph Worthington
WORKING 1793–

On July 8, 1793, Joseph Worthington, cabinet-maker, and Miss Betsey Arnold, "lately arrived from Cork," were married.[1] This is the first knowledge that we have of Worthington's being in Charleston. In 1793 he formed a copartnership (?) with Kirby. This association lasted two months. Immediately afterwards Worthington formed another copartnership (?) with Sinclair. It is not known how long this partnership lasted. In the directory of 1801 Worthington is listed as an upholsterer. His name appears for the last time in the directory of 1806, still as an upholsterer. Nothing is known of his subsequent career.

Worthington & Kirby
WORKING 1793

This copartnership (?) was of short duration. Worthington and Kirby advertised on January 1, 1793, in the *City Gazette and Daily Advertiser* that they were "lately from London" and that they would do "Cabinet Work and Upholstery in General"; they also advertised "Funerals furnished on the shortest notice." In the following month Kirby disappears, to be replaced by Sinclair.

Worthington & Sinclair
WORKING 1793–?

Sinclair replaced Kirby as the partner (?) of Worthington. In the advertisement telling of his association with Worthington, Sinclair is spoken of as being from Edinburgh.[1] It is not known how long they remained together, no notice having been discovered of the dissolution of the partnership.

Fig. 143 BELLFLOWER DETAILS
(see Fig. 102)

Fig. 144 IVORY BELLFLOWER
(see Frontispiece)

Fig. 145 DETAIL OF CHAIR *(see Fig. 121)*

Fig. 146 THISTLE INLAY *(see Fig. 106)*

Fig. 148 INCISED CARVING OF FOOT (see Fig. 31)

Fig. 149 DETAIL OF FRET (see Fig. 4)

Fig. 147 DESK AND BOOKCASE
Height 7'1¾"; width 42"; depth 23⅝"

ADDENDA

After the manuscript had been sent to the printer, the Charleston Museum acquired a very fine clothespress. Examination revealed that it bore a label of Robert Walker, a Charleston cabinet-maker (*see* Fig. 139). That the label was tacked in place instead of being glued on probably accounts for the fact that it has not been destroyed by glue-eating insects. So far this is only the second known labeled piece of Charleston-made furniture. Strangely enough, the only other known label also bears the name of Robert Walker (*q.v.*). Most interesting, however, is that with the exception of the drawer sides, which are of poplar, *all* of the secondary wood is of white pine—conclusive evidence that Charleston cabinet-makers of the late eighteenth and early nineteenth century did use white pine in the construction of their furniture (*see* White Pine).

It was during the last decade of the eighteenth and the first decade of the nineteenth century that the greatest number of cabinet-makers worked in Charleston. Apparently there was such a demand for furniture during this period that the cabinet-makers had difficulty in supplying the needs of their customers. In endeavoring to meet his needs Charles Watts (*q.v.*) inserted the following advertisement in *The Diary* (New York City) on January 28, 1797:

"Wanted from 8 to 15 Journeymen Cabinet and Chair-Makers, to go to Charleston, South Carolina where they will receive generous encouragement for further particulars, apply to Captain Joseph Baker, on board the Sloop Romeo, laying at the Coffee House Slip.

"I hereby oblige myself to pay to any good workman, who is capable of doing the general run of Cabinet-work seventy-five percent advance on the New London book of Cabinet prices, published in 1793. I will also advance the passage money for whoever chuses to come in the above line; and find work for any, or all, of the above number, for 6, 9, or 12 months; board, or find them it at 3-½ dollars per week. The money for the work shall be paid weekly, or when each job is finished. Charles Watts, Cabinet-Maker, Charleston." [1]

Two very interesting things can be deduced from the advertisement: first, the large number of cabinet- and chair-makers that any one cabinet-maker needed for his business (there were approximately sixty cabinet-makers working in Charleston at that time); second, the prosperity of Charleston and vicinity which made it possible for Watts to pay wages that were "seventy-five per cent advance" over the published tariff.

[1] *The Arts and Crafts in New York 1777–1799.* R. S. Gottesman, New-York Historical Society, 1954, p. 130.

Cabinet-makers' Receipts

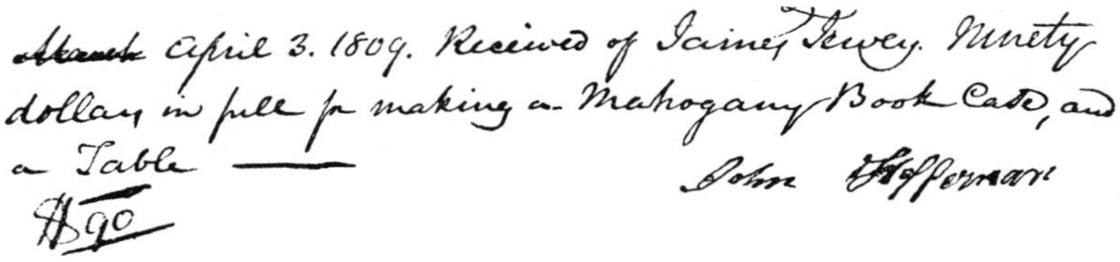

[handwritten receipt]
April 3. 1809. Received of James Tewey, Ninety
dollars in full for making a Mahogany Book Case, and
a Table ——
$90

[handwritten receipt]
March 29th
1810   Mr Daniel Huger Esqr
Bot of Thos Wallace
one Sett Dining Tables 38 8
                Matts   1 - 50
Recd Pay in full   39 50
              Thos Wallace

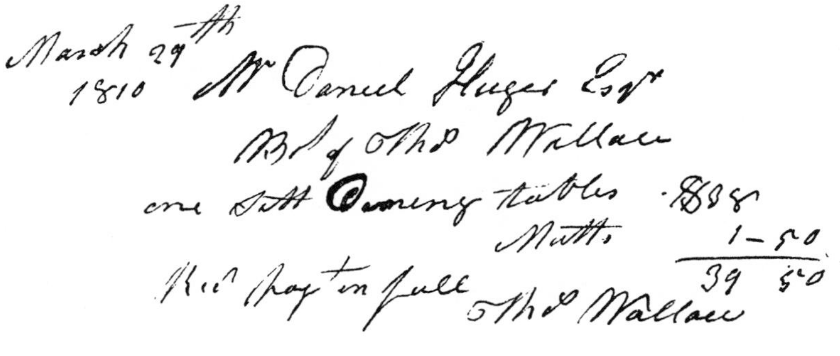

[handwritten receipt]
Mr   Huger.   To R. Smith. Dr
1810
Novr 22d — To a Bookcase --- $50 - 00
          „ a Bead cornice --- 6 - 00
          „ Repairing a close press 6 - 00
            Locks, and hinges, for ditto 1 - 00
                            $63 - 00
Recd payment in full for the above
account ——
              Richard. Smith.

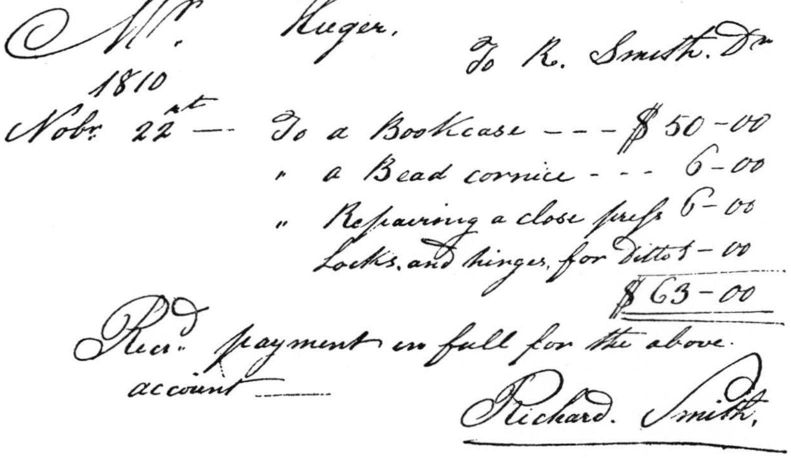

Received 25th August 1810 from Daniel Huger forty three dollars being in full payment for twelve black & gilt Chairs. Jacob Sass

RECEIPT FROM JACOB SASS, AUGUST 25, 1810

Daniel Huger Esqr.
August 7 1811 . . To Joshua Neville Dr.
A Secretary and wardrobe — $85
Ditto Ink and sand stand — 2.25
Ditto difference in patent lock — 2.50
$89.75
Recd Payment in full
Joshua Neville

RECEIPT FROM JOSHUA NEVILLE, AUGUST 7, 1811

Frazier Esqr
Bot of P. Moore
1809
June 14th a Carved post bedstead stained sides & ends $20
matts package & Drayage — — 1 —
$21 —
$21. Received payment in full
Entd 582 DB Philip Moore

RECEIPT FROM PHILIP MOORE, JUNE 14, 1809

[handwritten receipt]

RECEIPT FROM WILLIAM W. PURSE, NOVEMBER 8, 1822

[handwritten receipt]

RECEIPT FROM JACOB SASS & SON, OCTOBER 9, 1810

[handwritten receipt]

RECEIPT FROM ABRAHAM JONES, JULY 16, 1813

NOTES

ABBREVIATIONS

Dir.: Directory.
MCO: Register of Mesne Conveyance Office.
PC: Office of the Judge of Probate Court.
SCG: *South Carolina Gazette.*
SCHM: *South Carolina Historical and Genealogical Magazine* and *South Carolina Historical Magazine.*
USDC: United States District Court at Charleston, S. C.

Early Charleston. [1] McCrady, *Hist. of S. C.,* Vol. I, 95. [2] Wallace, *Short Hist. of S. C.,* 335. [3] Lawson, *History,* xiii, xv. [4] Carroll, *Hist. Coll. of S. C.,* Vol. II, 128, 129. [5] Sellers, *Chas. Business on the Eve of the Amer. Rev.,* 4. [6] Bridenbaugh, *Myths,* 67. [7] Phillips, *Hist. of Transportation,* 49. [8] Ravenel, *Chas., the Place and the People,* 385. [9] [Harrison], *John's Island Stud.* [10] Mereness, *Travels in the Amer. Colonies—1690–1783.* [11] Bowes, *Culture of Early Chas.,* 3, 10. [12] Jones, *Amer. Members of the Inns of Court,* xxvii.

Sources of Furniture: Charleston Cabinet-makers. [1] Mills, *Stat. of S. C.,* 427. [2] SCHM, Vols. 35–42.

English Importations. [1] Letter from Her Majesty's Customs & Excise, London, Feb. 9, 1953. [2] Wertenberger, *Golden Age of Colonial Culture,* 134. [3] SCG, Apr. 9–16, 1741; 2/2. [4] "Neptune" Chart of Charles Town, 1777; *London Magazine,* June, 1762 (*Chas. Year Book,* 1882, 341). [5] Sellers, *Chas. Business on the Eve of the Amer. Rev.,* 4. [6] Bowes, *Culture of Early Chas.,* 10. [7] Wallace, *Hist. of S. C.,* Vol. I, 396. [8] Carroll, *Hist. Coll. of S. C.,* Vol. II, 230. [9] Symonds, *The English Export Trade* (*Antiques,* Oct. 1935, 156). [10] PC, Inv. Book 67-A, 1732–1746, 189. [11] Dir. 1790, 48. [12] Dir. 1822, 41.

American Importations. [1] SCG, Apr. 13, 1769; 1/1. [2] Ibid. Jan. 24, 1774; 2/3. [3] Downs, *Amer. Furn.,* xxviii; Bridenbaugh, *Myths,* 59. [4] Swan, *Samuel McIntire,* 6. [5] S. C. State Gaz., June 20, 1797; 3/1. [6] S. C. Gaz. and Gen. Adv., Jan. 13, 1784 [Prime]. [7] Chas. City Gaz. and Adv., Nov. 29, 1798 [Prime]. [8] City Gaz. and Comm. Adv., Jan. 1, 1819; 1/5, 3/2. [9] Ibid. Jan. 1, 1819; 3/3. [10] Ibid. Mar. 27, 1819; 3/3. [11] Moore, *Hitchcock Chairs.* [12] SCHM, Vol. 43, 69. [13] Antiques, June 1941, 311. [14] Courier, Jan. 4, 1832; 1/3.

Other Importations. [1] City Gaz. and Daily Adv., Feb. 3, 1798; 3/1. [2] Ibid. May 16, 1798; 3/3.

Negro Cabinet-Makers. [1] Wills, Inv. & Mcl. Rec., Vol. 62–A, 1729–1731, 27. [2] S. C. and Amer. Gen. Gaz., June 1, 1771. [3] State Gaz. of S. C., Dec. 11, 1783; 2/3. [4] Courier, Nov. 16, 1824. [5] Ibid. Sept. 22, 1828.

Kinds of Furniture Used in Charleston. [1] Inv. Book Vol. 87–A, 1761–1763, 137. [2] Inv. Book Vol. 94–A, 1771–1776, 45. [3] Inv. Book Vol. 94, 1771–1774, 251.

Kinds of Furniture Not Made in Charleston. [1] Miller, *Amer. Antique Furn.,* Vol. I, 381.

Styles and Influences. [1] SCG, Aug. 12, 1732 [Prime]. [2] Bowes, *Culture of Early Chas.,* 93. [3] Letter from the Dean of the School of Architecture, Columbia University, n.d., Rec'd Dec. 13, 1952; and A.I.A. [4] SCHM, Vol. 47, 180. [5] Crevecoeur, *Letters from an Amer. Farmer.* [6] Bowes, *Culture of Early Chas.,* 64. [7] Drayton, *View of S. C.,* 217. [8] Wallace, *Hist. of S. C.,* Vol. II, 353. [9] Liancourt, *Travels through the U. S.,* Vol. I, 558. [10] Ravenel, *Chas., the Place and the People,* 365. [11] Adams, *Hist. of the U. S. of Amer.,* Vol. I, 149. [12] Phillips, *Hist. of Trans.,* 45; Gray, *Hist. of Agri. in the Sou. States,* Vols. I and II. [13] Albion, *The Rise of N. Y. Port,* 95. [14] Antiques, June 1941, 311. [15] SCHM, Vol. 43, 69.

Exports and Country Trade. [1] SCG, Mar. 14, 1768. [2] Columbian Museum and Savannah Daily Gaz., June 19, 1817; 3/3; Jan. 7, 1819; 3/1. [3] Easterby, *Journal of Sou. Hist.,* Vol. VII, 164. [4] Easterby, *S. C. Rice Plantation,* 362. [5] Chas. Year Book, 1883, 427. [6] Cole, *Wholesale Com. Prices in the U. S., 1700–1861,* 154. [7] SCHM, Vol. 43, 83. [8] Papers of Col. John Chestnut in the S. C. Hist. Soc. [9] Phillips, *Hist. of Trans.,* 135. [10] Inf. from Charles Navis, Antique Dealer in Richmond, Va.

Prices of Furniture. [1] Brackett, *Thomas Chippendale,* 112. [2] SCHM, Vol. 40, 61. [3] Vol. 100, 1776–1784, 145. [4] Easterby, *S. C. Rice Plantation,* 363.

Dearth of Local Furniture. [1] Chas. Year Book, 1880, 307. [2] Smith, *Dwelling Houses of Chas.,* 155. [3] SCG, Mar. 15–22, 1740; 3/1. [4] Baltimore Furniture, 14.

Woods. [1] Coll. of the S. C. Hist. Soc., Vol. V, 444. [2] Carroll, *Hist. Coll. of S. C.,* Vol. II, 63. [3] Letter from Dr. J. H. Easterby, S. C. Hist. Comm., Nov. 16, 1951. [4] Vol. 100, 1776–1784, 84.

West Indian Mahogany. [1] Letter from George N. Lamb, Sec., Mahogany Asso., Chicago, Jan. 2, 1951. [2] SCG, Aug. 12, 1732 [Prime]. [3] PC, Inv. Book 58, 1722–1724, 392. [4] SCG, Feb. 25–Mar. 1, 1749;

Mar. 19–26, 1750. 5 *Chas. Morn. Post and Daily Adv.*, Sept. 6, 1786; 3/4. 6 *Antiques*, Oct. 1942, 212. 7 *City Gaz. and Com. Adv.*, Mar. 27, 1819; 3/3.

Honduras Mahogany. 1 *SCG*, Mar. 29–Apr. 4, 1740; 3/3. 2 *State Gaz. of S. C.*, Dec. 20, 1787; 1/1. 4 Downs, *Amer. Furn.*, xxx.

Southern Red Cedar. 1 Little, *Important Forest Trees of the U. S.*, 774. 2 Lawson, *Hist.*, 55. 3 PC, Inv. Book 58, 1722–1724, 146. 4 PC, Inv. Book 65, 1732–1736, 112.

Walnut. 1 Elliott, *Botany of S. C. and Ga.*, Vol. I, 622. 2 PC, Inv. Book 58, 1722–1724, 146. 3 PC, Inv. Book 64, 1732–1736, 342. 4 Carroll, *Hist. Coll. of S. C.*, Vol. II, 237.

Cypress. 1 *SCHM*, Vol. 38, 133; Vol. 35, 61. 2 Browne, *Sylva Americana*, 146.

Red Bay. 1 Catesby, *Natl. Hist. of Carolina*, Vol. I, 63. 2 Michaux, *N. A. Sylva*, Vol. II, 150. 3 PC, Inv. Book 74, 1746–1748, 348.

White Pine. 1 *State Gaz. of S. C.*, Sept. 1, 1788; 1/1. 2 *The Times*, Dec. 19, 1801; 3/1. 3 *Ibid.* Dec. 31, 1801; 3/3. 4 *City Gaz.*, Mar. 1, 1805; 3/3.

Southern Red Maple. 1 PC, Inv. Book 65, 1732–1736, 112, 113.

White Oak. 1 *Baltimore Furniture*, 16. 2 Letter to Charleston Museum, May 16, 1951.

Sweet Gum. 1 Lawson, *Hist.*, 54. 2 PC, Inv. Book 79, 1751–1753, 489, 518.

White Ash. 1 *SCHM*, Vol. 36, 64, 84.

Mulberry. 1 PC, Inv. Book 74, 1746–1748, 22.

Holly. 1 Drayton, *Carolinian Florist*, 103.

Beds. 1 Vol. 61–A, 1726–1727, 24. 2 Vol. 79, 1751–1753, 84. 3 Inv. Book C, 1789–1800, 125.

Double Chests of Drawers. 1 Vol. 94–A, 1771–1774, 45. 2 *SCG*, July 9, 1772 [Prime]. 3 Vol. 65, 1732–1736, 175.

Clothespresses. 1 Cescinsky, *Old-World House*, 91. 2 *SCHM*, Vol. 40, 86.

Tables. 1 Brackett, *Thomas Chippendale*, 122. 2 Horner, *Philadelphia Furn.*, 140. 3 Inv. Book Vol. 73, 1741–1743, 63. 4 *Burroughs, Southern Antiques*, 79. 5 *SCG*, July 9, 1772. 6 Downs, *Amer. Furn.*, xxiii. 7 Jourdain, *Regency Furn.*, 24. 8 Inv. Book, Vol. 62–B, 1729–1731, 520. 9 *SCG*, Mar. 22, 1740 [Prime]. 10 *SCG*, Dec. 5, 1774; 3/3. 11 *City Gaz. & Com. Daily Adv.*, May 14, 1810; 3/2. 12 Dir. 1807, 22. 13 Downs, *Amer. Furn.*, 334.

Side Chairs. 1 Vol. 65, 1732–1736, 113. 2 Vol. 62–B, 1729–1731, 768. 3 *SCG*, Aug. 12, 1732 [Prime]. 4 *SCG*, Aug. 8, 1771 [Prime]. 5 *SCG*, July 9, 1772 [Prime]. 6 *SCHM*, Vol. 35, 20. 7 *S. C. State Gaz.*, Oct. 31, 1795 [Prime].

French Chairs or Armchairs. 1 Inv. Book, 1783–1797, 30.

Windsor Chairs. 1 Vol. 65, 1732–1736, 424. 2 *SCG*,

Jan. 19, 1759; 2/2. 3 *Courier*, Jan. 4, 1832; 1/3. 4 Chapman, *Hist. of Edgefield*, 192. 5 *Penn. Museum Bull.*, Nov. 1925, 37.

Sofas, Couches, and Settees. 1 Inv. Book 73, 1741–1743, 60. 2 *See* Magrath and Elfe.

Sideboards. 1 Eberlein and McClure, *Practical Book of Period Furn.*, 219; Lockwood, *Colonial Furn.*, Vol. I, 18. 2 Hopkins, *Sheraton Period*, Fig. 35. 3 Inv. Book C, 1789–1800, 38. 4 *S. C. State Gaz.*, Oct. 31, 1795, 190 [Prime]. 5 *Chas. City Gaz. & Adv.*, Dec. 10, 1796; 1/1; July 19, 1796, 202 [Prime]. 6 *Balt. Furn.*, 17. 7 Jourdain & Rose, *English Furn.*, 185. 8 *SCHM*, Vol. 41, 65.

Knife Cases and Urns. 1 Inv. Book, 1783–1797, 499. 2 *Antiques*, Oct. 1934, 133. 3 *Antiques*, Dec. 1934, 222.

Wine Coolers and Cellarettes. 1 Inv. Book 100, 1776–1784, 382. 2 Inv. Book 1783–1797, 499; Inv. Book D, 1800–1810, 97, 476. 3 Inv. Book 100, 1776–1784, 7. 4 Whilden, *Reminiscences*, (*Chas. Year Book*, 1896, 411).

Corner Cupboards. 1 Inv. Book 79, 1751–1753, 246.

Desk and Bookcases; and Secretary and Bookcases. 1 *SCG*, Jan. 27, 1732. 2 *Ibid.* Mar. 22, 1740. 3 Inv. Book 67–A, 1732–1746, 124. 4 Inv. Book 79, 1751–1753, 509. 5 Cescinsky, *Old-World House*, Vol. II, 336. 6 Hepplewhite, *Guide* (1794), 8. 7 *Times*, Nov. 2, 1801; 3/1.

Bookcases. 1 Bowes, *Cult. of Early Chas.*, 60. 2 Inv. Book 87–A, 1761–1763, 123. 3 Inv. Book 94–A, 1771–1774, 112.

Clocks. 1 *SCHM*, Vol. 41, 153.

Inlays and Bellflowers. Inv. Book 100, 1776–1784, 156. 2 *Times*, May 23, 1805; 3/2.

Japanned Furniture. 1 Inv. Book 60, 1724–1725, 65. 2 Inv. Book 61–B, 1726–1727, 542. 3 *City Gaz. & Daily Adv.* 4 Lockwood, *Colonial Furn.*, Vol. I, 87.

Brasses. 1 *SCG*, Dec. 18, 1749; Oct. 14, 1756. 2 *Times*, Dec. 11, 1801.

Polishes. 1 *SCHM*, Vol. 35, 20. 2 Cescinsky, *Old-World House*, Vol. II, 344. 3 *SCHM*, Vol. 43, 32.

Allen, Josiah. 1 MCO, Book B–8, 411. 2 *SCHM*, Vol. 34, 102.

Archbald, Robert. 1 USDC, Citizens Book A.

Artman, John. 1 Letters of Adm. (Intestate), 1815–1819, 291.

Axson, William. 1 *SCG*, Feb. 12, 1763 [Prime]. 2 *SCG*, Sept. 21–28, 1765; 3/3. 3 *S. C. Gaz. & Country Journal*, Apr. 26, 1768 [Prime]. 4 *SCG*, Apr. 25, 26, 1768 [Prime]. 5 *SCHM*, Vol. 45, 171. 6 Ravenel, *Architects of Charleston*, 26. 7 *Reg. St. Thomas and St. Denis's Parish*, 26. 8 *Ibid.* 48. 9 Easterby, *S. C. Society*, 106. 10 *SCHM*, Vol. 53, 15. 11 *SCHM*, Vol. 33, 282. 12 *Ibid.* Vol. 34, 78. 13 *State Gaz. of S. C.*, June 2, 1788.

Badger, Jonathan. [1] MCO, Book CC, 76. [2] Mcl. Rec., Vol. 75–B, 1746–1749, 705. [3] MCO, Book SS, 126. [4] Ibid. 313. [5] SCHM, Vol. 38, 34. [6] Account of Payment of Gen. Tax 1760–1769, 73, 94, 103, 104 (Museum Library). [7] SCHM, Vol. 27, 91. [8] Journal of Ct. of Gen. Sessions, 1769–1776, 51 (Museum Library). [9] Mcl. Rec., Vol. 91–B, 1767–1771, 677. [10] MCO, Book M–4, 106.

Barker, Thomas. [1] Mcl. Rec., Vol. 53, 1692–1693, 247. [2] SCHM, Vol. 8, 167. [3] Ibid. Vol. 14, 59.

Barksdale, Charles. [1] MCO, (Abst.) Book DD, 253. [2] SCHM, Vol. 20, 68. [3] Mcl. Rec., Vol. 75–A, 1746–1749, 158. [4] MCO, Book SS, 229. [5] SCHM, Vol. 21, 74. [6] Will Book 13, 1767–1771, 873. [7] Inv. Book 84, 1756–1758, 355.

Barrite, Gerred E. [1] MCO, Book O–9, 154. [2] Ibid. Book G–10, 316.

Baylis, William. [1] MCO, Book T–6, 38.

Beamer, James. [1] Wills, Inv. & Mcl. Rec., Vol. 53, 1692–1693, 206. [2] SCHM, Vol. 14, 4. [3] Will Book 1, 1671–1724, 25.

Becais, Claude. [1] Citizens Book 4–H, 223. (S. C. Archives Dept., Columbia, S. C.)

Besseleu, Lewis. [1] Reg. St. Thomas, 50. [2] Letters of Adm., 1827–1833, 67.

Binsky, Martin. [1] St. Philip's Par. Reg. 1720–1758, 190. [2] Will Book 8, 1757–1763, 180. [3] Inv. Book, Vol. 84, 1756–1758, 417.

Bird, Jonathan. [1] PC, Inv. Book, 1800–1810, 468.

Bradford, Thomas. [1] PC, Letters of Adm., 1797–1803, 149. [2] City Gaz., Mar., 29, 1792. [3] MCO, Book L–6, 201. [4] Ibid. Book L–6, 275. [5] PC, Inv. Book C, 1789–1811, 449.

Brewer, Charles. [1] Vol. 63, 1729–1731, 224 (Free Library).

Brickles, Richard. [1] Will Book 4, 1736–1740, 82. [2] St. Philip's Par. Reg. 1720–1758, 73, 163. [3] Mcl. Rec., Vol. 75–B, 1746–1749, 390.

Broomhead & Blythe. [1] MCO, Book L, 291.

Brown, Daniel. [1] Chas. Courier, Sept. 29, 1806; 1/2.

Brown, Hugh. [1] MCO, Book V–4, 32. [2] Ibid. Book I–4, 209. [3] Book 95, 1771–1775, 204 (Free Library).

Caine, Isaac. [1] Will Book 21, 1783–1786, 834.

Calder, Alexander. [1] SCHM, Vol. 24, 31. [2] USDC, Citizens Book A. [3] MCO, Book B–8, 89. [4] City Gaz. and Com. Adv., June 15, 1819; 3/1. [5] Will Book 45, 1845–1851, 484. [6] Health Dept. Rec.

Carwithen, William. [1] St. Philip's Par. Reg. 1720–1758, 160. [2] MCO, Book K, 146. [3] Ibid. Book S, 266. [4] Ibid. Book FF, 205. [5] Mcl. Rec., Book 83–B, 1754–1758, 632 (Free Library). [6] Jour. Ct. of Gen. Sessions, 1769–1776, 53 (Museum Library). [7] SCHM, Vol. 44, 45.

Charnock, Thomas. [1] MCO, Book A–8, 231. [2] Dir. 1822, 103.

Claypoole, George. [1] MCO, Book H, 17.

Claypoole, Josiah. [1] Penn. Gaz., May 18, 1738 [Prime]. [2] SCG, Aug. 9, 1742. [3] Ibid. Feb. 4, 1745. [4] Ibid. Apr. 11, 1748. [5] SCHM, Vol. 14, 158.

Coker, Thomas. [1] SCHM, Vol. 36, 87. [2] Ibid. Vol. 41, 153. [3] Ibid. Vol. 26, 155.

Cook (e), Thomas. [1] SCHM, Vol. 40, 60. [2] Ibid. Vol. 33, 282. [3] Ibid. Vol. 34, 83. [4] Will Book 20, 1783–1786, 387. [5] MCO, Book N–5, 359. [6] Letters of Adm., 1785–1791, 69. [7] Chas. City Dir. and Business Reg., 1790, 8.

Coquereau, Charles. [1] Citizens Book 4–C, 23 (Arch. Dept., Columbia, S. C.). [2] Weekly Reports of the Stewards of the Orphan House (S. C. Hist. Soc.) [3] Constitution and By-Laws of the Societe' Francaise of Charleston, S. C., 11.

Cowan, John. [1] Health Dept. Rec.

Culliatt, Adam. [1] Hirsch, Hug. of S. C., 84. [2] MCO, Book WW, 140, 145, 150. [3] Will Book 12, 1767–1771, 420. [4] SCHM, Vol. 10, 230.

Deans, Robert. [1] St. Michael's Coll. (S. C. Hist. Soc.). [2] MCO, Book WW, 526. [3] Ibid. Book B–3, 316. [4] Ibid. Book C–3, 426. [5] SCHM, Vol. 34, 194.

Delorme, John Francis. [1] City Gaz., Sept. 16, 1794. [2] Prime, Vol. II, 219. [3] Citizens Book 3–E, 494 (Arch. Dept., Columbia, S. C.). [4] SCG, Mar. 1, 1797. [5] City Gaz. and Com. Adv., Jan. 5, 1819.

Desel, Charles. [1] MCO, Book P–4, 457. [2] Ibid. Book H–5, 273. [3] SCHM, Vol. 31, 264; Tombstone Inscriptions. [4] Will Book 31, 1807–1818, 35. [5] PC, Inv. Book, 1800–1810, 450.

Desel, Samuel. [1] MCO, Book G–8, 201. [2] Dir. 1822. [3] Will Book 32, 1807–1818, 859.

Dobbins, John. [1] Mcl. Rec., Vol. 90, 1765–1769, 99. [2] St. Philip's Par. Reg. 1754–1810, 246. [3] MCO, Book O–6, 442. [4] Ibid. Book Z–6, 163.

Douglas, John. [1] MCO, Book Y–6, 75. [2] USDC, Citizens Book A. [3] MCO, Book I–7, 392. [4] PC, Letters of Adm., 1803–1808, 168. [5] PC, Inv. Book, 1800–1810, 373.

Duddell, James. [1] PC, Inv. Book D, 1800–1810, 208.

Duval, Lewis. [1] PC, Inv. Book 60, 1724–1726, 82. [2] Ibid. 9.

Eden, Joshua. [1] SCHM, Vol. 19, 81. [2] Jour. Ct. of Gen. Sessions, 1769–1776, 215, 318. [3] SCHM, Vol. 1, 135, 187. [4] PC, Letters of Adm., 1785–1791, 406. [5] SCHM, Vol. 27, 44. [6] PC, Will Book 28, 1800–1807, 276. [7] PC, Inv. Book, 1800–1810, 93.

Ehrenpford, John Godfrey. [1] USDC, Citizens Book A.

Elfe, Thomas. [1] Elfe Family Bible now (1955) in the possession of Mrs. John A. Zeigler of Moncks Corner, S. C. [2] Mcl. Rec., Vol. 75–B, 1746–1749, 497. [3] Ibid. 609. [4] SCHM, Vol. 35, 13. [5] St. Philip's Par. Reg. 1754–1810, 143. [6] Mcl. Rec., Vol. 75–B, 1746–1749, 731. [7] SCHM, Vol. 31, 9. [8] St.

Michael's Coll. (S. C. Hist. Soc.). [9] *Statutes at Large, S. C.*, Vol. 4, 63. [10] Mcl. Rec., Vol. 83–B, 1754–1758, 616. [11] Kershaw, *Hist. of St. Michael*, 95. [12] *SCG*, Apr. 20, 1765; 3/2. [13] MCO, (abst.) Book VV, 405. [14] *Ibid.* Book E–3, 621. [15] *Ibid.* Book D–3, '310. [16] Mcl. Rec., Vol. 91–B, 1767–1777, 961. [17] Jour. Ct. of Gen. Sessions, 1769–1776, 44 (Museum Library). [18] *SCHM*, Vol. 35, 14. [19] Inv. Book, Vol. 99–A, 1776–1778, 116.

Elfe, Thomas, Jr. [1] PC, Will Book 18, 1776–1784, 88. [2] *SCHM*, Vol. 11, 167. [3] *Statutes at Large, S. C.*, Vol. 6, 629. [4] MCO, Book P–5, 282. [5] *Ibid.* Book F–7, 74. [6] Dir. 1807, 90.

Ellis, Matthew. [1] PC, Letters of Adm., Vol. RR, 1797–1803, 446.

Emarrett, Peter. [1] Weekly Reports of the Stewards of the Orphan House (S. C. Hist. Soc.).

Fairchild, Robert. [1] *St. Philip's Par. Reg. 1720–1758*, 66. [2] MCO, (abst.) Book OO, 57. [3] *SCHM*, Vol. 23, 69, 70, 196. [4] Rec. Book 95, 1771–1775, 237 (Free Library).

Fairley, Hance. [1] USDC, Citizens Book A. [2] *SCHM*, Vol. 40, 65.

Finlayson, Mungo, [1] *SCHM*, Vol. 35, 16, 20, 66. [2] *Reg. St. Thomas*, 31. [3] *Ibid.* 60. [4] Letters of Adm., Book OO, 1775–1785, 312. [5] *SCHM*, Vol. 22, 23. [6] PC, Inv. Book 1789–1800, 122.

Finlayson, Mungo Graeme. [1] *St. Philip's Par. Reg. 1754–1810*, 360.

Fisher, John. [1] Ravenel, *Architects of Charleston*, 51. [2] *SCHM*, Vol. 38, 40; Vol. 39, 87. [3] Jour. Ct. of Gen. Sessions, 1769–1776, 296. [4] MCO, Book C–5, 208, 570. [5] *Statutes at Large, S. C.*, Vol. 6, 629. [6] Jour. of the Senate, 76. [7] S. C. Confiscated Estates.

Freling, Theodore. [1] PC, Letters of Adm. (Intestate), 1797–1803, 185. [2] Inv. Book C, 1789–1800, 418.

Frew, John. [1] *State Gaz. of S. C.* Sept. 25, 1795 [Prime]. [2] *SCHM*, Vol. 26, 49.

Fyfe, John. [1] *St. Philip's Par. Reg. 1754–1810*, 219. [2] MCO, Book P–4, 457. [3] *SCHM*, Vol. 11, 169.

Gilmer, James. [1] Inv. Book 94–A, 1771–1774, 348.

Gough, John. [1] MCO, Book H–5, 190.

Gouldsmith, Richard. [1] USDC, Citizens Book A. [2] MCO, Book K–9, 247.

Graham, Thomas. [1] *SCHM*, Vol. 23, 110. [2] MCO, Book E–8, 425. [3] *Ibid.* Z–8, 60. [4] *SCHM*, Vol. 47, 146.

Gros, John. [1] Salley, *Mar. Not. in Chas. Courier*, 47. [2] Tombstone Inscriptions [Huguenot Churchyard], 264. [3] MCO, Book Y–9, 241.

Hall, Peter. [1] *SCG*, Nov. 20, 1762. [2] *SCHM*, Vol. 35, 16.

Hammet, William. [1] Vol. 68, 1736–1739, 260 (Free Library).

Hampton, William. [1] *SCHM*, Vol. 38, 35. [2] MCO, Book C–6, 62.

Hancock, George. [1] USDC, Citizens Book A.

Harden, Joel. [1] Wills, Inv. & Mcl. Rec., Vol. 64, 1731–1733, 35.

Hefferman, John. [1] USDC, Citizens Book A. [2] Information from Miss Frances Jervey, 1936. [3] *SCHM*, Vol. 43, 98. [4] *Ibid.* Vol. 48, 198.

Holton, Thomas. [1] MCO, (abst.) Book A, 132. [2] *St. Philip's Par. Reg. 1720–1758*, 152. [3] MCO, Book I, 568. [4] Wills, Inv. & Mcl. Rec., Vol. 62–A, 1729–1731, 27. [5] *Ibid.* Vol. 62–B, 1729–1731, 963. [6] *Ibid.* Book 64, 1731–1733, 118.

How and Roulain. [1] Book 86–B, 1758–1763 (Free Library).

Hutchinson, Thomas. [1] MCO, (abst.) Book VV, 115. [2] *SCHM*, Vol. 53, 14. [3] *Chas. Year Book*, 1897, 394. [4] Sabine, *Loyalists of Am. Rev.*, Vol. II, 535. [5] *St. Philip's Par. Reg. 1754–1810*, 353. [6] PC, Will Book A, 1783–1786, 262. [7] Jour. of the Senate, 76.

Johnston, Edward. [1] PC, Letters of Adm, Vol. QQ, 357.

Jones, Abraham. [1] *Rules of German Friendly Soc.*, 100. [2] *Rules of Chas. Ancient Artillery Soc.*, 47. [3] MCO, Book A–9, 197; Book H–9, 449. [4] *German Friendly Soc., loc. cit.*

Jones, Robert W. [1] *St. Philip's Par. Reg. 1754–1810*, 107.

Jones, William. [1] *City Gaz. or Daily Adv.*, Apr. 9, 1791. [2] Will Book 24, 1786–1793, 1134 (Free Library). [3] PC, Inv. Book 1783–1797, 495.

Kirkwood, James. [1] *St. Philip's Par. Reg. 1720–1758*, 93. [2] MCO, Book WW, 568; 577. [3] *SCG*, Feb. 7–14, 1761. [4] *SCHM*, Vol. 15, 44. [5] *St. Philip's Par. Reg. 1754–1810*, 346.

Lacroix, Francis Joseph. [1] *SCHM*, Vol. 30, 117.

Lapiere, Gilbert Bernard James. [1] USDC, Citizens Book A. [2] Will Book 32, 1807–1818, 841 (Free Library).

Lardant, James. [1] *Statutes at Large, S. C.*, Vol. 2, 131–133. [2] *SCHM*, Vol. 9, 22. [3] Mcl. Rec. Book 53, 1692–1693, 367.

Larue, Francis. [1] Mcl. Rec., 1783–1812, 252.

Lee, Thomas. [1] Dir. 1806. [2] *Courier*, Mar. 2, 1814. [3] Letters of Adm. (Intestate), Book 1808–1815, 388.

Legare, Solomon, Jr. [1] *Statutes at Large, S. C.*, Vol. 4, 275. [2] Will Book 16, 1774–1779, 258. [3] *SCHM*, Vol. 17, 89.

Lejeune, Thomas. [1] *Constitution & By-Laws of Societe' Francaise of Charleston*, 1934, 11.

Lewis, William. [1] Health Dept. Rec.

Lining, Thomas. [1] *St. Philip's Par. Reg. 1720–1758*, 197. [2] *SCHM*, Vol. 23, 170. [3] *SCG*, Oct. 14, 1756; 2/2. [4] Minutes of Vestry of St. Philip's Church, May 14, 1750. [5] Acct. of Payment of Gen. Tax,

1760–1769, 45. 6 *St. Philip's Par. Reg. 1754–1810*, 304. 7 Inv. Book 87–B, 1761–1763, 634 (Free Library).

Lipper, Henry. 1 Letters of Adm. (Intestate), 1803–1808, 425. 2 PC, Inv. Book, 1800–1810, 468.

Liston, Robert. 1 Mcl. Rec., 83–B, 1754–1758, 616 (Free Library). 2 Mcl. Rec., 86–A, 1758–1763, 373. 3 *St. Philip's Par. Reg. 1754–1810*, 144. 4 Inv. Book, 85–B, 1758–1761, 572 (Free Library).

Litle, John. 1 Letters of Adm. (Intestate), 1815–1819, 373. 2 PC, Inv. Book, 1809–1819, 527.

Lupton, William. 1 *St. Philip's Par. Reg. 1720–1758*, 181.

Magrath, Richard. 1 *SCG*, July 9, 1772. 2 *Ibid.*, Apr. 3, 1775; 4/2.

Marlen, William. 1 *St. Philip's Par. Reg. 1754–1810*, 362.

Marshall, John. 1 Letters of Adm., Book QQ, 230. 2 MCO, Z–6, 277. 3 *Ibid.* Z–6, 282, 285. 4 *SCHM*, Vol. 47, 148.

May, John. 1 Information from Miss Frances Jervey from account book of James Jervey. 2 *SCHM*, Vol. 42, 32. 3 *Ibid.* Vol. 29, 246. 4 Will Book 48, 1856–1862, 502.

McGilvrey, Farquhar. 1 Day Book of James Poyas (Chas. Museum). 2 MCO, Book D–3, 33. 3 *SCHM*, Vol. 35, 16, 19, 66. 4 *Ibid.* Vol. 16, 131. 5 *Ibid.* Vol. 44, 173.

McIntosh, John. 1 USDC, Citizens Book A. 2 *SCHM*, Vol. 34, 158. 3 PC, Inv. Book, 1819–1824, 473.

McIntosh and Foulds. 1 Information from Miss Frances Jervey from account book of James Jervey.

Mills, Thomas. 1 *SCHM*, Vol. 22, 35. 2 Mcl. Rec. 90, 1765–1769, 99 (Free Library). 3 *SCHM*, Vol. 36, 10. 4 MCO, M–6, 1; K–6, 48.

Mintzing, Philip. 1 Letters of Adm., 1785–1791, 205.

Moncrief, Richard. 1 MCO, (abst.) Book VV, 585. 2 *SCG*, June 27, 1748; 1/2. 3 St. Michael's Coll. (S. C. Hist. Soc.), No. 35 Commisioners Bills. 4 Gen. Tax, 1760–1769, 73 *et seq.* 5 Jour. Ct. of Gen. Sessions, 1769–1776, 115, 193 (Chas. Museum). 6 *SCHM*, Vol. 11, 129. 7 Sabine, *Amer. Loyalists*, 477. 8 Will Book 23, 1786–1793, 517. 9 Inv. Book B, 1783–1797, 244. 10 *St. Philip's Par. Reg. 1720–1758*, 95, 104.

Moore, Philip. 1 *SCHM*, Vol. 5, 145. 2 *Ibid.* Vol. 33, 35. 3 *Ibid.* Vol. 33, 306. 4 MCO, Book B–7, 65. 5 Will Book 48, 1856–1862, 114 (Free Library).

Morison, Simon. 1 *Courier*, Oct. 5, 1839; 2/6. 2 Health Dept. Rec. 3 *Courier*, Oct. 5, 1839. 4 Will Book 42, 1839–1845, 26.

Muckenfuss, Michael. 1 *Rules of German Friendly Soc.*, 98, 99. 2 MCO, C–7, 282. 3 *Ibid.*, Z–6, 145. 4 *SCHM*, Vol. 32, 67. 5 Will Book 31, 1807–1818, 144. 6 PC, Inv. Book 1800–1810, 476.

Murphy, Josiah. 1 Records, Vol. 95, 19 (Free Library). 2 Inv. Book 94–A, 1771–1774, 213.

Neville, Henry W. and Joshua. 1 USDC, Citizens Book A. 2 Dir. 1822. 3 *Courier*, Aug. 17, 1828. 4 Health Dept. Rec.

Neville, James 1 MCO, Book S–8, 111.

Newton, Thomas. 1 *St. Philip's Par. Reg. 1720–1758*, 94, 181.

Norris, James C. 1 Dir. 2 Schirmer Records (S. C. Hist. Soc.).

Packrow, John. 1 MCO, Book XX, 13, 194; Book C–3, 667. 2 *SCHM*, Vol. 10, 235; Vol. 22, 35. 3 *St. Philip's Par. Reg. 1754–1810*, 319. 4 Will Book 27, 1793–1800, 712 (Free Library).

Pearce, Abraham. 1 Council Journal 32, 709. 2 *SCG*, Mar. 14, 1768 [Prime]. 3 *SCHM*, Vols. 35–39. 4 Sabine, *Loyalists of Am. Rev.*, Vol. II, 564.

Peigne, James L. 1 Health Dept. Rec. 2 *Ibid.*

Pfeninger, Martin [II]. 1 PC, Letters of Adm., 1778–1821, 252. 2 PC, Inv. Book, 1798–1800, 166.

Philips, John M. 1 *City Gaz. and Daily Adv.*, May 23, 1796 [Prime].

Porter, Benjamin R. 1 *State Gaz. of S. C.*, June 20, 1797. 2 *City Gaz. and Adv.*, Jan. 3, 1798.

Powell, John. 1 Will Book 23, 1786–1793, 546. 2 PC, Inv. Book, 1783–1797, 248.

Price, Thomas. 1 PC, Letters of Adm., 1797–1803, 17. 2 MCO, Book T–6, 382. 3 Inv. Book C, 1789–1800, 284.

Purse, W. W. 1 *Georgetown* [S. C.] *Gazette*, June 27, 1826. 2 MCO, Book N–9, 425.

Quackinbush, Laurence. 1 *SCHM*, Vol. 33, 39. 2 *Ibid.* Vol. 34, 53.

Ralph, John. 1 *SCHM*, Vols. 38 and 39. 2 MCO, Book D–5, 16, 20. 3 *Chas. Year Book*, 1897, 394. 4 Sabine, *Loyalists of Am. Rev.*, Vol. II, 569. 5 MCO, Book Y–5, 139. 6 Letters of Adm., 1775–1785, 358. 7 *SCHM*, Vol. 21, 121. 8 MCO, Book U–6, 108. 9 *St. Philip's Par. Reg. 1754–1810*, 369. 10 Letters of Adm., 1797–1803, 362. 11 Inv. Book D, 1800–1810, 107.

Ralph & Silberg. 1 *City Gaz. & Daily Adv.*, Oct. 1, 1793.

Redmond, Andrew. 1 *SCHM*, Vols. 39 and 40. 2 *Ibid.*, Vol. 1, 54. 3 Will Book 24, 1786–1793, 793.

Reside, William. 1 Dir. 1806, 43. 2 PC, Letters of Adm., 1797–1803, 5. 3 MCO, Book W–6, 301. 4 *Ibid.* Book B–7, 270. 5 Salley, *Mar. Not. in S. C. Gaz.*, 109. 6 Letters of Adm., 1797–1803, 299. 7 MCO, Book Q–7, 252. 8 Clerk of Court Decree Book, 1807–1811, 36.

Riley, John. 1 *SCHM*, Vol. 1, 58. 2 Letters of Adm., 1775–1784, 346. 3 *SCHM*, Vol. 24, 77. 4 *Ibid.* Vol. 27, 178.

Rosse, Paul. 1 USDC, Citizens Book A. 2 *Courier*, Sept. 29, 1806; 1/1.

Roulain, Abraham. [1] *Reg. St. Thomas*, 78. [2] *SCHM*, Vols. 37 and 41. [3] Jour. Ct. of Gen. Session, 1769–1776, 203 (Museum Library). [4] MCO, Book M–5, 220. [5] Will Book 22, 1786–1793, 281. [6] MCO, Book D–6, 200. [7] Inv. Book, 1783–1797, 127.

Roushan, James. [1] Wills, Inv. & Mcl. Rec. 64, 1731–1733, 80. [2] MCO, Book L, 56. [3] *SCHM*, Vol. 19, 163. [4] Mcl. Rec. 75–B, 1746–1749, 567. [5] Inv. Book 82–B, 1753–1756, 531. [6] Will Book 7, 1752–1756, 285.

Row, George Daniel. [1] MCO, Book A–7, 73.

Sass, Edward George. [1] Schirmer Records (S. C. Hist. Soc.). [2] *SCHM*, Vol. 33, 67. [3] Schirmer Records. [4] MCO, Book 9, 122. [5] *Ibid.* Book A–12, 573. [6] Tombstone Inscriptions (First Baptist), 16, 17. [7] Will Book 44, 1845–1851, 456.

Sass, Jacob. [1] *Chas. Courier*, Feb. 15, 1836. [2] *Ibid.* Feb. 18, 1836.

Saunders, Harry. [1] Letters of Adm., 1785–1791, 72.

Scull, Edward. [1] Wills, Inv. & Mcl. Rec. 62–B, 1729–1731, 832. [2] Will Book 5, 1740–1747, 328. [3] Inv. Book 67–A, 1732–1746, 96.

Sheridan, John J. [1] MCO, Book Q–13, 647.

Sigwald, Thomas. [1] Letters of Adm., 1797–1803, 147. [2] MCO, Book F–7, 36.

Silberg, Nicholas. [1] *City Gaz. & Daily Adv.*, June 11, 1796. [2] Salley, *Mar. Not. in S. C. Gaz.*, 95. [3] *St. Philip's Par. Reg. 1754–1810*, 370. [4] Will Book 28, 1800–1807, 231. [5] Inv. Book 1800–1810, 97.

Simmons, James. [1] Letters of Adm. 1785–1791, 300.

Smith, George Elias. [1] *SCHM*, Vol. 33, 51.

Smith, John. [1] *New Eng. Hist. & Gen. Register*, Vol. 64, 108.

Smith, Richard. [1] Information from Miss Frances Jervey. [2] *SCHM*, Vol. 33, 52. [3] *Ibid.* Vol. 34, 164.

Stewart, Charles. [1] *City Gaz.*, May 14, 1795. [2] *Reg. St. Thomas*, 42. [3] Arch. Dept., Columbia, S. C. [4] MCO, Book X–6, 70; U–6, 324. [5] *SCHM*, Vol. 44, 150.

Stewart, George. [1] Letters of Adm., Book OO, 1775–1785, 445. [2] Inv. Book A, 1785–1793, 337.

Stocks, Thomas. [1] MCO, Book TT (abst.), 399. [2] *SCHM*, Vol. 38, 35.

Tamerus, Christian. [1] MCO, Book T–7, 126. [2] *SCHM*, Vol. 32, 286.

Tennant, Thomas. [1] MCO, Book A–13, 501.

Thom, Jacob. [1] *SCHM*, Vol. 33, 37.

Townsend, Stephen. [1] *SCG*, Sept. 21, 1765; 3/3. [2] MCO, Book L–3, 339. [3] *Ibid.* Book S–3, 111. [4] Mcl. Rec. 91A, 1767–1771, 428. [5] *SCHM*, Vol. 35, 154. [6] MCO, Book F–7, 203. [7] Sabine, *Loyalists of Am. Rev.*, Vol. II, 588. [8] MCO, Book H–6, 30. [9] *SCHM*, Vol. 25, 157. [10] Letter from Rhode Island School of Design.

Townsend and Axson. [1] *SCG*, Feb. 5, 1763.

Vanall, Matthew. [1] Inv. Book 68, 1736–1739, 301.

Vinyard, John. [1] *SCHM*, Vol. 29, 335. [2] MCO, Book K–9, 7.

Walker, Robert. [1] Letters of Adm., 1797–1803, 189. [2] Dir. 1801. [3] MCO, Book X–7, 313; Book D–8, 168. [4] Will Book 33, 1807–1818, 1167. [5] Tombstone Inscriptions (Scots Presbyterian). [6] Will Book 39, 1826–1834, 1185. [7] Inv. Book, 1834–1843, 31.

Walker, William. [1] MCO, Book K–7, 157. [2] Letters of Adm., Book SS, 276. [3] Inv. Book E, 1809–1819, 48.

Wallace, Thomas. [1] *City Gaz. & Daily Adv.*, Feb. 19, 1796. [2] MCO, Book S–6, 444; Book C–7, 296; Book L–7, 286. [3] Tombstone Inscriptions (Scots Presbyterian), 465. [4] Will Book 33, 1807–1818, 1167. [5] Inv. Book F, 1819–1824, 44.

Warham, Charles. [1] *SCHM*, Vol. 12, 21. [2] MCO, Book WW, 290; Book GG, 178. [3] *Ibid.* Book Q, 126. [4] *S. C. Gaz. & Country Journ.*, Nov. 17, 1768. [5] Jour. Ct. of Gen. Sessions, 1769–1776 (Museum Library). [6] *SCHM*, Vol. 35, 73. [7] *Ibid.* Vol. 29, 316.

Watson, John. [1] *City Gaz. and Adv.*, Feb. 4, 1797. [2] *Ibid.* Jan. 1, 1798; 4/4. [3] Book 3–V, 37 (Arch. Dept., Columbia, S. C.). [4] MCO, Book M–6, 460. [5] Jervey, *Epitaphs from St. Michael's*, 290.

Watson, William. [1] *St. Philip's Par. Reg. 1720–1758*, 153. [2] MCO, Book K, 202. [3] *St. Philip's Par. Reg. 1720–1758*, 248. [4] Will Book 3, 1731–1737, 305.

Watts, Charles. [1] *City Gaz. & Adv.*, Mar. 24, 1795. [2] MCO, Book Q–6, 381; Book U–6, 44; Book H–7, 438, 441. [3] Will Book 32, 1807–1818, 510. [4] Inv. Book, 1809–1819, 62.

Wayne, William. [1] MCO, Book L–3, 101. [2] Prime, Vol. I, 177. [3] MCO, Book E–4, 456. [4] Mcl. Rec., 91–A, 1767–1771, 207. [5] Journ. Ct. of Gen. Sessions, 1769–1776, 64 (Museum Library). [6] *SCHM*, Vol. 35, 106. [7] *Ibid.* Vol. 38, 38. [8] MCO, Book B–5, 123. [9] *Ibid.* F–5, 268.

Welch, George. [1] *SCHM*, Vol. 28, 133. [2] *Ibid.* Vol. 34, 101, 160.

Weyman and Carne. [1] *S. C. Gaz. & Country Journal.*

Wheeler, Benjamin. [1] *SCHM*, Vol. 33, 284; Vol. 34, 83. [2] Will Book 20, 1783–1786, 387.

White, Gottlieb. [1] MCO, Book O–8, 206. [2] Dir.

Wilkie, George. [1] Letters of Adm., 1785–1791, 79. [2] Inv. Book A, 1785–1793, 337.

Williams, John. [1] *N. E. Hist. & Gen. Reg.*, Vol. 62, 322.

Wilson, John. [1] MCO, Book P–6, 214. [2] *SCHM*, Vol. 32, 281.

Woodin, Thomas. [1] *Statutes at Large, S. C.*, Vol. 4,

Act 962. [2]Mcl. Rec., Book 91–B, 1767–1771, 676. [3]MCO, Book H–4, 38, 166; Book Z–3, 333, 336, 344, 354. [4]*SCHM*, Vol. 21, 68. [5]Will Book, 1775–1779, 183.

Worthington, Joseph. [1]*State Gaz. of S. C.*, July 8, 1793; 3/3.

Worthington and Sinclair. [1]*City Gaz. and Adv.*, Feb. 26, 1793.

WORKS CONSULTED

MANUSCRIPT SOURCES

Account of Payment of General Tax 1760–1769. [In the Charleston Museum.]

Citizens Book. [South Carolina Archives Department, Columbia, S. C.]

Clerk of Court Decree Book, 1807–1811.

Day Book of James Poyas. [In the Charleston Museum.]

Elfe Family Bible, now [1954] owned by Mrs. John A. Zeigler of Moncks Corner, S. C.

Health Department Records, 1821–   , Charleston County, S. C.

Journal of the Court of General Sessions, 1769–1776. [In the Charleston Museum.]

Marceil, Elizabeth C. (compiler). Tombstone Inscriptions from Charleston Churchyards. Charleston, S. C. 1936. [Typewritten copy in the South Carolina Historical Society.]

Mesne Conveyance Office, Office of the Registrar: Deeds, Mortgages, etc., Charleston County, S. C.

Minutes of the Vestry of St. Philip's Church, Charleston, S. C.

Papers of Col. John Chestnut. [South Carolina Historical Society.]

Probate Court, Office of the Judge of Probate: Wills, Inventories and Miscellaneous Records, Charleston County, S. C.

Sass Coffin Plate Book. [South Carolina Historical Society.]

Schirmer, Jacob. Records October 1826–1886. [South Carolina Historical Society.]

St. Michael's Collection. [South Carolina Historical Society.]

United States District Court [Charleston]. Aliens admitted Citizens, Book A.

Weekly Reports of the Stewards of the Orphan House. [South Carolina Historical Society.]

PRINTED SOURCES

Adams, Henry. *History of the United States of America.* Vol. I. New York. 1889.

Albion, Robert Greenhalgh. *The Rise of New York Port.* [1815–1860.] New York. 1939.

Baltimore Furniture. Baltimore Museum of Art. Baltimore, Md. 1947.

Bowes, Frederick. *The Culture of Early Charleston.* University of North Carolina Press. 1942.

Bracket, Oliver. *Thomas Chippendale.* Boston and New York. 1925.

Bridenbaugh, Carl. *Myths and Realities.* Louisiana State University Press. 1952.

Browne, D. J. *The Sylva Americana; or a Description of the Forest Trees* . . . Boston. 1832.

Burroughs, Paul H. *Southern Antiques.* Richmond, Va. 1931.

Carroll, B. B. *Historical Collections of South Carolina.* Vol. II. New York. 1836.

Catesby, Mark. *The Natural History of Carolina, Florida, and the Bahama Islands.* . . . London. 1731–1748.

Census of the United States. *Heads of Families at the first Census of the United States taken in the year 1790. South Carolina.* Washington, D. C. 1908.

Cescinsky, Herbert. *The Old-World House.* Vols. I & II. London. 1924.

Chambers, Sir William. *Design of Chinese Building, Furniture, Dresses, Machines and Utensils.* London. 1757.

Chapman, John A. *History of Edgefield County* . . . Newberry, S. C. 1897.

Charleston Year Book, 1880, 1882, 1883, 1896, 1897. Charleston, S. C.

Chippendale, Thomas. *Director.* London. 1754.

Clute, Robert F. (arranged by). *The Annals and Parish Register of St. Thomas and St. Denis Parish, in South Carolina, from 1680 to 1884.* Charleston, S. C. 1884.

Cole, Arthur Harrison. *Wholesale Commodity Prices in the United States 1700–1861.* Harvard University Press. 1938.

Crevecoeur, J. Hector St. John. *Letters from an American Farmer,* . . . London. 1783.

Dalcho, Frederick. *An Historical Account of the Protestant Episcopal Church, in South Carolina* . . . Charleston, S. C. 1820.

Directories, City of Charleston, S. C.: 1790, 1801, 1802, 1803, 1806, 1807, 1809, 1813, 1816, 1819, 1822, 1829, 1841, 1849, 1852, 1855.

Downs, Joseph. *American Furniture.* New York. 1952.

Drayton, John. *A View of South Carolina.* Charleston. 1802.

Easterby, J. Harold. *The South Carolina Rice Factor as Revealed in the Papers of Robert F. W. Allston.* (*Journal of Southern History,* Vol. 7, May, 1941.)

———. *The Rules of the South Carolina Society* . . . Baltimore, Md. 1937.

———. *The South Carolina Rice Plantation.* University of Chicago Press. 1945.

Eberlein, Harold Donaldson, and McClure, Abbot. *The Practical Book of Period Furniture*. Philadelphia and London. [1914.]

Elliott, Stephen. *A Sketch of the Botany of South-Carolina and Georgia*. Vol. I. Charleston, S. C. 1821.

German Friendly Society, Rules of. Ninth ed. Charleston, S. C. 1908.

Congaware, George J. (compiler). *The History of the German Friendly Society of Charleston, South Carolina, 1766–1916*. Richmond, Va. [c. 1935.]

Gray, Lewis Cecil. *History of Agriculture in the Southern States to 1860*. Washington, D. C. 1933.

[Harrison, Fairfax]. *The John's Island Stud* (South Carolina) *1750–1788*. Richmond, Va. 1931.

Hepplewhite, A. and Co. *Cabinet-Maker and Upholsterer's Guide*. London. 1794. [Reprint 1898.]

Hibernian Society, Constitution and Rules of the. Charleston, S. C. 1818.

Hirsch, Arthur H. *The Huguenots of Colonial South Carolina*. Durham, N. C. 1928.

Horner, William Macpherson, Jr. *Blue Book* [of] *Philadelphia Furniture*. Philadelphia. 1935.

Jervey, Clare. *Inscriptions on the Tablets and Gravestones in St. Michael's Church and Churchyard, Charleston, S. C. . . .* Columbia, S. C. 1906.

Jones, E. Alfred. *American Members of the Inns of Court*. London. 1924.

Jourdain, Margaret. *Regency Furniture*. London. 1949.

Jourdain, Margaret, and Rose, F. *English Furniture*. London. 1953.

Kershaw, John. *History of the Parish and Church of St. Michael*. Charleston, S. C. [1915.]

La Rouchfoucauld-Liancourt, Francis Alexander Frederic, duc de la. *Travels through the United States of North America in the years 1795, 1796, 1797 . . .* London. 1799. 2 vols.

Lawson, John. *A New Voyage to Carolina . . .* London. 1709.

[Lesesne, Thomas P.] *Historical Sketch of Orange Lodge No. 14, A. F. M.* Charleston, S. C. [1939.]

Little, E. L., Jr. *Important Forest Trees of the United States*, 774. Dept. of Agri. Year Book. 1949. (Separate No. 2156).

Lockwood, Luke Vincent. *Colonial Furniture in America*. New York. 1921. 2 vols.

Lutheran Church, Rules and Regulations of. Revised. 1897.

McCrady, Edward. *A Sketch of the History and Rules of the Charleston Ancient Artillery Society*. Revised. Charleston, S. C. 1901.

———. *The History of South Carolina*. Vol. I. New York. 1897.

Magazine Antiques. Vols. 1–64. 1922–1953.

Mereness, Newton D. *Travels in the American Colonies*. New York. 1916.

Meriwether, Margaret Babcock, ed. *The Carolinian Florist of Governor John Drayton of South Carolina, 1766–1822*. The South Caroliniana Library. 1943.

Michaux, F. Andrew. *The North American Sylva*. Vol. II. Philadelphia, Pa. 1818.

Miller, Edgar G., Jr. *American Antique Furniture*. Baltimore, Md. 1937.

Mills, Robert. *Statistics of South Carolina*. Charleston, S. C. 1826.

Moore, Mabel Roberts. *Hitchcock Chairs*. Tercentenary Commission of the State of Connecticut. 1933.

"Neptune" Chart of Charles Town. 1777. London.

New England Historical and Genealogical Register. Vols. 62, 64.

Newspapers. Naturally every line of the papers listed below has not been read word for word but the vast majority of papers has been carefully examined for advertisements by cabinet-makers. In the few instances where the lack of time precluded a page for page examination, alternate issues of the paper were examined. It is not likely that many advertisements were overlooked by this method, since it was the almost invariable custom for an advertisement to run consecutively for several issues.

Charleston: *Charleston Courier*: 1803–1852.
Charleston Evening Gazette: 1785–1786.
Charleston Morning Post and Daily Advertiser: 1786–1787.
City Gazette (known at various times by the following additional titles: *The City Gazette, and the Daily Advertiser; The City Gazette, or the Daily Advertiser; the City Gazette & Daily Advertiser; City Gazette; City Gazette and Daily Advertiser; City Gazette and Commercial Advertiser*): 1787–1820.
South-Carolina Gazette: 1732–1775.
South Carolina Gazette; And Country Journal: 1765–1775.
State Gazette of South Carolina: 1785–1793.
Times: 1800–1809.

Savannah, Ga.: *Columbian Museum and Savannah Daily Gazette*.

Phillips, Ulrich Bonnell. *A History of Transportation in the Eastern Cotton Belt to 1860*. Columbia University Press. 1908.

Prime, Alfred Coxe. *The Arts and Crafts in Philadelphia, Maryland and Carolina, 1721–1800*. Vols. I-II. The Walpole Society. 1929, 1932.

Ravenel, Beatrice St. Julien. *Architects of Charleston*. Charleston, S. C. [1945.]

Ravenel, Mrs. St. Julien. *Charleston, The Place and the People*. New York. 1922.

Reveirs-Hopkins, A. E. *The Sheraton Period, Post Chippendale Designers, 1760–1820*. New York [c. 1922.]

Revill, Janie. *A Compilation of the Original Lists of Protestant Immigrants to South Carolina, 1763–1773*. Columbia, S. C. 1939.

Sabine, Lorenzo. *Biographical Sketches of Loyalists*

of the *American Revolution.* Vol. II. Boston. 1864.

St. Andrew's Society of the City of Charleston, South Carolina. Charleston, S. C. 1892.

St. Philip's Parish Register. *See* Salley and Smith.

St. Thomas & St. Denis Parish Register. *See* Clute.

Salley, Alexander S., Jr., ed. *Marriage Notices in Charleston Courier (1803–1818).* Columbia, S. C. 1919.

———— ed. *Marriage Notices in the South-Carolina Gazette and Daily Advertiser.*

———— ed. *Register of St. Philip's Parish, Charles Town, South Carolina, 1720–1758.* Charleston, S. C. 1904.

Sellers, Leila. *Charleston Business on the Eve of the American Revolution.* University of North Carolina Press. 1934.

Shecut, J. L. E. W. *Medical Essays.* Charleston, S. C. 1819.

Smith, Alice R. Huger, and Smith, D. E. Huger. *Dwelling Houses of Charleston, South Carolina.* Philadelphia and London. 1917.

Smith, D. E. Huger, and Salley, Alexander S., Jr., eds. *Register of St. Philip's Parish, Charles Town, or Charleston, S. C., 1754–1810.* Charleston, S. C. 1927.

Societé Francaise of Charleston, S. C., Constitution and By-Laws of the. Charleston, S. C. 1934.

South Carolina Historical Society, *Collections of:* Published by the Society. Vol. V. 1897.

————. *Historical and Genealogical Magazine* and *Historical Magazine.* Vols. I-LIV. Published by the Society. 1900–1953.

Statutes at Large of South Carolina. Vols. II, IV, VI.

Swan, Mabel M. *Samuel McIntire, Carver and The Sandersons, Early Salem Cabinet Makers.* Salem, Mass. 1934.

Symonds, R. W. *The English Export Trade in Furniture in Colonial America.* Antiques, Oct. 1935, 156–159.

Union Kilwinning Lodge No. 4 Charleston under the jurisdiction of the Grand Lodge of Ancient Freemasons of South Carolina, Rules or By-Laws of the. Revised. Charleston, S. C. 5858 [1858].

Wallace, David Duncan. *The History of South Carolina.* Vol. II. New York. 1935.

————. *South Carolina, A Short History.* University of North Carolina Press. 1951.

Wertenberger, Thomas J. *The Golden Age of Colonial Culture.* New York. 1942.

Whilden, William G. *Reminiscences of Old Charleston. Charleston Year Book,* 1896, 402–417.

Williams, George W. *St. Michael's, Charleston, 1751–1951.* University of South Carolina Press. Columbia, S. C. 1951.

Index

Allen, Josiah, *69*
Apprentices, 10, 11, 71, 86, 93, *95*, 102, 109, 112, 124
Archbald, Robert, *69*
Armchairs, 12, *53*
Artman, John, *69*
August, Charles, *69*
Axson, William, Jr., *69*

Badger, Jonathan, *70*
Ball and Claw Foot, 12, 49, *64*
Barker, Thomas, *70*
Barksdale, Charles, *70*
Barnes, James, *71*
Barrite, Gerred E., 11, 22, *71*
Barville, Mitchell, *71*
Baylis, William, *71*
Beamer, James, 25, *72*
Becaise [Becaisse], Claude, *72*
Beds, 12, 30, *41*, 82, 83, 87, 91, 105, 114, 120, 126, 131
Bellflowers, 17, *63*
Besseleu, Lewis, *72*
Biggard, John, 54, *72*
Binsky, Martin, *73*
Bird, Jonathan, *73*
Block front furniture, 12
Block, Nathaniel, *73*
Bonner, John, *73*, 106
Bookcases, *60*, 88, 96, 98, 113, 122, 126, 128, 132
Bradford, Thomas, *73*, 78
Brasses, *65*
Brewer, Charles, *74*
Brickles, Richard, *74*
Broomhead & Blythe, 30, 44, *74*
Brown, Daniel, *74*
Brown, Hugh, *74*
Brown, Michael, *75*
Bulkley & Co., *75*
Burke, Patrick, *75*
Burn, James, *75*

Cabinet-Makers:
  Charleston, *6*, 67
  English, 73, 82, 84, 93, 94, 96, 101, 103, 109, 121, 122, 126, 131
  French, 15, 17, 72, 80, 81, 96, 100, 101, 111
  German, 17, 81, 84, 111, 118, 123, 131
  Irish, 90, 96, 109
  Italian, 116
  Journeymen, 54, 71, 93, *95*, 99, 133
  Negro, *10*, 11, 20, 77, 87, 89, 91, 124

Numbers of, 6, 7, 9, 18, 19, 25, 126, 133
  Scottish, 17, 18, *56*, 69, 76, 80, 83, 100, 105, 106, 108, 125, 126, 127, 132
  Swedish, 120
Caine, Isaac, *75*
Calder, Alexander, *55*, 72, *75*, 102
Calder, James, *76*
Candle Stands, 88
Canter, Benjamin, *76*
Carman, Andrew, *76*
Carne, John, *76*, 130
Carwithen, William, 61, *77*
Cellarettes, *58*, 99
Chairs: Arm, 12, *53*
  Easy, 11, 12, *52*, 88, 103, 104, 129
  French, *53*, 82, 88, 104
  Hitchcock, 9
  Side, *51*, 88
  Windsor, 8, 9, *53*, 72, 97, 114, 115, 121, 123
Charleston: Description of, 4, 5, 14, 15
Charnock, Thomas, 11, *77*
Chests of Drawers, 12, 30, *44*, 74, 75, 77, 78, 121, 126, 127, 128, 131
Clarke, John, *77*
Claypoole, George, *78*
Claypoole, Josiah, 7, 24, 44, 48, 50, 59, *78*
Clements, Henry, 73, *78*
Clocks, 12, *61*, 77, 88
Clothespresses, 12, *46*, 88, 120, 133
Cocks, William, *79*
Coker, Thomas, *79*
Conclusion, *25*
Conflagrations, *22*
Cook (e), Thomas, *79*, 130
Cooley, William, *79*
Coquereau, Charles, *80*
Corner Cupboards, *59*, 125
Couches, 12, *55*, 88, 104
Country Trade, *18*, 20, 101, 110
Cowan, John, *80*
Culliatt, Adam, *80*
Cyrus, Richard, *80*

Deans, Robert, *80*
Delorme, John Francis, *81*
Desel, Charles, *81*, 82, 108
Desel, Samuel, *82*
Desk and Bookcases, 11, 12, *59*, 77, 78, 87, 88, 106
Desks, 12, 126, 128
Disher, Lewis, *82*

Dobbins, John, *82*
Double Chests of Drawers, 11, 12, 13, 16, 21, *42*, 82, 87, 88, 104, 108
Douglas, James, *83*
Douglas, John, *83*
Dressing Drawers, 44, 128
Dressing Tables, 12, 13, *50*, 75, 132
Duddell, James, *83*
Duval, Lewis, *83*

Early Charleston, *3*
Easy Chairs, 11, 12, *52*, 88, 103, 104, 129
Eden, Joshua, 11, *83*
Ehrenpford, J. G., *84*
Elfe, Thomas, 6, 11, 19, 21, 25, 33, 34, 41, 48, *84*, 127
Elfe, Thomas, Jr., *89*, 98, 126
Elfe & Fisher, 86, *89*, 91
Elfe & Hutchinson, 52, 85, *90*, 102
Ellis, Matthew, *90*
Emarrett, Peter, *90*
Exports: Furniture, *18*, 111
    Other than Furniture, 4, 15
Exports and Country Trade, *18*

Fairchild, Robert, *90*
Fairley, Hance, *90*, 91
Finlayson, Mungo, *90*, 91
Finlayson, Mungo Graeme, *91*
Finlayson & Fairley, *91*
Fire Screens, 88
Fisher, John, 10, 86, *91*, 124
Forthet, John, 82, *92*
Foulds [Fowles], William, *92*, 107
Freeman, James, *92*
Freling, Theodore, *92*
French Chairs, *53*, 82, 88, 104
Frew, John, *92*
Furniture:
    Ball and Claw Foot, 12, 49, *64*
    Beds, 12, 30, *41*, 82, 83, 87, 91, 105, 114, 120, 126, 131
    Block Front, 12
    Bookcases, *60*, 88, 96, 98, 113, 122, 126, 128, 132
    Candle Stands, 88
    Cellarettes, *58*, 99
    Chairs: Arm, 12, *53*
        Easy, 11, 12, *52*, 88, 103, 104, 129
        French, *53*, 82, 88, 104
        Hitchcock, 9
        Side, *51*, 88
        Windsor, 8, 9, 12, *53*, 72, 97, 114, 115, 121, 123
    Charleston-made, *39*, 120
    Chest-on-chests, 42
    Chest of Drawers, 12, 30, *44*, 74, 75, 77, 78, 121, 126, 127, 128, 131
    Clocks, 12, *61*, 77, 88

Clothespresses, 12, *46*, 88, 120, 133
Corner Cupboards, *59*, 125
Couches, 12, *55*, 88, 104
Dearth of Local, 22
Desk and Bookcases, 11, 12, *59*, 77, 78, 87, 88, 106
Desks, 12, 126, 128
Double Chests of Drawers, 11, 12, 13, 16, 21, *42*, 82, 87, 88, 104, 108
Dressing Drawers, 44, 128
Fire Screens, 88
Half Drawers, 44, 88, 104, 110
High Boys, 13
Importations: American, *8*, *53*, 75, 79, 115
    English, 7, 53
    Other, *10*, 81
Japanned, *64*
Kinds not made in Charleston, 12
Kinds used in Charleston, *11*
Knife Cases and Urns, 12, *57*
Low Boys, 13, 51
Plantation-made, 20
Prices of, 20, 41, 44, 48, 49, 50, 51, 53, 57, 58, 59, 60, 61, 96, 99, 101, 105, 107, 109, 113, 121
Schools, *16*
Secretary and Bookcases, *59*, 75, 125, 126
Secretary-Wardrobes, 35, *46*, 75, 127
Settees, 9, *55*, 97
Sideboards, 20, *55*, 75, 78, 83, 120
Side Chairs, *51*, 88
Sofas, 12, 21, *55*, 76, 79, 88, 104, 107, 120, 127
Sources of, *6*
Styles and Influences, *13*
Tables, *48*
"Venture," 8
Wardrobes, *46*, 120, 128
Wine Coolers, 12, *58*
Fyfe, John, 81, *93*

Gaskins, Henry, *93*, 130
Gifford, Andrew, 55, *93*
Gilmer, James, *93*
Gough, John, *93*
Gouldsmith, Richard, *93*
Graham, Thomas, *94*
Greenland, Walter, *94*
Griffen, Ephraim, *94*
Gros, John, *94*, 100

Half Drawers, 44, 88, 104, 110
Hall, Peter, 14, 50, *94*
Hamett, Thomas, *95*
Hammett, William, *95*
Hampton, William, *95*
Hancock, George, *96*
Harden, Joel, *96*
Hefferman, John, 35, *96*

Henry, Julian, *96*
High Boys, 13
Hitchcock Chairs, 9
Hodge, David, *96*
Holton, Thomas, 10, *96*
Hope, Thomas, *97*
How & Roulain, *97*
Humiston, Jay, *97*, 121
Humiston & Stafford, 54, *97*, 121
Hutchinson, Thomas, *97*

Importations: Of Furniture, *10*, 81
    Other than Furniture, 7, 15
Inlays, *63*

Japanned Furniture, *64*
Jasper, William, *98*
Jocelin, Henry, *98*
Johnston, Edward, *98*
Jones, Abraham, *98*, 99
Jones, Robert W., *99*
Jones, William, *99*
Jones & Harper, *99*

Keckley, John, *99*
Kinkaid, Alexander, *99*
Kirkwood, James, *99*
Knife Cases and Urns, 12, *57*

Labels, 16, *18*, 35, 60, 61, 115, 125, 133
Lacroix, Francis Joseph, *100*
Lafayette Beds, 71
Lamare, Esparee, *100*
Lapiere, Gilbert Bernard James, *100*, 101
Lardant, James, *100*
Larue, Francis, *100*
Lee, Thomas, 94, *100*
Legare, Solomon, Jr., *101*
Lejeune, Thomas, 100, *101*
Lewis, William, *101*
Lining, Thomas, *101*
Lipper, Henry, *102*
Liston, Robert, 34, 85, *102*
Litle, John, *102*
Little, William, *102*
Low Boys, 13, 51
Lupton, William, *103*
Luyten, William, 33, *103*

Magrath, Richard, 17, 43, 49, 51, 52, 55, *104*
Mahogany Sawmill, 25, 30
Main, James, *104*
Marlen, William, *105*, 131
Marshall, John, 52, 55, 58, 60, *105*
May, John, 66, *105*

May & Munro, *105*
Mazett, James, *106*
McClellan, James 44, 48, *106*
M'Donald & Bonner, *106*
McGillivray [McGilvrey], Farquhar, *106*
McIntosh [M'Intosh], John, 92, *106*, 107
M'Intosh & Foulds, 21, 92, *107*
Mills, Thomas, 82, *107*
Mintzing, Philip, *107*
Moncrief, Richard, *107*
Moore, Philip, *108*
Morison, Simon, *108*
Muckenfuss, Michael, 57, 58, *108*, 109
Murphy, Josiah, *108*

Naser, Frederick, *109*
Negro Cabinet-Makers, *10*, 11, 20, 77, 87, 89, 91, 124
Neville, Henry & Joshua, 11, *109*
Neville, James, *109*
Newton, Thomas, *109*
Norris, James C., *110*
Nutt, John, *110*

Packrow, John, *110*
Pearce, Abraham, 18, *111*
Peigne, James L., *111*
Pfeninger, Martin, Sr., 63, *111*
Pfeninger, Martin, [II], *112*
Philips [Phillips], Eleazer, 95, *112*
Philips [Phillips], John M., *112*
Plantation-made Furniture, *20*
Polishes, *65*
Porter, Benjamin R., *112*
Porter & Labach [Fabach], *112*
Powell, John, *112*
Price, Thomas, *113*
Prices of Furniture, 20, 41, 44, 48, 49, 50, 51, 53, 57,
    58, 59, 60, 61, 96, 99, 101, 105, 107, 109, 113, 121
Produce, 21, 76, 79
Prue, John, *113*
Purse, W. W., 35, *113*

Quackinbush, Laurence, *114*, 123

Ralph, John, *114*, 120
Ralph & Silberg, *114*, 121
Rawson, William R., *115*
Redmond, Andrew, 54, *115*
Reside, William, *115*
Riley, John, *116*
Rosse, Paul, *116*
Rou, George D., *116*, 118
Rou, M., Jr., *116*
Roulain, Abraham, 97, *117*
Roushan [Rousham], James, *117*
Row, George Daniel, *117*

Sass, Edward George, 118
Sass, Jacob, 18, 58, 75, *118*, 120
Saunders, Harry, *119*
Sawmill: Mahogany, 25, 30
Scull, Edward, *120*
Secretary and Bookcases, *59*, 75, 125, 126
Secretary-Wardrobes, 35, *46*, 75, 127
Settees, 9, *55*, 97
Sheridan, John J., 54, *120*
Sideboards, 20, *55*, 75, 78, 83, 120
Side Chairs, *51*, 88
Sigwald, Thomas, *120*
Silberg, Nicholas, 58, 114, *120*, 121
Simmons, James, *121*
Smith, George Elias, *121*
Smith, John, *121*
Smith, Richard, *121*
Sofas, 12, 21, *55*, 76, 79, 88, 104, 107, 120, 127
Stafford, Theodore, 97, *121*
Stewart, Charles, *122*
Stewart, George, *122*
Stocks, Thomas, *122*, 123
Styles and Influences, *13*
Swaney, William, *122*

Tables: Ball and Claw, 12, 49
    Breakfast, *49*, 72, 75, 88, 104, 127, 131
    Card, 11, *49*, 75, 88, 104, 105, 127, 128
    China, *49*, 104
    Chinese, 14, 50, 82, 94, 132
    Dining, 11, *48*, 88, 110, 127, 128, 131
    Dressing, 12, 13, *50*, 75, 132
    Early, *48*
    Pembroke, 36, *50*
    Slab, 11, 12, *50*, 78, 88
    Tea, 11, *48*, 76, 78, 88, 110, 120, 128
Tamerus, Christian, *122*
Tariffs, 7, 8, 29, 50
Teachester, John, *123*
Tennant, Thomas, *123*
Thom, Jacob, *123*
Thom & Quackinbush, *123*
Thompson, James H., *123*
Thompson, William, *123*
Tools, *66*
Townsend, Stephen, 10, 69, 91, 122, *123*
Townsend & Axson, 123, *124*
Tremain, John, *124*

Vanoll, Matthew, *124*
Venetian Blinds, 79, 86, 91, 127
"Venture" Furniture, 8
Vinyard, John, *125*
Walker, Robert, 18, 35, 36, 60, 61, *125*, 126, 129, 133

Walker, William, 57, *125*
Wallace, Thomas, 125, *126*, 128
Wallace & Watts, *126*, 128
Wardrobes, *46*, 120, 128
Warham, Charles, *126*
Watson, John, 92, 102, *127*, 128, 132
Watson, William, *127*
Watson & Woodill, 127, *128*, 132
Watts, Charles, 55, 126, *128*, 129, 133
Watts & Walker, *129*
Wayne, William, 60, *129*
Welch, George, *129*
Welch, John, *129*
Werner, John M., *130*
Weyman & Carne, 77, *130*
Wheeler, Benjamin, 79, *130*
White, Charles, *130*
White, George, *130*
White, Gottleib, *130*
Whitney, Jedediah, *131*
Wilkie, George, *131*
Will, Mathew, *131*
Will & Marlin, *131*
Williams, John, *131*
Wilson, John, *131*
Windsor Chairs, 8, 9, 12, *53*, 72, 97, 114, 115, 121, 123
Wine Coolers, 12, *58*
Woodill, John Anthony, 127, 128, *131*
Woodin, Thomas, *132*
Woods, 29
    Ash, *36*, 87, 99
    Cedar, *31*, 72, 81, 82, 83, 87, 108, 117, 121
    Cypress, 16, *33*, 87, 89, 102
    Hickory, *36*, 117
    Holly, 37, 125
    Mahogany, 19, 20, 74, 95, 111
    Mahogany: Honduras, *31*
        West Indian or St. Domingo, 7, 17, 29, *30*, 31
    Maple, 9, *35*
    Mulberry, 37
    Oak, *35*, 36, 53
    Palmetto, *36*
    Pine, 83, 99, 108, 121
    Pine: Long-leaf, *34*
        White, *34*, 114, 133
    Poplar, *34*, 102, 133
    Red Bay, *33*, 95, 125
    Satinwood, *36*, 125
    Sweet Gum, *36*
    Walnut, 12, *32*
Wood Rays, 36
Worthington, Joseph, *132*
Worthington & Kirby, *132*
Worthington & Sinclair, *132*